2021

Sport Media Vectors

Gender and Diversity, Reconstructing the Field

Edited by:
Laurel Walzak, Danica Vidotto, and Francesco Collura

First published in 2021
as part of the *Sport & Society Book* Imprint
doi: 10.18848/978-1-61229-000-3/CGP (Full Book)

Common Ground Research Networks
60 Hazelwood Drive
University of Illinois Research Park
Champaign, IL 61820

Library of Congress Cataloging-in-Publication Data

Names: Walzak, Laurel, editor. | Vidotto, Danica, editor. | Collura, Francesco, editor.
Title: Sport media vectors : gender and diversity, reconstructing the field
/ edited by Laurel Walzak, Danica Vidotto, Francesco Collura.
Description: Champaign, IL : Common Ground Research Networks, 2021. |
Series: Sport & Society | Includes bibliographical references and index.
| Summary: "In this book, Walzak, Collura and Vidotto bring together an
invited collection of writing from emerging scholars about sport, sport
media and equity. Authors span from undergraduates and Masters students
to doctoral candidates. All are passionate and excited about the
possibilities for equity and radical change that needs to happen across
the sport and sport media landscape to make sports truly equitable. This
collection reflects the authors' investments and interest in sports.
Each author investigates and reflects on a key social justice issue
related to sport and sport media. The authors turn to social media,
traditional broadcast, and personal experiences to explore their areas
of interest. The content in this book ranges from exploring and
analyzing an individual athlete to Muslim Sportswomen, leagues and
teams, to autobiographical narratives. This critical social justice
scholarship in sport and sport media offers a critique by young
academics who are interested in pushing the status quo and shaking up
the historical, social-cultural, and political foundations of sports
locally, nationally, and globally"-- Provided by publisher.
Identifiers: LCCN 2021035051 (print) | LCCN 2021035052 (ebook) | ISBN
9780949313539 (Hardback) | ISBN 9781863352604 (Paperback) | ISBN
9781612290003 (Adobe PDF)
Subjects: LCSH: Sports--Social aspects. | Mass media and sports. |
Discrimination in sports. | Racism in sports. | Sex discrimination in sports.
Classification: LCC GV706.5 .S7354 2021 (print) | LCC GV706.5 (ebook) |
DDC 306.4/83--dc23
LC record available at https://lccn.loc.gov/2021035051
LC ebook record available at https://lccn.loc.gov/2021035052

Table of Contents

Introduction to Sport Media Vectors: Gender Equity and Diversity: Challenging Narratives in Sport and Sport Media, Emerging Scholars' Writing and Investigations
    Francesco Collura (PhD Candidate), X University, Toronto, Ontario, Canada
    Danica Vidotto, Ph.D, University of Toronto, Toronto, Ontario, Canada

"Serving" Looks: An Investigation of Eugenie Bouchard's Self-Representation on Instagram
    Analisa Raimondo (BA), X University, Toronto, Ontario, Canada

"Who Is the Purple-Haired Man?": Queer Erasure in Audience Sentiment toward Megan Rapinoe
    Grace Esford (MPC), X University, Toronto, Ontario, Canada

The In/Visibility of Black Muslim Sportswomen
    Sabrina Razack (PhD Candidate), University of Toronto, Toronto, Ontario, Canada
    Asma Khalil (PhD Student), University of Toronto, Toronto, Ontario, Canada
    Hibaq Mohamed (MSc), University of Toronto, Toronto, Ontario, Canada

Muslim Women's Experiences of Sport and Sport Culture in Toronto
    Laurel Walzak (BA, MBA) The Creative School, RTA School of Media, Sport Media, X University, Toronto, Ontario, Canada
    Danica Vidotto, Ph.D, University of Toronto, Toronto, Ontario, Canada

"We Are the Movement"
    Shireen Ahmed (MA), X University, Toronto, Ontario, Canada

An Investigation of How Women's Basketball in North America Has Been Silenced by the NBA and Men in the Sports Industry
    Dana Daschuk (Undergraduate Student), X University, Toronto, Ontario, Canada

ACKNOWLEDGEMENTS

The coeditors wish to acknowledge the Canadians in sport and sport media who, over the course of coediting this collection, continue to selflessly advocate for inclusion in sport and who have created and/or provided a spot and a voice at the table for all (and in Shireen Ahmed's case, "built her own table"). You know who you are.

Shireen Ahmed is a freelance writer, public speaker, mentor, and award-winning sports activist who focuses on Muslim women and the intersections of racism and misogyny in sports. Her work has been featured and discussed in numerous media outlets. She is on the advisory board of FARE Network (UK), Hijabi Ballers (Canada) and is also part of the screening committee with the Canadian Sport Film Festival. She mentors aspiring sports journalists and hopes to unite her love of the film *Bend It Like Beckham* with her academic work. Shireen is a columnist and contributor to TSN and is cocreator and cohost of the "Burn It All Down" feminist sports podcast team, the first feminist sports podcast that analyzes sports and sports culture from an intersectional feminist and antioppression lens. When she isn't watching soccer or serving her cat, she drinks coffee as a tool of resistance. She was one of the 2019 TEDxToronto Speakers. Shireen is pursuing a Master of Media Production at "X" University and is a part of the GXSLab team as a media consultant.

Francesco "Frankie" Collura is a PhD candidate in the joint Communication and Culture program at "X" University* and York University. *Frankie Collura is in favour of using "X" University in support of renaming her university, which was named after Egerton Ryerson, a key architect of Canada's Indian Residential School system. Frankie's research explores the experiences of LGBTQ+ athletes in soccer at all levels, with a particular focus on soccer players in Italy, England, Canada, and the United States. In his free time, Frankie pays homage to his Italian heritage by cooking Mediterranean dishes for his family.

Dana Daschuk is a current undergraduate student at the "X" University School of Journalism. Dana has dedicated a concentration of her studies to sports and the representation of women in sports. After completing her undergraduate degree, she hopes to study law and pursue a career as a sports attorney and agent. Her research explores the power dynamic of the sports industry and how it has silenced the female narrative, continuing to perpetuate hegemonic masculinity in sports. Dana's work, both academically and personally, aims to demonstrate the importance of having more women in sports. Dana grew up competing in a variety of sports and at one point was pursuing a professional wakeboarding career before sustaining an injury. In her free time, Dana focuses strongly on a healthy lifestyle, with a plant-based whole food diet, training daily, and watching basketball and football.

Grace Esford is a graduate of the Master of Professional Communication program in the Faculty of Communication and Design at "X" University. Her area of research is at the intersection of communication, gender, and sport, which is inspired by her professional career in video production, sports livestreaming, and content creation. Grace's research aims to understand audience sentiment toward professional athletes and how fourth-wave feminism offers marginalized voices agency through the use of the internet. This research seeks to inform policy action for social media network sites in order to make virtual spaces safe for all. Apart from researching, Grace has a passion for working on video sets and being a freelance video editor. She enjoys playing soccer in the summer and ice skating in the winter.

Devin Gotell, informally known among his athletic colleagues as "The Great Ghost," is a three-time Paralympic Swimmer and 2015 Toronto Para Pan Am Games gold medalist, multimedalist, and multifinalist. Devin is a current undergraduate student at "X" University. At "X," Devin studies within the Arts and Contemporary Studies program, with a specific focus on Disability Study. This interdisciplinary field allows Devin to fuse historical context into modern-day movements in order to interrogate present-day events. This unique multidisciplinary approach means that Devin sees immense value in the art of storytelling and personal perspectives of marginalized groups, particularly those who identify as disabled. As an individual with oculocutaneous albinism type I (lacking pigment, or melanin, in the eyes, hair, and skin) and a proud Paralympian, Devin values the personal story and believes that the personal narrative of marginalized individuals is one of the keys to breaking down the social and political barriers that these groups face within Canadian society. Devin still enjoys swimming whenever he can and, as an avid Steve Irwin and David Attenborough fan as a child, always had a particular passion and respect for nature and biology growing up. Devin also enjoys fictional history novels such as Bernard Cornwell's *The Last Kingdom* and loves to ponder the philosophy of alternate historical events.

Lydia Ferrari Kehoe is a former Irish international swimmer and holds a bachelor's degree in specialist sports journalism from the University of Derby. She completed her dissertation, entitled "Media Portrayal of Female Swimmers: An Analysis of Inequalities in British Online Coverage (Case Study of *the Guardian* Newspaper)," in 2020. Her work illuminated the many discrepancies that exist within modern media coverage of swimming. She currently works as a communications officer in Swim England—the national governing body for aquatic sports in England—as well as a freelance journalist.

A passion for swimming and journalism has merged and positioned Lydia within the heart of the sport media field, facilitating an unyielding desire to produce equitable and fair sports reporting. Her research areas span topics of gender, sport, and media, and her aspirations for the future include continuing to build a career within sport media and expanding her academic research. Lydia has also recently made a return to the pool, where she hopes to compete internationally on behalf of her country again.

Asma Khalil is a PhD student in the Faculty of Kinesiology and Physical Education at the University of Toronto. Her research explores issues of identity, social support, and inclusion/alienation within Western sport spaces. Specifically, her master's thesis used a postcolonial, feminist approach to understanding the sport experiences of young Muslim women actively competing in Ontario. For this research, Asma has received the master's dissertation award from the International Institute of Qualitative Methods, the Marie Parkes Fellowship for Research in Women's Health and Physical Activity, and the Barbara Drinkwater Award. Asma is passionate about working within the community to bring about change. She currently serves on the advisory board for Hijabi Ballers, a project dedicated to celebrating Muslim women in sport, and on the executive committee of Black Muslim Initiative, a grassroots organization dedicated to understanding issues at the intersection of anti-Black racism and Islamophobia.

Hibaq Mohamed is an MSc student in the Exercise Science program at the University of Toronto. An intersectional, feminist sports scholar, Hibaq's research examines how COVID-19, related facility closures, and recreation program cancellations affect marginalized communities in Toronto using the neighbourhood of Rexdale as a case study. Hibaq's work aims to identify barriers to sport and recreation participation to inform future program planning and inclusion for historically marginalized communities in Toronto. Hibaq spends her spare time learning new recipes and watching movies.

Analisa Raimondo is a recent media production graduate at the RTA School of Media at Ryerson University. Analisa's focus at Ryerson has been in live event and broadcast production, and she hopes to pursue a career in international sport media. Her research examines how female athletes construct their online identities in regard to dominant sociocultural ideals. Analisa's work aims to deconstruct existing discourses surrounding female athletes and provide insight into how they can be adapted to fit the changing forms of representation that are a result of social media. In her free time, she enjoys watching her favourite sports (Go Leafs Go!), spending time outdoors, and playing new video games!

Sabrina Razack is a PhD candidate at the University of Toronto and completed her master's thesis examining the player experiences of National Women's Cricketers in Canada. Her current research examines the intersections of media, race, gender, class, and culture. She intends to study how digital platforms contribute to the formation, operation, and/or challenges of social movements and activism. Sabrina is an award-winning curriculum writer and developed Beyondaboundary.com to create units on critical sport and social issues.

Danica Vidotto, Ph.D., at the Ontario Institute for Studies in Education in collaboration with the iSchool Knowledge, Media, Design Institute at the University of Toronto. Danica's doctoral thesis investigates adolescent female athletes and social media. Approaching this research through an intersectional feminist sport media framework, Danica's research unpacks how adolescent female athletes produce and consume social media content as a possible tool to confront and disrupt current media discourses around women in sports and sport media. Danica is a qualified Ontario educator and has taught students from kindergarten through graduate school.

Laurel Walzak is an associate professor of the RTA School of Media Program, in the Faculty of Communication and Design, "X" University.* She joined "X" University* in summer 2016. * Laurel Walzak is in favour of using "X" University in support of renaming her university, which was named after Egerton Ryerson, a key architect of Canada's Indian Residential School system. She founded the Global Experiential Sport Lab, GXSLab www.gxslab.com a research lab, which exists within FCAD's Catalyst Research Hub in Toronto, and which serves as the connection between scholarly research and industry practice in sport and sport media. GXSLab focuses on the intersection and knowledge transfer between globalization, digitization, and commercialization. Laurel commits to a culture of diversity and inclusion, empowers students with and through experiences, provides engagement and hands-on learning with industry, and is focused on ensuring her work has global impact and mobilizes change.

Laurel was the recipient of the "X" University 2020 Alan Shepard Gender Equity and Inclusion Award and is cohost and cofounder of a global podcast "SportTokz with SportProfz" (www.sporttokz.com).

Introduction

Sport Media Vectors: Gender Equity and Diversity: Challenging Narratives in Sport and Sport Media, Emerging Scholars' Writing and Investigations

In this book, Walzak, Collura, and Vidotto bring together an invited collection of writing from emerging scholars about sport, sport media, and equity. We are excited about this work as authors range from undergraduates and master's students to doctoral candidates from Canada, and one author is from Ireland. All of us are passionate and excited about the possibilities for equity and radical change that need to happen across the sport and sport media landscape to make sports truly equitable. This collection reflects the authors' investments and interest in sports.

In the fall of 2019, Danica Vidotto and Francesco "Frankie" Collura met and began working with Laurel Walzak and the Global Experiential Sport Lab (GXSLab) at "X" University. Walzak founded the GXSLab in the fall of 2018 and resolutely supports the values of committing to a culture of diversity and inclusion and empowering students through hands-on learning experience/s. These values of GXSLab are consistent with Walzak's leadership and advocacy, as she consistently looks for and provides openings, connections, and championship for "up and coming" students and young scholars to grow, build, and use their presence and voice in sport. The GXSLab is the connection between scholarly research and industry practice in sport and sport media. Since we joined the lab, we have been engaged in sport-based projects that encompass the GXSLab's three pillars: sports fans/audiences; gender equity and diversity; and emerging fields (such as Esports). In the summer of 2020, during the COVID-19 pandemic, civil unrest after the murder of George Floyd and the Black Lives Matter protests, a pause on our work for the lab, and uncertainty looming before us, we came together as a collective. Bringing together our research interests, the main pillars for the GXSLab, and the many opportunities that the GXSLab affords to young academics, we decided to develop a book by emerging scholars that could be used to shed light on an array of topics that deal with sports and social justice. "Gender Equity and Diversity: Challenging Narratives in Sport and Sport Media, Emerging Scholars Writing and Investigations" contributes upcoming voices with the hopes of expanding conversations in sport, sport media, and social justice to show just how these issues are being thought about and worked through by those newly entering the intersectional feminist sport media field.

Each author investigated and reflected on a key social justice issue related to sport and sport media. The authors turn to social media, traditional broadcast, and personal experiences to explore their areas of interest. The content of this book ranges from exploring and analyzing an individual athlete to Muslim sportswomen, leagues and teams, to autobiographical narratives. This critical social justice scholarship in sport and sport media offers a critique by young academics who are interested in pushing the status quo and shaking up the historical, social–cultural, and political foundations of sports locally, nationally, and globally.

In chapter one, *"Serving" Looks: An Investigation of Eugenie Bouchard's Self-Representation on Instagram*, Analisa Raimondo provides a case study of Canadian tennis player Eugenie Bouchard. Raimondo's chapter explores how Bouchard presents her feminine athletic identity on Instagram. Raimondo's chapter demonstrates tensions of agentic self-representation where dominant sociocultural ideals remain strong despite sportswomen bypassing media gatekeepers on social media.

Grace Esford pens chapter two titled *"Who Is the Purple-Haired Man?": Queer Erasure in Audience Sentiment toward Megan Rapinoe.* Esford examines online discourses that emerged from the comments section of a Guardian Football YouTube video featuring the United States Women's National Soccer athlete Megan Rapinoe. Esford unpacks the microaggressions, discrimination, and hate about Rapinoe that reinforce the dominance of heterosexuality and masculinity in sports.

Chapters three to five investigate Muslim sportswomen in sports and sport media. Sabrina Razack, Asma Khalil, and Hibaq Mohamed's chapter, *The In/Visibility of Black Muslim Sportswomen,* investigates the portrayal of Black Muslim sportswomen in the sport media landscape. Through an examination of feminist sport media texts, this chapter uncovers the intersectional relationship between racial identities and Muslim sportswomen. Laurel Walzak and Danica Vidotto write the next chapter, *Muslim Women's Experiences of Sport and Sport Culture in Toronto.* Walzak and Vidotto examine Muslim women's experiences participating as a Hijabi Baller, a Toronto local sports organization for Muslim women. Shireen Ahmed's chapter *We Are the Movement* examines how Muslim sportswomen can shift the dialogue and change the narratives about Muslim sportswomen in media. These chapters offer insight into an underserved, underrepresented, and "othered" cohort in the sporting world.

Chapter six, *An Investigation on How Women's Basketball in North America Has Been Silenced by the NBA and Men in the Sports Industry,* is written by Dana Daschuk. Her chapter explores gender equality and female representation in sport media by investigating the 2020 WNBA finals on traditional broadcast networks. Through an exploration of the quality of coverage and promotion of the WNBA by the NBA, Daschuk outlines the control and silencing of women's basketball.

Lydia Ferrari Kehoe writes chapter seven, *Where Equality Should Flow: Swimming as a Catalyst for Nongendered and Equality-Driven Media Coverage in Sport.* A national swimmer herself, Ferrari Kehoe's interest in the natural parity of swimming where athletes often compete and train side by side or consecutively has her exploring swimming as a potential way to promote equal and nongendered reporting in sport media.

Lastly, chapter eight, *The Ghost from Antigonish: The Social Construction of Disability in Our Nation* was written by Devin Gotell. In this personal reflection, Gotell explores his story as a three-time Paralympic swimmer. Gotell turns to Joseph Campbell's "Hero's Journey," or Monomyth, to "interrogate the ways in which disabled people are socially constructed in Canadian society." Gotell's personal narrative helps "humanize marginalized groups" in an attempt to "use the personal story as a tool to see how we are all connected."

FINAL THOUGHTS

These chapters were written by emerging scholars who are challenging norms and bringing a fresh perspective to the fifty-year history of sport media scholarship and the centuries of literature in sports. We hope that each chapter is able to provide you with newfound knowledge on the many areas that need to be addressed to achieve equity in sport. Our goal as feminist sport-based researchers is to continue to share the narratives of marginalized sporting communities. In doing so, we continue shaping discussions about who is welcomed and who is celebrated in sports with the intention of creating equitable sporting spaces for all. Learning from voices that have often been silenced, and in some cases that remain silent, is necessary to build an inclusive sporting culture where everyone is welcome.

CHAPTER 1

"Serving" Looks: An Investigation of Eugenie Bouchard's Self-Representation on Instagram

Analisa Raimondo

INTRODUCTION

In an age of Instagram "influencers" and internet celebrities, many female athletes are turning to social media as a way to further their careers and build a fan base. An "influencer" is a social media user who has gained a significant online following and leverages this online fame to make a profit. Although many influencers are popular because of their social media, celebrities and athletes use social media in a similar way. One such athlete, Eugenie Bouchard, has amassed a significant social media following and exemplifies the Instagram influencer lifestyle. Eugenie "Genie" Bouchard is a Canadian tennis player, who first rose to prominence in 2014 after advancing to the Wimbledon Final. Since her initial breakthrough performances, she has struggled to remain consistent and has fallen in the rankings. Despite these struggles, she has managed to remain relevant, as shown by her multitude of followers. Mainstream media storytellers, such as tabloids and sport news websites, acknowledge and even criticize her use of social media. Like many other female athletes, mainstream sport media representation of Bouchard undermines and trivializes her status both as an athlete and as a woman. This is a result of the dominant male perspective in the sport media industry; sport stories are told by White males to White males, leading to narratives that enforce masculine hegemony (Cooky, Messner, and Musto 2015). While the sport media industry undoubtedly focuses on male sports, there are women who have managed to be successful and receive media attention. However, they find themselves trying to simultaneously conform to traditional feminine ideals while embracing the traditionally masculine athleticism that is required to be a successful athlete. There is a lack of accurate and meaningful representation of female athletes in the mainstream media channels such as broadcast and print, and sportswomen continue to be marginalized in sport media.

The rise of social media, however, has allowed athletes to write their own stories, constructing and presenting their self-identities to the world without media gatekeepers. Sportswomen are able to share their participation in sport and sporting culture in ways that have the potential to challenge the mainstream sport media (Heinecken 2015). This idea goes beyond representation in sport media; the participatory nature of social media and the internet points toward changes in the way we as humans communicate (Barney et al. 2016). Despite a greater level of agency on social media platforms, female athletes are still subject to the dominant ideologies that are perpetuated by the male-dominated mainstream media. Female athletes, like Bouchard, face scrutiny for their use of social media. However, social platforms put more power into the hands of athletes themselves. This is important to consider because the ways in which female athletes exemplify hegemonic values in their own self-representation differs from how the mainstream media perpetuates them (Thorpe, Toffoletti, and Bruce 2017).

In this chapter, I analyze Bouchard's self-representation on Instagram and how it relates to and exemplifies various feminist theories. Using a feminist sport scholarship lens as well as third-wave and neoliberal feminist theories, I perform a qualitative analysis to highlight the recurring themes throughout Bouchard's Instagram posts. I explain how they both perpetuate and subvert the dominant perspectives that are a result of masculine hegemony in sport media. This chapter demonstrates the importance of self-representation and perspective in the media. Social media has given female athletes a platform to control their own representation and tell their own stories. By examining the self-representation of a prominent female athlete, I highlight how feminist discourses are adapting to accommodate the shift in representation that is caused by social media.

MASCULINE HEGEMONY

In order for female athletes to be represented meaningfully and accurately, stories need to be told from their perspective. This is not the case in the sport media industry, where masculine hegemony is perpetuated, and storytelling is dominated by the patriarchal White male perspective. Masculine hegemony refers to the ideologies that result in "male power and privilege in our society," including in sporting spaces (Fink 2015, 337). In a study examining coverage of women's sports, Cooky, Messner, and Musto (2015, 278–79) described the sport media industry as "a place set up by men to celebrate men's sensational athletic accomplishments." In televised sports news, mostly White men spend most of the time talking about men (Cooky, Messner, and Musto 2015). The content is not created by or for women. Sport media is a space where masculine hegemony prevails, and there is a severe lack of consideration of other perspectives. Men's sports are considered the default, and anything that challenges this default is treated as if it is different or unusual. When one considers that 95 percent of sports news anchors are male and that only 3.2 percent of coverage is dedicated to women's sports (Cooky, Messner, and Musto 2015), one finds it difficult to imagine accurate and thoughtful representations of sportswomen. Sportswomen continue to be underrepresented, and when their stories are told it is most likely not by someone who may have shared experiences with them. This leads to inaccurate representations of female athletes, perpetuating a lack of interest in women's sports.

This idea is described by Fink (2015, 336) as a "circular quality to the 'production-reception relationship,'" where consistent misrepresentation and low-quality content uphold the existing disinterest in women's sports. Women's sports get a lower quality of coverage than do men's sports, both in production and content, making the viewing experience less attractive to the viewer. Broadcasts for men's sports are often more engaging from a production standpoint and focus more on the sport itself than the athlete's personal lives, creating a more enjoyable experience for viewers (Fink 2015). When the quality of the coverage is not attractive to viewers, as is the case with many women's sports broadcasts, they are less likely to show interest, and this is used as justification to claim there is no market for women's sports (Cooky, Messner, and Hextrum 2013). This begins the circular process whereby women's sports continue to be undermined and underreported. Women's sports are not provided with the opportunity to succeed, and female athletes are not given a platform. The issues with this type of representation go beyond its effects on the perception of women's sports. The messaging of sport media is extremely significant because "the majority of coverage is located within the realm of *news* media, which is grounded in ideas of objectivity, impartiality, and balance" (Bruce 2012, 126). When audiences view and consume sport-related content, there is, to an extent, an assumption that some portion of what they are seeing is grounded in reality. Sport content is presented in a way that makes it appear unmediated (Bruce 2012). It is often presented in a similar style to news content, which means audiences are less likely to view it with a critical eye (Bruce 2012). Although audiences may differentiate opinion from fact, they may be unable to recognize issues surrounding representation and diversity. If the audience sees only men's sports, they may be less likely to question the lack of inclusion of women's sports and will continue to accept the hegemonic masculinity that they see (Bruce 2012). This lack of critical thought is what contributes to Fink's (2015) description of the circular process that leads to the continuous suppression of women's sports.

The portrayal of female athletes by the media is not representative of both their status as athletes and their status as women. Although the study by Cooky, Messner, and Musto (2015) found that over the past 25 years representations of female athletes are becoming less sexualized, other researchers (see MacPherson and Kerr 2020; Fink 2015; Bruce 2016) have continued to see one-dimensional portrayals of women. Thorpe, Toffoletti, and Bruce (2017) note that "when women's sport does receive media attention, female athletes are routinely aestheticized, sexualized and trivialized" (4). These portrayals undermine women's status as athletes and uphold masculine hegemony through standards that are not applied to men's sports. Furthermore, the aestheticization and sexualization of female athletes is indicative of efforts to control the narrative around them. By portraying female athletes as highly sexualized and aestheticized, the media is creating a standard that sportswomen may feel required to achieve to fit in.

FEMALE ATHLETE REPRESENTATION

The attempts by mainstream media to portray women as highly sexualized and aestheticized are evidence of what Clasen (2001, 36) describes as "a paradox grounded in traditional dualisms of Western culture." The female/athlete paradox is based on the idea that in Western culture, gender and sex are defined "along two overlapping dualisms: masculinity/femininity and male/female" (Clasen 2001, 36), where each is the counterpoint to the other. Masculine and feminine are seen as opposites to each other, as if the differences are Black and White. The issue with this line of thinking is that the assumption is created that "females will always be feminine while males will always be masculine" (Clasen 2001, 37), and there is no overlap between the two. It feeds into the cultural idea of the gender binary and forces athletes to embody either/or with strict expectations for each. When considering how this translates to sports, conceptions of traditional sports are almost always related to the ideas of masculinity in Western culture (Clasen 2001). The association between hegemonic masculinity and sports implies that one cannot be an athlete while embodying what is traditionally feminine. Female equals feminine, and athlete equals masculine; therefore one cannot be both female and an athlete. There are also further implications regarding the hierarchy of the binary; "male and masculine traits are typically defined as better than female and feminine characteristics" (Clasen 2001, 36). Portraying women as hyperfeminine is meant to undermine their status as athletes and trivialize their participation in sport. Many female athletes respond to the paradox by exemplifying it. To compensate for displaying traditionally masculine characteristics that are required to compete at the highest levels of sport, they embody traditionally feminine ideals (Clasen 2001). This idea is emphasized by Krane et al. (2004, 315), where female athletes "live in two cultures, the sport culture and their larger social culture, wherein social and sport ideals clash." In sport culture, sportswomen are expected to perform at high levels, thus exemplifying what is considered traditionally masculine. In social culture, and in the media, they are expected to adhere to traditional gender roles. This separation emphasizes the paradox. Neither identity coexists; they are separate cultures where women are expected to act a certain way.

Traditional expectations and ideals about femininity are exemplified in the mainstream media, but the rise of social media has caused a shift in discourses surrounding female athlete representation. In contrast to the *either/or* perspective created by the paradox, Bruce (2016, 368–69) presents the *both/and* approach that is embraced by third-wave feminists, with a discourse that revolves around the idea that female athletes can be both "pretty *and* powerful" and that neither is more acceptable than the other. A female athlete can compete at the highest levels of sport and still embrace her sexuality and femininity. *Pretty and powerful* and *both/and* discourses each consider that it is possible for self-representation to be both oppressive and empowering. However, they recognize that there is a degree of agency. There are still issues with the current ideas of representation; femininity functions as a tool that is still required in some sport spaces. Female athletes leverage their femininity and use it as "a resource to continue competing and maintain a public profile" (Bruce 2016, 369). However, it is important to recognize the existing structural and cultural barriers that are in place. As discussed earlier in this chapter, female sports are reported on and covered significantly less than their male counterparts. Mainstream media still continue to trivialize and misrepresent female athletes, but social and digital media are allowing female athletes to present themselves in a space where they have more control than they do in mainstream channels.

SOCIAL MEDIA AND REPRESENTATION

Social media has become a significant part of the sport media industry. It is a space where traditional sport content exists; however, it is also space where athletes are able to present themselves and construct their own identities. In contrast to traditional media, athletes can, to an extent, control the narrative around themselves and share their own perspectives. This change in the power dynamic, including female athletes "speaking their own sporting truths, and being able to communicate them widely, is a result of the exponential growth of internet use for communication and sharing" (Bruce 2016, 369). Sportswomen have created a space for themselves on social media, and they are leveraging this space and platform to further their careers. Thorpe, Toffoletti, and Bruce (2017) suggest that female athletes' use of social media allows them to bypass media gatekeepers and has the potential to challenge the hegemonic norms of the sport media industry. When female athletes have access to their own platforms, there is a way for them to share their perspectives and more accurate representations of sportswomen.

Social media's impact goes beyond female athlete representation; Baer (2015, 18) explains that digital media has "altered, influenced, and shaped feminism in the twenty-first century by giving rise to changing modes of communication [and] different kinds of conversations." Digital platforms provide a space for feminist discourse, through both discussion and self-representation. In what Baer (2015, 18–19) describes as a "provocative and risky space," the body is made significant through the "politicization of the personal." The body has always been discussed in feminist activism. However social media has increased its significance. Instead of traditional forms of media, the body is shared from the perspective of women themselves. Their own choices about how to present their body can be seen as a form of resistance (Baer 2015). Whether female's online identities are ambivalent sharing or intentional resistance, the discourse centres around personal perspectives instead of constructed messaging from the mainstream media. But digital platforms are also paradoxical; although they are a site of empowerment and self-representation, they are also a site of surveillance. Although social media allows female athletes to have choice and agency when presenting themselves, they are still performing and being observed. This idea is most notably presented by Butler (1988, 520), where gender and gender identity are a "performative accomplishment compelled by social sanction." Butler, and other feminist theorists, distinguish between biological sex and gender. Gender is constructed on the basis of sociocultural ideas and is not strictly dictated by biological sex. When female athletes are presenting themselves on social media, many still maintain traditional gender constructs because social media is a site of surveillance. The digital space is still one where they are watched, and it does not exist separately from social culture.

It is important to consider how female athletes are presenting themselves when engaging in discourse regarding female athletic "empowerment" because despite a lack of mediated constructions they are still subject to cultural ideologies (Meân and Kassing 2008). The hegemonic values that are perpetuated by the male-dominated, mainstream media still occupy digital spaces. Research conducted by MacPherson and Kerr (2020, 5) found that through social media, athletes face "online public shaming" as a response to their transgressions, where fan comments directed to female athletes centred around objectification of females and are grounded in hegemonic masculinity. Social media allows for two-way communication, so it is not unlikely to expect fan response; however, this study shows that these responses are gendered. In many cases, negative responses to female athletes are much more likely to be sexual, whereas negative responses to male athletes reinforce traditional notions of masculinity (MacPherson and Kerr 2020).

Many sportswomen, like Bouchard, have amassed a significant following on social platforms. They have "the chance to control their own content and engage the passion of their fans, creating communities of interest," where they demonstrate an interest in both their personal and their professional lives (Bruce 2012, 133). Having a large following on social platforms is indicative of interest in an athlete and could potentially prove to mainstream media gatekeepers that there is an interest in female athletes and women's sports (Bruce 2012). The mainstream media now recognize social and digital media as a legitimate source of news and information sharing (Lowrey and Mackay 2008). Recognition of the online communities built by female athletes could lead toward more representation of women's sports in the mainstream media. These spaces are still largely male dominated, but they indicate that it is possible for women's sports to attract an audience. Additionally, there is the potential for female athletes to profit from the increased interest shown by their followings, through sponsorships and brand deals. The increased control that is afforded by social media means female athletes are the ones benefiting from their representation, instead of those who are in control of the mainstream media. This type of freedom is favoured by neoliberal feminism. Neoliberal feminism advocates for agency and independence, including from an economic standpoint (Thorpe, Toffoletti, and Bruce 2017). Women who are independently financially successful are seen to have overcome societal barriers that are caused by masculine hegemony. Female athletes who use social media are seen to be gaining independence from the mainstream media, regardless of how their representation is affected by social culture.

EUGENIE BOUCHARD

Eugenie Bouchard is a 26-year-old Canadian White, cis-gender, tennis player. Throughout her career, she has struggled with consistency and faced some difficulty. Her career-high world ranking of No.5 in 2014 came after advancing to the Wimbledon Final and two other Grand Slam semifinals but has since experienced a decline in success. Various factors contributed to her loss of form, including a concussion (and subsequent lawsuit), which, by 2018, had left her out of the top 100 rankings for the first time since 2013. Since then, she has continued to have mixed results: 2019 saw a 13-game losing streak and a No. 262 ranking by the end of the season. She finished the shortened 2020 season on an upswing but failed to qualify for any of the high-ranking tournaments. Despite her fall from the top, Bouchard has managed to remain in the public eye.

Bouchard's sustained fame has been achieved largely through the significant social media presence she holds across platforms such as Instagram, Facebook, and Twitter. On her personal Instagram account, she has shared over 1,000 posts and has amassed over 2 million followers (@geniebouchard). She uses this account as a space to share content from both her on and off-court life and engage with her fans. Bouchard's use of Instagram is similar to how many other female athletes use social media. Many female athletes employ social media strategies that emphasize their "athleticism, bodily confidence, an exotic lifestyle" in a manner similar to that of an Instagram influencer (Thorpe, Toffoletti, and Bruce 2017, 9). Bouchard's status as an Instagram influencer points toward a shift in representation of female athletes caused by social media. Sport and athletic performance are no longer the sole way to gain or maintain a following. As seen in Figure 1, Bouchard presents both tennis- and nontennis-related content. Pictures of her training on the tennis court or holding a tennis racquet are spread throughout photos of her posing, selfies, and branded content. Despite the varying content, her profile describes her as an "Athlete" with no mention of any other identity.

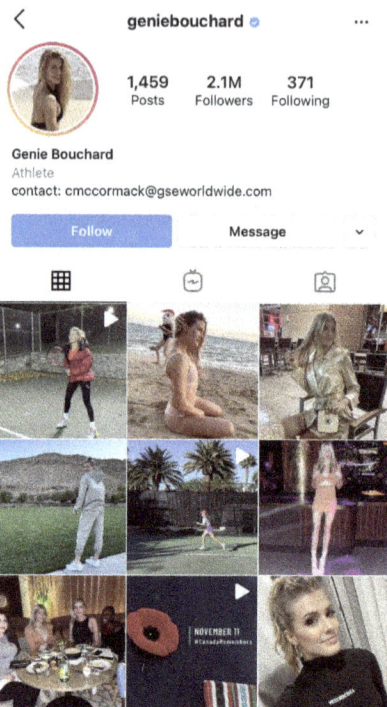

Figure 1: Screenshot of Genie Bouchard's Public Instagram Account
Source: Bouchard's Instagram (Taken December 7, 2020a)

It is important to note that Bouchard fits into the ideal standard of Euro-Western beauty. Euro-Western beauty idealizes thin, White, heterosexual, and often blonde women who perform femininity. Although Bouchard faces difficulties as a female athlete in a male-dominated landscape, her experiences likely differ from those who do not conform to the traditional ideals of beauty and femininity. Female athletes who do fit into idealized beauty are more likely to be economically successful and popular than those who do not (Barnett 2013). A significant amount of existing research concerning women in sports revolves around White women, who are seen as the "default." However, it is because this is what has been deemed acceptable by media producers and audiences (Bruce 2015). Despite fitting the ideal, Bouchard still finds it challenging to use social media to represent herself. In an August 2020 interview with *TENNIS.com*, she explained she felt the need to stop posting pictures of herself in a bikini because of backlash from fans and followers. Bouchard explained that she has received criticism for her bikini posts, stating "apparently if you post that, it means you don't play tennis or something" (*TENNIS.com* 2020). Although she does not explicitly mention it, she is conflicted about how to represent herself as both female/feminine and athletic. Since she does receive avid attention in the mainstream media, she has become aware of how she is perceived.

Additionally, social media allows for two-way communication. Bouchard receives comments from fans and social media "trolls" directly on her Instagram posts. A study by MacPherson and Kerr (2020) found that Bouchard faces online harassment, and a significant amount of it is sexual. After a poor on-court performance, followers responded by telling her to "retire from tennis and do porn" or "go for modelling [because] tennis is meant for hard workers" (MacPherson and Kerr 2020, 5). Bouchard is often sexualized in the mainstream media, and these responses may be a result of media representations of her. Throughout Bouchard's career, she has been the topic of discussion in many tabloids, where her body, personal life, romantic relationships, and tennis performance are scrutinized. Bouchard has appeared in the *Sports Illustrated* Swimsuit Issue twice, in 2017 and 2018. The "Swimsuit Issue" is dedicated to showcasing celebrities, athletes, and models wearing swimwear, often posing provocatively in a display of heterosexiness. However, fan reactions seem to differ when Bouchard herself shares content via social media. Considering that she has spoken about facing criticism on Instagram, I would argue that Bouchard's own representation is affected by the ideas perpetuated by the mainstream media.

METHODOLOGY

This chapter examines how Bouchard's Instagram self-representation tactics subvert and perpetuate the dominant perspectives that are present in the male-dominated sport media industry. I employ a qualitative virtual ethnographic approach to collecting and analyzing the digital artifacts. A virtual ethnography privileges an understanding of the individual in context with society (Creswell 2013) and, specifically, transcending the physical world to the digital world (Hine 2000). In this way, I attempt to make sense of Bouchard's life through her social media profile. Thinking alongside Markham (2005, 795), I use the photographic and digital text on Bouchard's social media to understand how Bouchard "perform[s] and negotiate[s] the self." Data was collected through images, videos, comments, and captions. I looked at Bouchard's Instagram posts from September, October, and November 2020. During this time, Bouchard posted 24 times. I considered each of these posts, first, by separating the posts into tennis and nontennis content and, then, by noting the content and captions. All posts during this time were considered, and I present those that best exemplify the themes patterns that I found in Bouchard's posts.

I analyze how Bouchard uses Instagram as a tool for her self-representation, as well as if and how Bouchard's self-representation reflects the dominant ideologies that are perpetuated by the mainstream media. Using a feminist sports scholarship lens, I examined the overall patterns and types of content Bouchard posted to understand how she negotiates with and constructs her self-representation. I then explored the recurring ideas throughout her posts and how they contribute to and can be analyzed using the theories and discourses presented throughout this chapter. Using the "pretty and powerful" discourse theories of Bruce (2016), I complicate and contextualize the meaning of Bouchard's self-representation. Analyzing Bouchard's Instagram profile is a way to understand how self-representation is influenced by and differs from traditionally mediated representations of female athletes and the resulting ideologies.

FINDINGS

As mentioned previously, Bouchard's Instagram page merges tennis-related content with lifestyle content. For the purpose of this study, tennis content is qualified as all posts relating to Bouchard's training and on-court content, whereas everything else is considered non-tennis related. There is a relatively even split between the two types of content; she tends to make multiple posts for each tournament, which counterbalances the non-tennis-related content. The tennis content is a mixture of on-court action shots, videos of training, and posed photos on or around the court. She shares the ups and downs of her career, often including playful, self-deprecating captions. This can be seen as a way for her to delegitimize herself as an athlete. She is putting herself down, both when sharing tennis and nontennis content, and undermining her own status as both an athlete and a feminine-performing woman. This is similar to some media representations of women; mainstream media representations of female athletes trivialize their athletic accomplishments and their status as women (Clasen 2001; Thorpe, Toffoletti, and Bruce 2017). Perhaps Bouchard's self-deprecating captions are her response to how the traditional media represents her. Although her captions come across as fun or sarcastic, they are suggestive of her lack of confidence in her own abilities and avoidance of presenting herself as too serious or too arrogant.

The tennis content comes across less as a serious recounting of events and more as casual sharing. The off-court content is varied; she documents many different aspects of her personal life, posting selfies, photos with friends and family, sharing her glamorous lifestyle, and the occasional beach or poolside bikini photo. Additionally, throughout the personal and athletic content, she posts sponsored advertisements. The time between advertisements varies, but they are not worked directly into her regular postings. They stand out as carefully composed messages with obvious product placement. The captions are written to carefully describe the product but sometimes feature comments that come across as more organic, such as mentioning how "cute" the colour of a product is (Bouchard 2020c). Additionally, every sponsored post uses the hashtag "ad" to disclose and differentiate between her own content.

Beyond a general analysis of the types of Instagram posts that Bouchard makes, I found significant recurring themes, the main ones being: (1) Bouchard consistently performs femininity both in her tennis and non-tennis posts. (2) She uses her femininity as a resource to remain relevant and capitalize on her persona. (3) She uses her Instagram as a "tool" to prove she is an athlete through an emphasis of her muscularity and documentation of tennis tournaments and practice. Through these findings, it becomes evident that Bouchard does negotiate with her femininity through self-representation.

Performing Femininity

Throughout most of her Instagram posts, Bouchard exemplifies heterosexual femininity. As discussed earlier in this chapter, Bouchard fits into the ideal beauty standards. Although she does share content related to her athleticism, many of her posts highlight her feminine physique and feature her posing for the camera. Often, the backgrounds of the photos showcase her luxurious lifestyle and activities, but most of the time she is meant to be the primary subject of the photo. She frequently posts casual "selfies" in which she directly looks into the camera in practiced manners. Many of these photos are performances of "heterosexiness," where she conforms to traditional gender representations. Bouchard has admitted to trying to refrain from posting "butt pictures" (*TENNIS.com* 2020) yet still dresses in trendy, feminine outfits. In a post from October 24, 2020, she can be seen smiling, wearing a short satin dress, carefully posed in front of the camera. She is not being provocative but is performing femininity by dressing in traditionally feminine ways, emphasizing her slender frame.

Additionally, many of her on-court photos do not highlight her athleticism through pictures and videos of her playing or action shots. She can be seen leaning on the net smiling, standing with her tongue sticking out in a joking manner, or simply posing directly for the camera. I would argue that her Instagram page is not meant to be a serious representation of her tennis career. Although she does share tennis-related content, her Instagram brand aligns more closely with what is traditionally expected of female athletes. The focus is more on social culture and her luxurious lifestyle than on her athletic career.

Femininity as a Resource

Bouchard's regular posting has allowed her to amass over 2 million Instagram followers despite her lacklustre career. Although she does receive attention for her tennis-related posts, she has created a separate brand to showcase her lifestyle in a similar fashion to Instagram "influencers." Her online persona is not meant to represent her athleticism; instead, she is diversifying her appeal by emphasizing her own femininity and creating an idealized image of herself. She is embracing Instagram as a platform and a tool to increase her popularity. Her personal branding has kept her in the public eye; despite her lack of success in tennis, she remained relevant by employing tactics that offered the potential for an audience regardless of her status as an athlete. These tactics, mainly her emphasized femininity and glamorous lifestyle, create an appeal that extends beyond her on-court performance and has become a significant part of her career.

Bouchard is able to directly capitalize on her Instagram persona through sponsored "brand deals." Brand deals are a method of influencer marketing; brands approach influencers to post about their products and services. Influencer marketing has become a significant aspect of the marketing industry, as internet celebrities continue to sustain their popularity and influence (Hudders, De Jans, and De Veirman 2020). In Bouchard's case, brands are paying for their product or service to be showcased in a post to her some two million followers in hopes that she will influence them to purchase. Some of these brand deals, such as energy drinks, are relevant to her athleticism. Others, however, are more closely related to the Instagram influencer persona she has created, such as dating apps and electronic toothbrushes. Regardless of the content of these posts, they are a result of the following she has gained as a result of her online persona.

Instagram as a Validation "Tool"

Although Bouchard performs femininity, she also uses her social media account to reaffirm her status as a professional athlete. Her content adheres largely to traditional gender roles, but she still displays athleticism and performs in ways that are seen as traditionally masculine. One post, where she can be seen midmovement with her muscles flexed, uses the hashtag "grinding" (Bouchard 2020b). She is drawing attention to the fact that she is still working and competing. This post highlights her muscular physique and athletic skill, contrasting with the previously discussed posts in which the tennis court is simply another backdrop for a posed photo. She also contrasts traditional femininity and masculinity within individual posts. In a post from November 13, 2020, she is seen leaning against a counter, laughing. She is wearing a form-fitting dress, a full face of makeup, and her long blonde hair hangs down her chest. In this pose, her muscular legs are revealed and pointed toward the camera. In the caption, she points this out saying, "yes i'm flexing my quads so what" (Bouchard 2020d). In a somewhat self-deprecating manner, she is intentionally highlighting her own muscularity. At the same time, she is implying that it requires an effort for her to present herself as athletic and muscular.

In addition to posts highlighting her muscularity, she documents some of her practice and training. She posts videos of her working on skills and action shows, as well as posed photos where the captions specify she was at practice. These photos, in a way, prove that she is working hard to improve her skills. As mentioned earlier, she has faced criticism for her frequent Instagram posts, but photos of her practicing function as proof that she is still dedicated to tennis. These posts contrast with her nontennis content, where her femininity is often highlighted and further emphasize Bouchard's attempts to negotiate her self-representation.

DISCUSSION

The findings noted in the foregoing indicate that although Bouchard presents both traditionally masculine and feminine characteristics, she faces difficulty with her own representation. Her efforts to explicitly reference both her athleticism and femininity exemplify many of the issues related to the female/athlete paradox. She performs femininity in most of her Instagram posts; however, her deliberate attempts to present her more masculine characteristics (e.g., muscular quadriceps) suggest that she is struggling to fit into the sporting space. This may be a result of her struggling career, but it is also partially a result of her performing hegemonic femininity. This is an example of the female athlete paradox at play. However, in many cases, female athletes feel they must compensate for masculinity by performing hyperfemininity (Hardy 2015). Bouchard does the opposite; she emphasizes her muscularity in order to reaffirm her status as an athlete.

The discussion surrounding female athlete representation has become paradoxical in itself. Attempts to subvert the female/athlete paradox by showing that women can possess traditionally masculine traits undermine those who choose to and want to present as feminine. This discourse feeds into the hierarchy that is implied by the dualisms of femininity and masculinity (Clasen 2001), thus perpetuating the idea that female and feminine are somehow less desirable than masculinity. Female athletes like Bouchard who choose to embrace their own femininity should not be criticized simply because their self-representation aligns with social norms. This view fails to recognize that there is a level of agency when self-representing (Bruce 2016). Assuming that all female athletes who embrace their femininity feel obligated or required to do so undermines their own agency, as if they are more oppressed or not "woke." Although it is possible that Bouchard feels compelled to perform a certain way, she still chooses what she shares with her followers. Additionally, placing blame on female-presenting athletes fails to acknowledge the broader social structures and ideologies that may lead to their feeling obligated to perform in such a way. Embracing masculinity entirely can also be disempowering because it limits femininities (Dworkin and Messner 2002), once again implying that there is something inherently wrong with femininity. Even if the criticism is because performing femininity is a result of social norms, in order to subvert the female/athlete paradox the discourse around female athlete representation must shift to be accepting of all types of self-representation.

It is evident that Bouchard does exemplify the "pretty and powerful" discourse presented by Bruce (2015). She is challenged by her own representation, but she also embraces her femininity and sexuality while competing at a high athletic level. Her career performance is not exceptional, but she is still a professional athlete. The "pretty and powerful" discourse also embraces the both/and perspective favoured by third-wave feminists. Bouchard's femininity can be seen as both empowering and oppressive. She perpetuates the social norms caused by hegemonic masculinity but does so in a way that presents her femininity as a positive part of her identity. Her own representation differs from the mainstream media because she controls the narrative. She curates each post to create her own image.

Social media allows athletes to have more control of their own image. Bouchard uses her femininity as a resource to remain relevant. The online persona she embodies allowed her to retain a following despite her struggling career. Instead of relying on the mainstream media to stay in the public eye, she was able to do so herself. Even though her self-sexualization and hyperfemininity can be seen as oppressive because she is able to capitalize on it herself, it differs from mainstream media representation. This idea aligns with neoliberal feminism, which places an emphasis on women who are economically successful (Thorpe, Toffoletti, and Bruce 2017). In Bouchard's case, she capitalizes directly on her femininity through sponsored posts. This is a direct result of the power social media affords female athletes when they control the channels of their representation. Bouchard has sponsorships related to her athletic performance, but these sponsored posts are a result of the personal brand she created using social media. However, this is also a result of the privilege afforded to female athletes who present as feminine and fit into traditional beauty standards. Female athletes who are masculine perceived are "labeled as social deviants" and are thus unable to benefit from positive media attention and sponsorships (Krane et al. 2004, 316). Bouchard capitalizing on her ideal femininity without acknowledging her privilege perpetuates this, which is another way her self-representation is both oppressive and empowering. Her use of social media elevates herself, and those who also embody ideal femininity, but it does not change the perceptions of female athletes regardless of how they choose to present.

CONCLUSION

This chapter provides an example of a female athlete who is using social media to negotiate with her own representation. As the discourse surrounding female athletes shifts to consider how social media affects and alters representation, it is important to look to the athletes themselves to understand exactly how representation is changing. In a media landscape where female athletes are not given equal representation, social media stands out as a place where they can make their voices heard and construct their own identities and stories.

In this chapter, I consider how Bouchard's self-representation relates to third-wave and neoliberal feminist theories, as well as how she reflects dominant sociocultural ideologies. Bouchard exemplifies the "pretty and powerful" discourse presented by Bruce (2016) and in some ways subverts the female/athlete paradox. She is able to control what she posts and the narrative around herself. But despite her increased agency when posting on social media such as Instagram, I would argue that Bouchard is still largely influenced by dominant sociocultural ideas. Although she does exemplify the "pretty and powerful" discourse, my research indicated that Bouchard uses social media as a way to validate herself as both feminine and an athlete. On Instagram she performs femininity, uses her femininity as a resource, and validates her athleticism. These efforts to directly reference both her femininity and athleticism indicate that she is aware of how she is perceived online and in the media. She demonstrates some of the issues related to the female/athlete paradox. Although many female athletes feel they must compensate for their traditionally masculine characteristics by performing hyperfemininity (Hardy 2015), Bouchard instead compensates for her femininity by highlighting her muscularity and athleticism.

Despite the challenges Bouchard and many other female athletes face when trying to self-represent on social media, it is still valuable because they are given a tool to share their own stories. Female athletes are largely underrepresented in the mainstream media (Cooky, Messner, and Musto 2015), so social media is one of the ways in which they can gain recognition from mainstream audiences. Social media is still subject to hegemonic masculine ideologies, but there is an increased level of agency. Bouchard has built a large following and is able to capitalize on her followers through sponsorships and brand deals. This type of financial success, which is favoured by neoliberal feminists, would not be possible without the increased agency that is afforded by social media. Female athletes face many challenges around their representation, but social media is pointing toward a shifting media landscape. Bouchard is one of many female athletes who is finding a platform and sharing her unique perspective.

REFERENCES

Baer, Hester. 2015. "Redoing Feminism: Digital Activism, Body Politics, and Neoliberalism." *Feminist Media Studies* 16 (1): 17–34. http://doi.org/10.1080/14680777.2015.1093070.

Barnett, Barbara. 2013. "The Babe/Baby Factor: Sport, Women, and Mass Media." In *Routledge Handbook of Sport Communication*, edited by Paul M. Pedersen, 350–58. London: Routledge. https://doi.org/10.4324/9780203123485.ch35.

Barney, Darin, Gabriella Coleman, Christine Ross, Jonathan Sterne, and Tamar Tembeck, eds. 2016. *The Participatory Condition in the Digital Age*, vii–xxxix. Minneapolis: University of Minnesota Press. http://www.jstor.org/stable/10.5749/j.ctt1ggjkfg.

Bouchard, Eugenie (@geniebouchard). 2020a. "Genie Bouchard." Instagram profile, December 7, 2020. https://instagram.com/geniebouchard/.

———. 2020b. "k where's the baseline to #grinding." Instagram photo, September 14, 2020. https://www.instagram.com/p/CFIJzeiJ_eb/.

———. 2020c. "My morning routine always starts with." Instagram photo, September 2, 2020. https://www.instagram.com/p/CEoyxwIJJLP/.

———. 2020d. "yes i'm flexing my quads so what." Instagram photo, November 13, 2020. https://www.instagram.com/p/CHjMMhvr8Kc/.

Bruce, Toni. 2012. "Reflections on Communication and Sport: On Women and Femininities." *Communication & Sport* 1 (1–2): 125–37. https://doi.org/10.1177/2167479512472883.

———. 2015. "Assessing the Sociology of Sport: On Media and Representations of Sportswomen." *International Review for the Sociology of Sport* 50 (4–5): 380–84. https://doi.org/10.1177/1012690214539483.

———. 2016. "New Rules for New Times: Sportswomen and Media Representation in the Third Wave." *Sex Roles* 74 (7): 361–76. https://doi.org/10.1007/s11199-015-0497-6.

Butler, Judith. 1988. "Performative Acts and Gender Constitution: An Essay in Phenomenology and Feminist Theory." *Theatre Journal* 40 (4): 519–31. https://doi.org/10.2307/3207893.

Clasen, Patricia R. W. 2001. "The Female Athlete: Dualisms and Paradox in Practice." *Women and Language* 24 (2): 36–41.

Cooky, Cheryl, Michael A. Messner, and Robin Hextrum. 2013. "Women Play Sport, But Not on TV: A Longitudinal Study of Televised News Media." *Communication & Sport* 1 (3): 203–30. https://doi.org/10.1177/2167479513476947.

Cooky, Cheryl, Michael A. Messner, and Michela Musto. 2015. " 'It's Dude Time!': A Quarter Century of Excluding Women's Sports in Televised News and Highlight Shows." *Communication & Sport* 3 (3): 261–87. https://doi.org/10.1177/2167479515588761.

Creswell, John W. 2013. *Qualitative Inquiry & Research Design: Choosing among Five Approaches*. Los Angeles: Sage.

Dworkin, Shari L., and Michael A. Messner. 2002. "Introduction: Gender Relations and Sport." *Sociological Perspectives* 45 (4): 347–52. https://doi.org/10.1525/sop.2002.45.4.347.

Fink, Janet S. 2015. "Female Athletes, Women's Sport, and the Sport Media Commercial Complex: Have We Really 'Come a Long Way, Baby'?" *Sport Management Review* 18 (3): 331–42. https://doi.org/10.1016/j.smr.2014.05.001.

Hardy, Elizabeth. 2015. "The Female 'Apologetic' Behaviour within Canadian Women's Rugby: Athlete Perceptions and Media Influences." *Sport in Society* 18 (2): 155–67. http://doi.org/10.1080/17430437.2013.854515.

Heinecken, Dawn. 2015. "So Tight in the Thighs, So Loose in the Waist." *Feminist Media Studies* 15 (6): 1035–52. https://doi.org/10.1080/14680777.2015.1033638.

Hine, Christine. 2000. *Virtual Ethnography*. London: Sage.

Hudders, Liselot, Steffi De Jans, and Marijke De Veirman. 2020. "The Commercialization of Social Media Stars: A Literature Review and Conceptual Framework on the Strategic Use of Social Media Influencers." *International Journal of Advertising* 40 (3): 327–75. https://doi.org/10.1080/02650487.2020.1836925.

Krane, Vikki, Precilla Choi, Shannon Baird, and Kerrie Kauer. 2004. "Living the Paradox: Female Athletes Negotiate Femininity and Muscularity." *Sex Roles* 50 (5/6): 315–29. https://doi.org/10.1023/B:SERS.0000018888.48437.4f.

Lowrey, Wilson, and Jenn Burleson Mackay. 2008. "Journalism and Blogging." *Journalism Practice* 2 (1): 64–81. https://doi.org/10.1080/17512780701768527.

MacPherson, Ellen, and Gretchen Kerr. 2020. "Online Public Shaming of Professional Athletes: Gender Matters." *Psychology of Sport and Exercise* 51. https://doi.org/10.1016/j.psychsport.2020.101782.

Markham, Annette. 2005. "The Methods, Politics, and Ethics of Representation in Online Ethnography." In *The Sage Handbook of Qualitative Research*, edited by Norman K. Denzin and Yvonna S. Lincoln. 3rd ed. Thousand Oaks, CA: Sage.

Meân, Lindsey J., and Jeffrey W. Kassing. 2008. " 'I Would Just Like to Be Known as an Athlete': Managing Hegemony, Femininity, and Heterosexuality in Female Sport." *Western Journal of Communication* 72 (2): 126–44. https://doi.org/10.1080/10570310802038564.

Pantic, Nina, and Eugenie Bouchard. 2020. "Genie Bouchard on Making the Most of Her Opportunities." *TENNIS.com* Podcast, August 2020. https://open.spotify.com/episode/6G6Ordc4pc8FC9HsC9Fv7G?si=k-Oh4fkdSBCWQwvKfms-9Q.

Thorpe, Holly, Kim Toffoletti, and Toni Bruce. 2017. "Sportswomen and Social Media: Bringing Third-Wave Feminism, Postfeminism, and Neoliberal Feminism into Conversation." *Journal of Sport and Social Issues* 41 (5): 359–83. shttps://doi.org/10.1177/0193723517730808.

"Who Is the Purple-Haired Man?": Queer Erasure in Audience Sentiment toward Megan Rapinoe

Grace Esford

INTRODUCTION

At the conclusion of the 2019 Fédération Internationale de Football Association (FIFA) Women's World Cup match, chants of "equal pay" echoed from the crowd in the Parc Olympique Lyonnais stadium in France. The United States of America (USA) captured their fourth World Cup title with a 2–0 win over the Netherlands. With an attendance of 57,900 (FIFA 2019b) people and viewership at an "average live audience of 82.18 million" (FIFA 2019a), all eyes were undoubtedly on the United States Women's National Team (USWNT). This action from the crowd made headlines and contributed to the social movement that the USWNT squad would harness in the face of their ongoing equal pay for equal play lawsuit with the United States Soccer Federation (U.S. Soccer).

The figurehead of this global sports movement centred on equal pay for equal play was the previous co-captain of the USWNT Megan Rapinoe. Rapinoe was born in Redding, California, on July 5, 1985. Her rise to soccer stardom began with being a tri-sport athlete in high school, running track and playing basketball, but her main talent was on the soccer pitch. After significant success in college at the University of Portland, Rapinoe had stints at a variety of professional clubs, such as the Chicago Red Stars of the Women's Professional Soccer, Sydney Football Club in Australia's W-League, Seattle Sounders Women in the Women's Professional Soccer League, and Olympique Lyonnais before settling with Seattle Reign in 2013, which is where she has played since. Her international career with Team USA has been most notable, playing for the senior national team in the 2009 and 2013 Algarve Cups (*Sports Illustrated* 2013), the 2012 Summer Olympics in London (Rapinoe 2012), and the 2015 and 2019 FIFA World Cups (U.S. Soccer 2021).

Adding to numerous wins and accolades, the 2019 FIFA World Cup Tournament saw Rapinoe capture not only a gold medal with the team, but also the World Cup Final Player of the Match, the Golden Boot award for top goal scorer in the tournament, and the Golden Ball award voted on by a variety of media representatives. In showing resilience throughout her career by overcoming injuries and in her activism for women and lesbian, gay, bisexual, pansexual, transgender, genderqueer, queer, intersex, agender, asexual and other queer-identifying (LGBTQIA+) individuals, Rapinoe has established herself as a cultural icon and the centre of the USWNT's sport media profile in their fight for equal pay.

This chapter will focus on Guardian Football's YouTube video titled *Megan Rapinoe on Equal Pay, Celebrating in the USA and Winning the Women's World Cup* posted on July 8, 2019. In the fifty-second video clip, Rapinoe discusses her excitement to return to the USA after the USWNT's time in France and reflects on the crowd chanting "equal pay" during the final match. Her lasting impression was that the chorus "went so far beyond anything sport" (Guardian Football 2019). The subsequent online discourse that emerged in the comment section of this video contributes to the promotion of hegemonic masculinity in sport media, leading to queer erasure in the contemporary context on the popular social media platform. Queer erasure is an embedded hostility toward and omission of the queer experience based on the priority of heteronormative Euro-Western culture. This comes in the form of "homophobia and transphobia, as well as heterosexism" (Lugg 2015, 94). In relation to queer erasure in public school, which acts as an example of larger societal reasoning, Lugg (2015, 94) explains:

> While homophobia and transphobia are the overt suppression of, and violence against, queer identity and queer information, heterosexism is a more subtle form of bias. Heterosexism merely assumes everyone in the public school building is non-queer and gender-conforming—without question. More simply, homophobia and transphobia are biases with a fist; heteronormativity is bias with a smile.

Queer erasure has taken on a variety of meanings during different political climates, from experiencing police repression and urban planning aimed at gentrification beginning in the 1970s (Rosenthal 2017) to facing biases when search engines are positioned to filter out positive LGBTQIA+ material in the 2010s (Anderson and Roth 2020). For this content analysis, the ensuing echo chamber in the comment sections that contribute to erasing of the LGBTQIA+ experience means that queer perspectives are hidden, with the potential for YouTube's popularity metrics to camouflage diverse voices altogether.

Disguised as statements opposing equal pay, the sentiments from commenters uphold a gender hierarchy in sport media with an emphasis on what Bruce (2015) calls appropriate femininity and heteronormativity. When aspects like microaggressions, homophobia, and misgendering occur, queer erasure is supported and allows commenters to symbolically annihilate (Tuchman, Daniels, and Benét 1978) queer representation in sport media. This case study is important because it highlights hegemonic masculinity as still being embedded in sport media. The microaggressions toward Rapinoe in the comment section of YouTube videos are situated in appropriate femininity, namely, that sports are a man's world and that compulsory heterosexuality is required if a female athlete is to be included in sport media. These tactics have come to form an "appropriate" female soccer player, leaving no space for athletes who do not embody an "idealized femininity."

When YouTube viewer comments emerge that target Rapinoe in sexist and homophobic ways, commenting on her appearance as different from the norm and misgendering her, the equal pay debate becomes a vehicle for these negative comments to emerge. The comments are largely situated in gender discrimination and hate and are not at all about the content of the video in question. The cause of equal pay and women's place in sports is used as a scapegoat to erase Rapinoe from sport media.

The Hegemonic Masculinity of Sport Media

Defining Queer

As a starting point to define queer in this chapter, Jagose's (1996) definition offers insight into the destabilization of societal structure that queerness embodied. In this reading, queer is "those gestures or analytical modes which dramatize incoherence in the allegedly stable relations between chromosomal sex, gender and sexual desire" (Jagose 1996, 3). Weston (1993, 348) explains that queer "defines itself by its difference from hegemonic ideologies of gender and sexuality." The importance of difference in the term queer centres on what Warner (1991, xxvi) attributes to an act of defying "the regimes of the normal."

Despite these interpretations, establishing a definition for the word queer may be contradictory to the word itself. Halperin (1995) argues that the more queer and queer studies are normalized within academic institutions, the further it moves from being queer. Butler (1994, 21), too, signalled that "normalizing the queer would be, after all, its sad finish." However, creating a foundation for how this word will be used in this chapter is of importance.

To define the use of queer in this chapter, Carter and Baliko's (2017) attribution of queer will be used. This definition positions queer as an all-encompassing term that goes on to include individuals who "identify as lesbian, gay, genderqueer, two-spirit bisexual, intersex and trans" (Carter and Baliko 2017, 697). Despite the intent of this term being used as a means to include all individuals in a diverse and nonheterosexual way, it is acknowledged that it can result in dismissing and rendering insignificant the multitudes of lived experiences and the differences in the expression of sexual or gender identity. The term "queer" is used to encapsulate "practices, acts, or as speech, and as representations bodies that do not signify 'normal'" (Eng 2006, 52).

Situated in the focus on binaries in Western society (Derrida and Bass 1981) with a gender hierarchy established between male and female, females are always positioned in response to the leading term ("male") and become derivative through this established binary opposition (Scott 1986, 37). As a result of such binaries, the hierarchy of sexuality is established in Euro-Western society and places anyone who deviates from monogamous, heterosexual relationships to be nonnormative. Even with this grounding in Western culture, Katz (1995) notes that heterosexuality is dependent on homosexuality in order to reinforce its position of privilege in society.

The Invisibility of Queerness

Gender marking is involved with queer erasure when individuals who may not externally embody binary gender stereotypes are incorrectly gendered. The blatant disrespect for individuals who do not identify as cisgender is enacted across sport media and is embodied within the comment section of the video in this analysis. Compulsory heterosexuality contributes to queer erasure through the pairing of gender and sexuality. With the prioritization of heterosexual athletes throughout sport media, this leaves no room for queer individuals to exist in this area of culture. With appropriate femininity (Bruce 2015) coupled with compulsory heterosexuality, this indicates that when women are featured in sport media, preference is given to athletes that align with White heterosexual feminine stereotypes (Bruce 2015). In soccer, this is the unwritten visual code of the girl-next-door look: high ponytails, thin, and White (Bremner 2002; Cavalier and Newhall 2018; Schultz 2014; Shugart 2003). This stereotype of an idealized female soccer player can be seen in mainstream media and films like *She's the Man* and *Bend It Like Beckham*.

This teams up with compulsory heterosexuality to instill a reading of female athletes in the gendered roles of trophy or motherhood in addition to athletes. But first and foremost, they are female, and gender expectations accompany their position in sports. With this perspective, people who are Black, Indigenous, and people of colour (BIPOC), queer, or disabled are repeatedly unwelcomed while sport media "continue to privilege a narrative that favours [w]hite, male, heterosexual athletes" (McGuire, Armfield, and Earnheardt 2015, 113).

The choice for queer erasure in sport media comes as a result of the hegemonic masculinity of sport media and the "invisibility of queerness and awareness of what it means to be queer and the diversity of queer culture within the larger heterosexual culture" (Carter and Baliko 2017, 696). Despite more openly queer sports figures in mainstream culture who have emerged as strong athletes and champions of LBGTQIA+ rights, queer individuals embody a "contradictory place within Western society, being simultaneously visible and invisible" (Carter and Baliko 2017, 696). Even with more visibility and "inclusive perspective on homosexuality" being adopted by some media outlets (Magrath, Cleland, and Anderson 2017, 303), the "heterosexist nature of media coverage" remains intact (Magrath, Cleland, and Anderson 2017, 301).

Although the 2015 *Obergefell v. Hodges* civil rights case ruled that same-sex couples have the right to marry in all 50 states in the USA, the acceptance of queer athletes across sport media is imperative for this area of culture to truly embody feminist goals and change the hegemonic masculinity of sports. Loftus' (2001) sociological research showed a positive change in the U.S. public's attitudes toward LBGTQIA+ individuals, but they still face significantly high levels of discrimination, specifically lesbian women and gay men in Western society (Magrath, Cleland, and Anderson 2017). Within sports, these individuals have been targeted with physical violence and harassment based on the cultural understanding that sports are no place for anyone who is queer (Anderson 2002).

As a result of the heteronormativity of sports, sport media favours and prioritizes those individuals who exalt heterosexuality. The patriarchal power structure of sport media means there is an embedded "alchemy of erasure" (Moreira 2014, 50) for queer athletes. Yep (2003, 2) states:

> The language and law that [regulate] the establishment of heterosexuality as both an identity and an institution, both a practice and a system, is the language and law of defense and protection: heterosexuality secures its self-identity and shores up its ontological boundaries by protecting itself from what it sees as the continual predatory encroachment of its contaminated other, homosexuality.

When aspects like covert homophobia and incorrect gender marking occur for individuals who do not embody Western cisgender traits, queer erasure becomes a prevalent theme that symbolically annihilates (Tuchman, Daniels, and Benét 1978) queer representation in sport media. This can be seen in action for androgynous athletes or queer female athletes who may wear their hair shorter and do not adhere to codes of Western femininity and compulsory heterosexuality.

Elimination of LGBTQIA+ Representation

Queer erasure in sport media comes as a result of a gender hierarchy and the preservation of sport as a site of heterosexuality in culture. When compulsory heterosexuality and hypermasculinity are prioritized in sport culture, both candid and covert homophobia become intertwined in the institution of sports (Kian, Anderson, and Shipka 2015). Adding to this, the focus on gender marking in sport media contributes to the compulsive othering for all individuals who are non-cisgender males in this sphere. When these tactics, both concealed and obvious, are used by sport media creators, this leads to the symbolic annihilation (Tuchman, Daniels, and Benét 1978) of queer representation in sport media.

Tuchman, Daniels, and Benét (1978) outlines three stages of annihilation that occur: omission, trivialization, and condemnation. When these tactics are used in mass media, Tuchman describes that women are underrepresented or represented in stereotypical ways that indicate their dependence on men throughout mass media. This tactic of symbolic annihilation has contributed to other marginalized groups like LGBTQIA+ folks being rendered invisible too. This annihilation means that gender and sexual discrimination are enacted when queer folks are not incorporated into cultural content ranging from film and television to music and books. This supports an understanding that mass media is a place of heteronormativity and that those outside this cultural norm are not welcomed. To combat this seemingly passive but impactful form of marginalization in mass media, the digital space that is a backbone to fourth-wave feminism has allowed for more diverse voices to be heard and this symbolic annihilation to be reduced (Venzo and Hess 2013).

Heterosexuality in Sports

Throughout the history of sports and sport media, these areas of culture have been solidified as a nostalgic site for "doing masculinity" (Pfister 2013, 173). Traditional gender roles made women's entry into the arena of sports difficult (Ezzell 2009). Many argued that it was important to keep "competition and motherhood" (Pfister 2013, 169) separate as a means of social control. Medical experts even argued that women's reproductive ability would be compromised if they engaged in sport (Ezzell 2009). Clearly, the prioritization for women to reproduce confirms a paternalistic and heterosexist outlook on women who wanted to engage in sports at any level. This extends and is promoted by the "institutionalized sexism of sports reporting" (Ezzell 2009, 114).

The condescending approach to discrimination meant women were seen in the singular role of homemaker and child bearer, which was contrary to the existing qualities of hegemonic masculinity embedded in sports culture (Ezzel 2009; Messner 2002). Baron Pierre de Coubertin, the founder of the modern-day Olympics, even said "women should not soil the Olympic Games with their sweat" (Pfister, Habermann, and Ottesen 2004, 5). This statement speaks volumes for the naturalized sexism of sports. Hegemonic masculinity is an ideology that "places women in a lower social position" and where women are "considered off-limits in certain areas, sport being one of the most obvious" (Whisenant, Pedersen, and Obenour 2002, 486).

In summary, this indicates that if you are outside of the prioritized norm of sport media, that being a White, cisgender, male, able-bodied, and heterosexual individual, then you are *othered* (Bruce 2013; Moreira 2014). This category of acceptance is exclusive and narrow and noninclusive of anyone who may be different from the heterosexual norm. This proves that in order to be deemed significant within culture, you have to be a White, cisgender, male, able-bodied, heterosexual individual. With the understanding that sports equate to masculinity, there is already a refusal engrained in sports accepting anyone who embodies femininity and queerness because of the contrary nature of their experience that intersects with hypermasculine sports. This *othering* process is upheld when sports coverage highlights privileged athletes and ignores those in a marginalized position.

Women's Roles in Sport Media

Within sport media, anyone outside of the prioritized norm is seen as invisible and insignificant. With sports as a "site of culture" (Bruce 2013, 129) that "valorizes elite, able-bodied, heterosexual, and professional sportsmen" (128), this overt masculinity "drives the decisions and actions of media workers" (129), leading to their ideal athlete being significantly featured across media. This comes to fruition in recent statistics that state that women's sports make up a mere 4 percent of all sport media coverage (Canadian Women & Sport 2020). With numbers this low, it is clear that women in sport media constitute such a small fraction of content and are strategically placed on the periphery by content creators, writers, and broadcasters.

Female broadcasters still face large amounts of gender bias in their roles, with Luisi, Adams, and Kilgore's (2020, 1) study demonstrating that participants believed female broadcasters "were not as credible or exciting" compared with male broadcasters. In Lapchick's (2018) findings there was a decrease in sports reporters who were women from 12.7 percent in 2014 to 11 percent in 2018. Not only are women in sports receiving less viewership but women employed in *sport media* are marginalized as well. As a result, viewers do not prioritize content by women or about women.

Women's underrepresentation throughout society is multifaceted and extreme. The gender hierarchy is evident in "intersecting traditions, culture, structure and institutions, and interwoven in social arrangements and individual lives" (Pfister 2013, 175). These proliferating moments of underrepresentation that instill hegemonic masculinity are epitomized in the Televised Sports Manhood Formula (TSMF), established through a content analysis by Messner, Dunbar, and Hunt (2000). The ten themes that emerged in this analysis demonstrated how White, male, cisgender, heteronormative individuals are highlighted and promoted within television, but this is also evident in other sport media formats like print and social media. When watching sports, themes like "White Males Are the Voices of Authority," "Aggressive Players Get the Prize; Nice Guys Finish Last," and "Women Are Sexy Props or Prizes for Men's Successful Sport Performances or Consumption Choices" are perpetuated and used to stabilize sports as a man's area (Messner, Dunbar, and Hunt 2000).

Other themes like "Gender Marking," "Compulsory Heterosexuality and Appropriate Femininity," and "Comparison to Men's Sports" emerge (Bruce 2013). The overall control of and strong opposition to femininity in sports, "offers a vehicle for reproducing dominant conceptions of masculinity by alleviating fears of feminization among middle-class men" (Denham 2009, 145). However, Bruce (2015) adds to this thematization by highlighting that the pretty *or* powerful discourse has changed to pretty *and* powerful in the modern context for female athletes. This comes as a result of the internet and social media's positive shift in the way sportswomen are represented in sport media (Bruce 2015).

The Fight for Equal Pay

In the Beginning of USWNT versus U.S. Soccer Federation

The chronicle of the battle between USWNT and U.S. Soccer began back in 2016, with high-profile players Carli Lloyd, Hope Solo, Alex Morgan, Becky Sauerbrunn, and Rapinoe formally filing a complaint about unequal pay and bonuses with the Equal Employment Opportunity Commission (EEOC) (Gajanan 2019). This federal agency called on The Equal Pay Act of 1963, which constitutes employees receive "equal pay in certain situations where members of the opposite sex are doing 'equal work'" (Sullivan 1978, 545). Even though there has been a decline in the gender pay gap since the 1970s, the "residual discrimination" (Blau, Gielen, and Zimmermann 2012, 5) that women experience on the basis of gender remains intact.

In 2017, a collective-bargaining agreement was reached between the USWNT players and U.S. Soccer after significant negotiations. On the list of demands, the USWNT players stated they required "better base pay, bonuses and travel provisions" in addition to gaining "some control of certain licensing and marketing rights" (Dwyer 2017, 4) Since five players on the 2016 USWNT formally sued U.S. Soccer on a wage discrimination complaint that was filed in 2016, there has been limited progress for the team in gaining pay equity (Dwyer 2017). Megan Rapinoe, one of the original five players who was involved with the 2016 lawsuit, has made use of public appearances and social media as a means to engage and win the court of public opinion in the fight for equal pay for equal work in her professional soccer career (Thomas 2016).

Complaints of experiencing inadequate accommodations, receiving "lower sponsor-appearance fees" (Thomas 2016, 9), playing through harmful field conditions in the form of artificial turf, and, most importantly, the claims of receiving less pay than the United States Men's National Team (USMNT) per diem were the backbone of the lawsuit. Although this battle is ongoing, settling this gender discrimination lawsuit will set the course for the future for *all* female athletes' pathway to progress in gaining gender equality. I argue how this issue of gender discrimination in sports will be key in ensuring female athletes are supported by their sporting federations and the public moving forward.

At the conclusion of 2020, this lawsuit stands with a proposed settlement reached between the USWNT and U.S. Soccer. USWNT cited improper working conditions come as a result of gender discrimination. These include playing matches on real grass rather than artificial grass surfaces and comparable hotel accommodations to what the U.S. Men's National Team receives. Sadly, however, the equal pay for equal play battle continues (*Sports Illustrated* 2020). For these athletes, the gender pay gap in sports salaries comes as a result of systemic issues in women's sports and sport media constructed by the hegemonic masculinity of sports. This results in the cycle of *claims* of female athletes being physically weaker than male athletes, leading to less media coverage and, in turn, to fewer endorsement deals, and, finally, to low economic return. This cycle is continuous and proliferates in the argument for why female athletes should not receive equal pay for equal play.

The movement of equal pay is not unique to the twenty-first century. Despite the increasing entry of women into the labour force, a pattern of pay equity did not reflect the rising numbers of women in the workforce. What is of note is that the push for equal pay has escalated as a result of the growing presence of fourth-wave intersectional feminism and social media–oriented social justice warriors captivated by the likes of Rapinoe and her social media presence. Even in the realm of lawmakers, West Virginia Senator Joe Manchin backed the pay equity fight by introducing a significant bill (Zerunyan 2018) that "would withhold federal funding for the men's 2026 World Cup . . . until the pay dispute was resolved" (Gajana 2019, 22).

The Waves of Feminism

Fourth-wave feminism stems from the lineage of the previous waves of feminism.

First-wave feminism began in the last nineteenth and early twentieth centuries with a focus on gaining suffrage and granting rights for different opportunities for women and was led by middle-class, White, cisgender women. With the ongoing debates on what it meant to be ladylike and to be a lady in society, the second wave of feminism began in the 1960s and well into the 1990s (Rampton 2015). This marked a pushback against traditional notions of sexuality and the reproductive rights of women. This was also marked by the era of civil rights movements and antiwar sentiment forming in the Western world, leading to radical movements and modern protests. This wave sought to incorporate women of colour in addition to middle-class, White women.

In third-wave feminism, "constructs were destabilized, including the notions of 'universal womanhood,' body, gender, sexuality and heteronormativity" (Rampton 2015, 4). In the 1990s, this was marked by the incorporation of both the complexities and the multiple intersections of womanhood in order to destabilize boundaries that had been built up in society. In this era, advocating that women could be both pretty and powerful was a hallmark. The fourth wave of feminism began in 2008 (Baumgardner 2011) and uses the internet as a backbone in order to achieve intersectional justice (Bruce 2015). Here, new discourses can emerge within the internet culture, which allows for people to be empowered to create social change and for original content to be easily distributed. Through the internet, activism is now accessible for many.

Present Day Issues

In the time line of the grievances, the USWNT has combated the dismissal of their lawsuit by federal Judge R. Gary Klausner in May of 2020 and a variety of sexist statements from U.S. Soccer's previous President Carlos Cordeiro. Court documents from the lawsuit demonstrated that discriminatory statements were used to combat the lawsuit, one of which was as follows: "The point is that the job of MNT player (competing against senior men's national teams) requires a higher level of skill-based on speed and strength than does the job of WNT player (competing against senior women's national teams)" (*Alex Morgan et al. v. U.S. Soccer Federation, Inc.* 2020, 12).

These statements resulted in Cordeiro stepping down from the position and Cindy Parlow Cone taking over the presidency, demonstrating a serious growing investment in women's soccer from the public. Despite making deep runs into the World Cup tournaments, capturing four World Cup trophies, and being ranked number one out of 142 FIFA-recognized national teams (FIFA 2020), U.S. Soccer, and USWNT have not reached a compromise that will allow USWNT to be accurately financially compensated.

The USWNT was strategic to capitalize on using their international platform throughout their 2019 World Cup tournament campaign and turned their lawsuit into an international conversation about the dollar value that their labour constitutes in the eyes of U.S. Soccer (Masters 2020). Through fervent tweeting sessions, opportunistic media coverage, and statements of unity from teammates, the current players on the

USWNT were able to clearly state their objective of reaching pay equity with the USMNT in order to leave the structure of payment in a better position for players in the future.

Naming significant success and popularity in their cause for equal pay, the USWNT still has an uphill battle with the lawsuit. Where the adversity comes in is that the men and women players have different contracts, the women receiving less in performance bonuses in the collective-bargaining agreement they have but with the security of benefits. What is key is that the lawsuit will have to prove that the financial disparity between the women's and men's sides comes as a result of gender discrimination (Gajana 2019).

METHODOLOGY

For this chapter, a content analysis will be used to analyze a digital artifact and interpret the meaning behind sentiments. A content analysis is used to "examine data, printed matter, images, or sounds—texts—in order to understand what they mean to people, what they enable or prevent, and what the information conveyed by them does" (Krippendorff 2004, xviii). Additionally, it is "a research technique for making replicable and valid inferences from texts (or other meaningful matter) to the contexts of their use" (Krippendorff 2004, 18). Drisko and Maschi (2015, 2) state that the importance of a content analysis is that an analyst can "identify and document the attitudes, views, and interests of individuals, small groups, or large and diverse cultural groups." This is of importance for this chapter because the prominent sentiment formed by commenters will come to classify either the small group's support, opposition, or neutrality toward Megan Rapinoe in sport media.

The text that will be examined is the communication section of a video on the social media platform YouTube. Using the comment section for the YouTube video "Megan Rapinoe on Equal Pay, Celebrating in the USA and Winning the Women's World Cup," published by Guardian Football on July 8, 2019, queer erasure in the comments section toward professional athlete Megan Rapinoe will be examined. This will be conducted to discover the prevalent sport media sentiment toward her at the conclusion of winning the FIFA Women's World Cup in 2019. The research questions that are the focus for this content analysis are as follows:

1. What are the prominent sentiments from YouTube commenters toward Megan Rapinoe?

2. How do these comments contribute to the queer erasure of female athletes in sport media?

Using www.hadzy.com, an online random sample generator for YouTube comments, the first ten comments that were generated through this random sample were analyzed. Identifying the sentiment patterns will allow for the isolation and thematization of the meaning behind the comments that sought to erase Rapinoe's presence as a queer female athlete.

This is a brief video, only 50 seconds long. The video was about an interview with Rapinoe that focused on the post-World Cup win, her reaction to the tournament, and the question of equal pay for equal play that she and the USWNT support. The B-roll features Rapinoe greeting fans for autographs on the street of Lyon, France, in addition to her interview shots. There is also a prerecorded video from the stands of the gold medal match where fans began to chant "equal pay."

The video was liked by 432 viewers and disliked by 965 viewers, with 604 comments on the video too. The Guardian Football channel, which falls under The Guardian channel, has 175k subscribers. This video was selected because Rapinoe is the only player interviewed, and the interview clips that were selected take a positive angle toward the equal pay debate, illustrated by Rapinoe in her own words.

A random sample was used because "each unit of the population has an equal probability of inclusion in the sample" (Bryman and Bell 2016, 190). Random sampling is also used to ensure no bias is included by the analyst if they were to select the comments to analyze (Bryman and Bell 2016).

The text will be coded using Weber's (1990) strategy. The basic unit of text that will be classified is the sentence because the comments are often only one sentence long. These comments will be coded either positive evaluation, negative evaluation, or neutral evaluation (Weber 1990). After the random sample has been coded, the text will be analyzed through the lens of themes that contribute to hegemonic masculinity.

Coding Manual

Evaluation Types:

1. Positive evaluation
2. Negative evaluation
3. Neutral evaluation

Themes:
1. Physical appearance
2. Appropriate femininity
3. Sports are a man's world
4. Economics
5. Homophobia
6. Sexism
7. Emasculation
8. Infantilization
9. Combination of one or more themes

Random Sample with Coding

Table 2.1: Coded YouTube Comments

Comment	Author's Username	Date	Evaluation Type	Theme
She/he whatever needs to spend some time in economics class rather than gender studies.	Rivu Dutta	July 9, 2019 4:53:19 am	2	4
Who is the purple-haired man? What is he doing on a celebration for the Women's World Cup champions?	orionh3000	July 9, 2019 6:37:05 pm	2	1
Why is everyone bagging on this nice lad. I think he has nice hair.	Robert Litsenberger	July 8, 2019 6:31:24 pm	2	1
They don't deserve equal pay because most women around the world don't play soccer, so it's a watered down league. Plus, these women got smoked by a team of 14 yr old boys. Then toss in the endless drama and the spoiled bratty child attitude. ... . Really, these so called women are lucky to be on tv.	First Last	July 8, 2019 11:41:07 am	2	9
But if the women get paid equally, it might emasculate the men in the audience. For example, look at this comment section.	OnlyARide	July 8, 2019 11:57:26 am	3	7
Nice hair cut dude . . .	Logan 5	July 8, 2019 9:12:34 am	2	1
This team does not represent the USA It represents the LGBTQ movement. Majority of Americans do not accept homosexuality as normal. This is a disgrace. Disgusting.	Joshua Huihui	July 8, 2019 10:48:52 am	2	5

Equal pay for women, I'm fine with that. Tell her to start acting like a woman.	carolinasown	July 8, 2019 10:52:43 am	2	2
Id10t. Equal pay? Girls kickball made 75 million dollars. Guys team made 4 billion dollars. He belongs on the guys team, as waterboy.	Harry Paul Garcia	July 10, 2019 2:09:15 pm	2	9
Congratulations purple-haired lesbian. . . . on winning ball game played by little kids. History will remember this day forever!	Anthony Hubbard	July 8, 2019 1:42:19 pm	2	1

Source: Data Collected from "Megan Rapinoe on Equal Pay, Celebrating in the USA and Winning the Women's World Cup," Guardian Football 2019.

Findings

In examining the comment section of Guardian Football's YouTube video titled "Megan Rapinoe on Equal Pay, Celebrating in the USA and Winning the Women's World Cup," there are 615 comments listed (Guardian Football 2019). On the basis of the random sample, the comments almost exclusively combat Rapinoe's statements advocating for equal pay and her existence in a traditionally masculine sport. Overwhelmingly, comments claim she is a "disgrace," "disgusting," and undeserving of equal pay; that she can receive equal compensation only when she plays with the men.

The clear majority of statements indicate commenters are unsatisfied with Rapinoe's outward exhibition of her advocacy for equal pay. What appears in this random sample of comments is that commenters have decided to make use of gender marking Rapinoe as a male as well as comment on her physical appearance in an attempt to slight her, which displays both sexist and homophobic tactics.

These comments come to textually support that hegemonic masculinity is still very much embedded in sport media. They also call on themes of appropriate femininity, compulsory heterosexuality, and comparison to men's sports to be deemed relevant. With an emphasis that Rapinoe is not in a traditional role as a female athlete (i.e., "He belongs on the guy's team, as waterboy"), the theme of "sports are a man's world" is established and advocated by commenters as a justifiable reason for insulting Rapinoe's accomplishments. She is demoted to the position of a sideline staff member despite her cocaptaincy on the USWNT and numerous accolades at the highest level of soccer.

The emphasis on Rapinoe's hair in four of these comments also contributes to framing Rapinoe as diverting from notions of appropriate femininity (Table 2.1). Rapinoe's short, cropped hair dyed a light shade of pinkish-purple for the World Cup tournament becomes a target in these comments, indicating that commenters are uncomfortable with her choice of outward appearance. Rapinoe defies the visual codes of female soccer players (Bremner 2002; Cavalier and Newhall 2018; Schultz 2014; Shugart 2003). Her existence as a queer woman in the space of hegemonic masculinity challenges these notions of what a "normal" woman must look like to be included in sport media.

What is of note in these comments pulled from the random sample is that one comment falls under the evaluation type as neutral (Table 2.1). The comment comes across as sarcastic in tone and is reflexive of the echo chamber that has occurred. It is neither a positive evaluation of the video or a negative one. It calls on the participants in the comment section to reflect on their feelings of emasculation when Rapinoe is the focus of this sport media video. This demonstrates that not all comments contribute to homophobia or sexism, but the infrequency of these neutral or positive comments in the random sample shows how difficult it is for alternative perspectives to emerge in the comment sections of videos of this nature.

YouTube Echo Chamber Effect Involving Marginalized Athletes

Despite YouTube's Official Rules & Policies page being a public-facing record of how the company monitors their website and what is permitted, harmful comments still exist and are authorized. The Policies Overview page outlines what personal perspectives can be incorporated on their site: "Viewers and Creators around the world use YouTube to express their ideas and opinions freely, and we believe that a broad range of perspectives ultimately makes us a stronger and more informed society, even if we disagree with some of those views" (YouTube 2020). The freedom of speech and presentation of different perspectives on the social media platform is emphasized here. However, on scrolling down the Rules & Policies page, one finds contradictory statements on what is permitted: "Our Community Guidelines define what we do and don't allow on YouTube. They exist so that we can protect the community from things such as harmful content, harassment, and spam. They apply to everyone, and to all types of content on YouTube—such as videos, comments, links, and thumbnails" (YouTube 2020).

In YouTube's Community Guidelines (YouTube 2020), these forms of explicit homophobic and sexist comments violate their hate speech policy by targeting Rapinoe, who is an openly queer woman. YouTube qualifies hate speech in their guidelines to be: "Hate speech is not allowed on YouTube. We remove content promoting violence or hatred against individuals or groups based on any of the following attributes: age, caste, disability, ethnicity, gender identity and expression, nationality, race, immigration status, religion, sex/gender, sexual orientation, victims of a major violent event and their kin, veteran status" (YouTube 2020). From there, viewers are encouraged to report comments if the language violates the community guidelines. The onus on users' identifying when comments violate these guidelines meant to make YouTube a safe space means that comments are not screened before they are accepted as comments on videos. Here, an echo chamber is effectively created.

Avnur (2020, 578) describes an online echo chamber to be "news feeds on our social media accounts that contain information from like-minded sources." Echo chambers reinforce thoughts for a user because users seek other information from others or groups that will support and insulate their ideas from external sources or thought (Avnur 2020). The comment section on this video in analysis successfully demonstrates that alternative perspectives that are contrary to popular opinions have a difficult time emerging.

Brugnoli et al. (2019, 1) attribute echo chambers to the creation of "homogeneous and polarized communities" in social media, which is evident in the comment section in question. When a user searches for content online that aligns with their belief system, ideas proliferate between users, supporting each other and resulting in a snowball effect in accumulating a similar disposition. This sharing of information is uninterrupted "without the mediation of journalists or experts in the field" (Brugnoli et al. 2019, 1). Echo chambers are also classified by users' need for challenge avoidance and their need for reinforcement (Brugnoli et al. 2019). Since negative comments exist in the comment thread, the addition of more negative comments is easy for users because of the "reinforcement seeking mechanisms" (Brugnoli et al. 2019, 1) that are unaffected by sources outside of their thoughts.

Through a combination of echo chambers proliferating in YouTube comment sections and the affordances of the platform's layout (viewers see the top 2 or 3 comments), these comments effectively create a bias when watching video content. Gibson (1982) asserts that the constraints and control in these behaviours mean viewers may be influenced by the most liked comments in the privileged top comment section, and in this case, take a biased stance when watching the video (Schultes, Dorner, and Lehner 2013). A pitfall to balancing the echo chamber is that comments that counter the homophobic and sexist language are lost in the comment section for this video due to YouTube's strategy of keeping the most popular comment at the top of the comment section (Burgess and Green 2018).

Schultes, Dorner, and Lehner (2013, 659) have attested that "user comments are the most popular but also extremely controversial form of communication on YouTube." Their 2013 study supports "the claim that users frequently communicate their emotions in comments" (Schultes, Dorner, and Lehner 2013, 671), which is of concern for this video when a publicly out, queer, female athlete becomes the target of hate online. The "juvenile, aggressive, misspelled, sexist, homophobic" (Owen and Wright 2009, 1) comments persist because users know that they can attack anyone online correspondingly with the support an echo chamber provides.

As the result of the user's confirmation bias, this comment section solidifies the creation of an echo chamber and allows like-minded users to assemble behind similar comments to breed a textual thread of hate. The exposure to information that counters Rapinoe's rally for equal pay demonstrates the need for those who have opposite opinions to voice them and for YouTube to take into account the way their comment popularity filtering allows for echo chambers to emerge. When disagreements in the comment sections occur, those subject to the effect of an echo chamber are immune "to reasoning to an unfavoured conclusion" (Avnur 2020, 587).

Despite YouTube's Community Guidelines being in place, the hateful comments toward Megan Rapinoe snowball on this video. This means that hegemonic masculinity is still abundantly present in sport media and results in Rapinoe being misgendered, discounted, and harassed as a queer athlete. The comment section masks these sentiments by rejecting the equal pay for equal play cause. Both microaggressions and visible homophobia are cited by commenters as reasons for why the USWNT should not receive equal pay.

Considering YouTube conveys these notes on how to conduct on their platform as "guidelines," the rules or guidelines are not strictly enforced on the platform, which is how comments of this nature can be placed in the comment section of videos without being contested. Since Rapinoe operates at the intersectional axis of being a woman and being queer (Kaskan and Ho 2016), she is subjected to these microaggressions in more than one way (Sue 2010).

CONCLUSION

The specific ways in which Rapinoe becomes subjected to microaggressions in the comment section are framed in appropriate femininity, sports as a man's world, and compulsory heterosexuality. Rapinoe's quintessential lavender pixie cut hair for the tournament stood out as a form of cultural resistance and pushback toward appropriate femininity. The comment section emphasized her hair, and the negative tone taken toward it is congruent with sport media's emphasis on what constitutes femininity: "physical or emotional characteristics that reflect ideals of [w]hite, middle-class femininity" (Bruce 2015, 366). Rapinoe's physical appearance does not align with the values of traditional White, male sport media producers or consumers and the importance placed on the female athlete's body as a place of masculine consumption in sport media.

The combination of comments on the appropriateness of her hair in addition to the misgendering of Rapinoe offers an intersectional area to investigate. Since she does not comply with the appropriate femininity outlined in sports, Rapinoe is masculinized (Bruce 2015), and her gender is erased in the comments. In the process, her queerness is also erased because, under the structure of sports, heterosexuality remains mandatory. The idealized image of a sportswoman perpetuated by sport media is White, thin, heterosexual, cisgender, and wearing a ponytail in soccer (Cavalier and Newhall 2018). Rapinoe counters the focus on physical appearance and diverts from the idealized norm of female athletes with her short, dyed hair. The rejection of anyone outside the privileged circle of White, male, cisgender, heterosexual athletes is apparent in the comments about Rapinoe and her hair.

The misgendering is seen as a tactic to enforce a cisgender and heterosexual vision of athletes (Yep 2003). The comments are used as a means to both erase the queerness of the athlete and undermine female athletes in this case. Bruce (2015, 366) states: "Compulsory heterosexuality is evident in a media preference for, and highlighting of, sportswomen with sexual or emotional relationships with men." The misgendering of

Rapinoe is used as a strategy to state that sports are no place for someone who does not identify as a heterosexual cisgender man, which continues to uphold the hegemonic masculinity of sports in the process.

This research is important because it signals that when comments that vilify queer female athletes are posted by YouTube users, the heterosexuality and hegemonic masculinity ingrained in sport media is reinforced. This homophobic thinking is strengthened and tolerated when it goes unchecked. Hegemonic masculinity is not destabilized and is perpetuated. Not only does this contribute to sexism and homophobia aimed at queer female athletes, but this type of thinking and active commenting remains a justified action by users of YouTube. This demonstrates not only that sport media support these discriminatory comments as a permissible perspective on queer female athletes, but that the YouTube antiharassment and hate speech policies are ineffective when it comes to creating a safe digital space.

REFERENCES

Alex Morgan et al. v. U.S. Soccer Federation, Inc. Case No. 2:19-cv-01717-RGK-AGR, Defendant's Memorandum of Points and Authorities in Opposition to Plaintiffs' Motion for Partial Summary Judgement, 12 (2020).

Anderson, Eric. 2002. "Openly Gay Athletes: Contesting Hegemonic Masculinity in a Homophobic Environment." Gender & Society 16 (6): 860–77. https://doi.org/10.1177/089124302237892.

Anderson, April, and Andy Lee Roth. 2020. "Queer Erasure: Internet Browsing Can Be Biased against LGBTQ People, New Exclusive Research Shows." Index on Censorship 49 (1): 75–77. https://doi.org/10.1177/0306422020917088.

Avnur, Yuval. 2020. "What's Wrong with the Online Echo Chamber: A Motivated Reasoning Account." Journal of Applied Philosophy 37 (4): 578–93. https://doi.org/10.1111/japp.12426.

Baumgardner, Jennifer. 2011. F 'em!: Goo Goo, Gaga, and Some Thoughts on Balls. Berkeley, CA: Seal Press.

Blau, Francine D., Anne C. Gielen, and Klaus F. Zimmermann. 2012. Gender, Inequality, and Wages. New York: Oxford University Press.

Bremner, Kyla. 2002. "Gender, Sexuality and Sport." Canadian Woman Studies 21 (3): 6. https://www.proquest.com/openview/092ab62d7b027414f19123294468a4f5/1?pq-origsite=gscholar&cbl=44042.

Bruce, Toni. 2013. "Reflections on Communication and Sport: On Women and Femininities." Communication & Sport 1 (1–2): 125–37. https://doi.org/10.1177/2167479512472883.

Bruce, Toni. 2015. "New Rules for New Times: Sportswomen and Media Representation in the Third Wave." Sex Roles 74 (7-8): 361–76. https://doi.org/10.1007/s11199-015-0497-6.

Brugnoli, Emanuele, Matteo Cinelli, Walter Quattrociocchi, and Antonio Scala. 2019. "Recursive Patterns in Online Echo Chambers." Scientific Reports 9 (1): 20118. https://doi.org/10.1038/s41598-019-56191-7.

Bryman, Alan, and Edward A. Bell. 2016. Social Research Methods. Fourth Canadian ed. New York: Oxford University Press.

Burgess, Jean, and Joshua Green. 2018. YouTube: Online Video and Participatory Culture. 2nd ed. Cambridge: Polity Press.

Butler, Judith. 1994. "Against Proper Objects: Differences—More Gender Trouble: Feminism Meets Queer Theory." The Psychoanalytic Quarterly 6 (2/3): 1.

Canadian Women & Sport. 2020. "Women in Sport: Fuelling a Lifetime of Participation" https://womenandsport.ca/wp-content/uploads/2020/03/Fuelling-a-Lifetime-of-Participation-Report_Canadian-Women-Sport.pdf.

Carter, Claire, and Krista Baliko. 2017. " 'These Are Not My People': Queer Sport Spaces and the Complexities of Community." Leisure Studies 36 (5): 696–707. https://doi.org/10.1080/02614367.2017.1315164.

Cavalier, Elizabeth S., and Kristine E. Newhall. 2018. " 'Stick to Soccer:' Fan Reaction and Inclusion Rhetoric on Social Media." Sport in Society 21 (7): 1078–95. https://doi.org/10.1080/17430437.2017.1329824.

Denham, Bryan E. 2009. "Masculinities and the Sociology of Sport: Issues and Ironies in the 21st Century." In Sociology of Sport and Social Theory, edited by Earl Smith, 143–52. Champaign, IL: Human Kinetics.

Derrida, Jacques, and Alan Bass. 1981. Positions. Chicago: University of Chicago Press.

Drisko, James W., and Tina Maschi. 2015. Content Analysis. New York: Oxford University Press. https://doi.org/10.1093/acprof:oso/9780190215491.001.0001.

Dwyer, Colin. 2017. "In 'Important Step,' U.S. Women's Soccer Team Reaches New Labor Deal." npr, April 6, 2017. https://www.npr.org/sections/thetwo-way/2017/04/06/522843140/in-important-step-u-s-womens-soccer-team-reaches-new-labor-deal.

Eng, Heidi. 2006. "Queer Athletes and Queering in Sport." In Sport, Sexualities and Queer/Theory, edited by Jayne Caudwell, 61–73. New York: Routledge.

Equal Pay Act of 1963. 1963. Monthly Labor Review 86 (8): 947. https://www.eeoc.gov/statutes/equal-pay-act-1963.

Ezzell, Matthew B. 2009. " 'Barbie Dolls' on the Pitch: Identity Work, Defensive Othering, and Inequality in Women's Rugby." Social Problems 56 (1): 111–31. https://doi.org/10.1525/sp.2009.56.1.111.

FIFA (Fédération Internationale de Football Association). 2019a. "FIFA Women's World Cup 2019™ Watched by More than 1 Billion." October 18, 2019. https://www.fifa.com/womensworldcup/news/fifa-women-s-world-cup-2019tm-watched-by-more-than-1-billion.

———. 2019b. "FIFA Women's World Cup France 2019™ Match Report." July 7, 2019, https://resources.fifa.com/image/upload/eng-52-0707-usa-ned-fulltime-pdf-3044630.pdf?cloudid=owdlkbnw1p9sf7wnlhfs.

———. 2020. "FIFA World Ranking—Women's Ranking." Last modified December 18, 2020. https://www.fifa.com/fifa-world-ranking/ranking-table/women/.

Gajanan, Mahita. 2019. "The USWNT Seeks Nearly $67 Million in Damages In Equal Pay Lawsuit Against U.S. Soccer. Here's What to Know About the Case." Last modified February 21, 2020. https://time.com/5653250/uswnt-equal-pay-lawsuit/.

Gibson, James J. 1982. "Notes on Affordances." In Reasons for Realism. Selected Essays of James J. Gibson, edited by Edward S. Reed and Rebecca Jones, 401–18. London: Lawrence Erlbaum Associates.

Guardian Football. 2019. "Megan Rapinoe on Equal Pay, Celebrating in the USA and Winning the Women's World Cup." July 8, 2019. Video, 0:50. https://www.youtube.com/watch?v=DpB6CqwnLnU.

Halperin, David M. 1995. Saint Foucault: towards a gay hagiography. New York: Oxford University Press.

Jagose, Annamarie. 1996. Queer Theory. Melbourne: Melbourne University Press.

Kaskan, Emily R., and Ivy K. Ho. 2016. "Microaggressions and Female Athletes." Sex Roles 74 (7): 275–87. https://doi.org/10.1007/s11199-014-0425-1.

Katz, Jonathan. 1995. The Invention of Heterosexuality. New York: Dutton.

Kian, Edward M., Eric Anderson, and Danny Shipka. 2015. " 'I Am Happy to Start the Conversation': Examining Sport Media Framing of Jason Collins' Coming out and Playing in the NBA." Sexualities 18 (5–6): 618–40. https://doi.org/10.1177/1363460714550915.

Krippendorff, Klaus. 2004. Content Analysis: An Introduction to Its Methodology. 2nd ed. London: Sage.

Lapchick, Richard. 2018. "The 2018 Associated Press Sports Editors Racial and Gender Report Card." https://43530132-36e9-4f52-811a-182c7a91933b.filesusr.com/ugd/7d86e5_9dca4bc2067241cdba67aa2f1b09fd1b.pdf.

Loftus, Jeni. 2001. "America's Liberalization in Attitudes toward Homosexuality, 1973 to 1998." American Sociological Review 66 (5): 762–82. https://doi.org/10.2307/3088957.

Lugg, Catherine. 2015. US Public Schools and the Politics of Queer Erasure. New York: Palgrave Macmillan US.

Luisi, Tony, Kelly L. Adams & LaShawnda Kilgore. 2020. "Roughing the caster! Sexism and perceived female sports broadcasters' credibility." Atlantic Journal of Communication 29 (4): 262-74. https://doi.org/10.1080/15456870.2020.1754822

Magrath, Rory, Jamie Cleland, and Eric Anderson. 2017. "Bisexual Erasure in the British Print Media: Representation of Tom Daley's Coming Out." Journal of Bisexuality 17 (3): 300–17. https://doi.org/10.1080/15299716.2017.1359130.

Masters, Hannah L. E. 2020. "Red Card on Wage Discrimination: US Soccer Pay Disparity Highlights Inadequacy of the Equal Pay Act." Vanderbilt Journal of Entertainment and Technology Law 22 (4): 895–922. https://scholarship.law.vanderbilt.edu/jetlaw/vol22/iss4/7/.

McGuire, John, Greg G. Armfield, and Adam C. Earnheardt. 2015. The ESPN Effect: Exploring the Worldwide Leader in Sports. New York: Peter Lang.

Messner, Michael A. 2002. Taking the Field: Women, Men, and Sports. Minneapolis: University of Minnesota Press. http://www.jstor.org/stable/10.5749/j.ctttssgq.

Messner, Michael A., Michele Dunbar, and Darnell Hunt. 2000. "The Televised Sports Manhood Formula." Journal of Sport and Social Issues 24 (4): 380–94. https://doi.org/10.1177/0193723500244006.

Moreira, Robert P. 2014. "Marta Past Messi: (Re)Definitions of Gender and Masculinity, Patriarchal Structures and Female Agency in International Soccer." Soccer & Society 15 (4): 503–16. https://doi.org/10.1080/14660970.2013.828592.

Owen, Paul, and Christopher Wright. 2009. "Our Top 10 Funniest YouTube Comments—What Are Yours?" Guardian News and Media, November 3, 2009. https://www.theguardian.com/technology/blog/2009/nov/03/youtube-funniest-comments.

Pfister, Gertrud. 2013. "Developments and Current Issues in Gender and Sport from a European Perspective." In Gender Relations in Sport, edited by Emily A. Roper, 162–80. Rotterdam: Sense.

Pfister, Gertrud, Ulla Habermann, and Laila Ottesen. 2004. Women at the Top: On Women, Sport and Management. Copenhagen: Institute of Exercise and Sport Sciences.

Rampton, Martha. 2015. "Four Waves of Feminism." Last modified July 14, 2019. http://gdelaurier.pbworks.com/w/file/fetch/134554611/Four%20Waves%20of%20Feminism%20_%20Pacific%20University.pdf.

Rapinoe, Megan. 2012. "Megan Rapinoe on Winning Gold, Soccer's Future." Interview by Melissa Gross. All Things Considered, npr, August 15, 2012. Audio, 6:04. https://www.npr.org/2012/08/15/158887977/soccer-star-rapinoe-on-winning-gold.

Rosenthal, Gregory. 2017. "Make Roanoke Queer Again: Community History and Urban Change in a Southern City." The Public Historian 39 (1): 35–60. https://doi.org/10.1525/tph.2017.39.1.35.

Schultes, Peter, Verena Dorner, and Franz Lehner. 2013. "Leave a Comment! An In-Depth Analysis of User Comments on YouTube." Information Systems and Applied Computer Science 659–73. https://aisel.aisnet.org/cgi/viewcontent.cgi?article=1041&context=wi2013.

Schultz, Jaime. 2014. Qualifying Times: Points of Change in U.S. Women's Sport. Champaign, IL: University of Illinois Press. Accessed December 15, 2020. http://www.jstor.org/stable/10.5406/j.ctt5vk0cg.

Scott, Joan W. 1986. "Gender: A Useful Category of Historical Analysis." The American Historical Review 91 (5): 1053–75. https://doi.org/10.2307/1864376.

Shugart, Helene A. 2003. "She Shoots, She Scores: Mediated Constructions of Contemporary Female Athletes in Coverage of the 1999 US Women's Soccer Team." Western Journal of Communication 67 (1): 1–31. http://www.uky.edu/~addesa01/documents/SheShootsSheScores.pdf.

Sports Illustrated. 2013. "Alex Morgan, U.S. Women Beat Germany for Algarve Cup Title." Last modified March 13, 2013. https://www.si.com/soccer/2013/03/13/us-women-germany-algarve-cup.

———. 2020. "USWNT, U.S. Soccer Settle Working Conditions Claims, Setting Stage for Appeal on Equal Pay." December 1, 2020. https://www.si.com/soccer/2020/12/01/uswnt-us-soccer-working-conditions-settlement-equal-pay-appeal.

Sue, Derald Wing. 2010. Microaggressions in Everyday Life: Race, Gender, and Sexual Orientation. Hoboken, NJ: Wiley.

Sullivan, Charles A. 1978. "The Equal Pay Act of 1963: Making and Breaking a Prima Facie Case." Arkansas Law Review 31 (4): 545–606. https://papers.ssrn.com/sol3/papers.cfm?abstract_id=2373936.

Thomas, Louisa. 2016. "Equal Pay for Equal Play: The Case for the Women's Soccer Team." The New Yorker, May 27, 2016. https://www.newyorker.com/culture/cultural-comment/the-case-for-equal-pay-in-womens-sports.

Tuchman, Gaye, Arlene Kaplan Daniels, and James Benét. 1978. Hearth and Home: Images of Women in the Mass Media. New York: Oxford University Press.

US Soccer. 2021. "Megan Rapinoe." Accessed January 20, 2021. https://www.ussoccer.com/players/r/megan-rapinoe.

Venzo, Paul, and Kristy Hess. 2013. " 'Honk against Homophobia': Rethinking Relations between Media and Sexual Minorities." Journal of Homosexuality 60 (11): 1539–56. https://doi.org/10.1080/00918369.2013.824318.

Warner, Michael. 1991. "Introduction: Fear of a Queer Planet." Social Text 9 (4): 3. https://www.jstor.org/stable/466295.

Weber, Robert Philip. 1990. Basic Content Analysis. 2nd ed. Vol. 49. London: Sage.

Weston, Kath. 1993. "Lesbian/Gay Studies in the House of Anthropology." Annual Review of Anthropology 22 (1993): 339–67. https://doi.org/10.1146/annurev.an.22.100193.002011.

Whisenant, Warren A., Paul M. Pedersen, and Bill L. Obenour. 2002. "Success and Gender: Determining the Rate of Advancement for Intercollegiate Athletic Directors." Sex Roles 47 (9): 485–91. https://doi.org/10.1023/A:1021656628604.

Yep, Gust A. 2003. "The Violence of Heteronormativity in Communication Studies: Notes on Injury, Healing, and Queer World-Making." Journal of Homosexuality 45 (2–4): 11–59. https://doi.org/10.1300/J082v45n02_02.

YouTube. 2020. "Community Guidelines." Accessed January 17, 2021. https://www.youtube.com/intl/ALL_ca/howyoutubeworks/policies/community-guidelines/.

"YouTube Comments Search." Hadzy. Accessed January 20, 2021. https://hadzy.com/.

Zerunyan, Nicole. 2018. "Time's Up: Addressing Gender-Based Wage Discrimination in Professional Sports." Loyola of Los Angeles Entertainment Law Review 38 (3): 229. https://digitalcommons.lmu.edu/elr/vol38/iss3/2/.

CHAPTER 3

The In/Visibility of Black Muslim Sportswomen

Sabrina Razack, Asma Khalil, and Hibaq Mohamed

INTRODUCTION

The recent worldwide racial injustice protests that were sparked by the murder of George Floyd and Breonna Taylor and the beatings unleashed on Dafonte Miller have necessitated an examination of scholarship related to Black Muslim sportswomen. Several academics (Ratna and Samie 2017; Samie 2017; Ahmad and Thorpe 2020; Samie & Sehlikoglu 2015; Samie and Toffoletti 2018; Sehlikoglu, 2012) have interrogated previous knowledge of Muslim sportswomen as reductionist and essentialist, noting that the primary focus overwhelmingly centres on barriers to participation or gendered Islamophobia. The preoccupation with the "veiled oppressed Muslim" sportswoman has dominated studies that uncritically investigate the "sameness" in the oppression against women in sporting cultures that consequently inhibit collective solidarities against patriarchal systems (Ratna 2018; Samie 2017). The glaring omission from Muslim sport studies (Ahmad et al. 2020; Samie 2017) is the lack of attention to intersections of racial identities within Muslim sportswomen. The more recent critical studies effectively establish discourses that complicate representations of Muslim women as a monolith, yet Black Muslim women are rarely integrated, reflected, or investigated in such sport studies.

In the limited studies of Black Muslim sportswomen, an antiracist methodology and/or critical race theory (CRT) are inadequately adopted as an approach (Bahrainwala and O'Connor 2019; Samie and Toffoletti 2018). This chapter will further explore the framing of Black Muslim sportswomen. First, we will briefly discuss anti-Black racism and head coverings. The media framing of Black Muslim women and Black Muslim sportswomen is also explored. The second section analyzes the media production and resistance of dominant representations of Black Muslim sportswomen. The chapter concludes with a call to action for researchers and the media to adopt a more intersectional approach and recognition of racial identities within Muslim communities.

Hijab Discourses

Much of the discourse surrounding Muslim women has centred on the hijab. This has often led to discussions of the function and conditions under which Muslim women choose to veil. Rarely, if ever, is there a discussion of race and the various forms of veiling. Hijab is influenced by, and often becomes a signifier of, different racial or ethnic cultural groups. From a loose draping of a dupatta in Pakistani communities to an undercap and chiffon scarf in Arab communities to the colourful, printed turbans in various Black cultures, it is clear that the hijab is a signifier not only of Islam but also of the racially diverse communities that make up the ummah[1] (Tarlo 2010; Almila 2016). By ignoring these differences, we not only erase entire communities but privilege one understanding and representation of the hijab. This leaves no room for interrogating how anti-Black racism functions in both Muslim and non-Muslim communities, resulting from different forms of veiling. For example, there have been documented experiences of Black Muslim women being victims to de-veiling by law enforcement officers (Taylor 2019). Despite laws that grant Muslim women the right to veil while incarcerated, some police officers have incorrectly interpreted the African style of hijab (turban or high bun) as a fashion statement rather than a religious one (Wheeler 2020; Taylor 2019). Within Muslim diasporic communities, different styles of veiling have resulted in anti-Black racism. In 2017, a high school in Maine garnered national media coverage because it became the first school in the United States to provide sport hijabs for its Muslim student-athletes. Two Black athletes, Fadumo Adan and Sulwan Ismail-Ahmed, were featured proudly wearing their hijabs (Sharp 2017). However, there was a backlash from the Muslim community owing to the athletes' choice in wearing the hijab with a short-sleeved jersey. Despite varying interpretations of Islamic guidelines of modesty, it is widely accepted that covering of the arms falls under the requirements of hijab. In a similar situation, Black Muslim model Fatma Yusuf was targeted by Arab Muslim influencers, including Melanie Elturk and Mariah Idrissi, following a hijab ad campaign for Banana Republic that featured her wearing a hijab with short sleeves (Wheeler 2020). Melanie Elturk, the founder of Haute Hijab, stated "there are guidelines to hijab outside of just covering hair . . . it's important we keep the essence of hijab intact for ourselves and our future generations" (Ifteqar 2019). This sentiment is particularly relevant to the discussion of anti-Black racism, as Haute Hijab features hijabi models who wear the turban style and/or have their neck and arms exposed on their website. This surveillance and policing of Black Muslim women's bodies, by Muslims and non-Muslims alike, is pervasive and has only been exacerbated by online forums and social media (Karim 2006; Muslim Census 2020). These types of comments from within the broader Muslim community are often framed as advice or guidance toward Black Muslim women. This indicates a Muslim privilege based on assumptions of cultural readings of an Arab or South Asian Islam as wholly acceptable and Black Islam as backward and/or in need of correction from others within and outside of the Muslim faith.

Islamophobia and Anti-Blackness

In the eyes of the state and the media, Muslim equals brown (Wheeler 2020, para. 13).

In the West, "9/11" symbolizes the destruction of the World Trade Centres in New York City that transformed the worldview of Muslims (Karim 2006). A racialized bearded Muslim man and the veiled Muslim woman became the signifier of an identity to be feared or saved. A veiled woman has come to represent a widespread belief that covering is the ultimate display of oppression that connects to a religious order inclusive of Hadiths[2] and the Qurān that supposedly perpetuate a submissive, patriarchal fixed state (Karim 2006; McMurray 2007; Samie 2017; Wheeler 2020). Black Muslim women became ostensibly invisible under the guise of Muslim genealogy that connects to the Middle East, Northern African, South Asian, and Southeast Asian countries. The classification of racialized Muslims warrants some attention. The racialization of diasporic Muslim majority communities is subjugated through racial and colonial hierarchies (Wheeler 2020). The complex global Muslim diasporic communities privilege lighter and White-passing subjectivities. Therefore, the categorization or the use of the term 'brown' is an insufficient umbrella classification. This chapter will adopt the term Muslim diasporic communities specified by region and is interested in the racialization of Muslim diasporic communities, particularly Black Muslim women. We also recognize the limitations associated with the term women. An examination of Nonbinary and LGBTQ2S+ Muslim diasporic communities is outside the scope of this chapter. The erasure of Black Muslim women will be centred and linked with several case studies that integrate an examination of critical sports studies. An analysis of Black Muslim sportswomen will illuminate the pervasiveness of anti-Black racism and interrogate scholarship that functions to evade race and racist discourses. Wheeler (2020, para. 15) claims that:

> Not only do Black Muslim women face intersecting misogynoir and gendered Islamophobia from non-Muslims, they often face misogynoir from other Muslims. Struggles over who gets to represent Islam to the non-Muslim public are often rooted in anti-Blackness, with Black Muslim women bearing the brunt of the criticism.

There is a dearth of research on Black Muslim women, and even less when referencing Black Muslim sportswomen. Critical intersectional scholarship of Muslim sportswomen (Ahmad et al. 2020; Ahmad and Thorpe 2020; Samie 2017) fails to integrate CRT or approaches inclusive of Blackness and Black identities. Therefore, it is incumbent on scholars to integrate the literature of Black women and Black sportswomen. A further examination is required to provide insight and build a framework that operates to conceptualize the experiences of the Black Muslim sportswomen and investigate how race affects religious sport studies. This work is heavily inspired by CRT, grounded in the four principles that are reviewed for the ease of readers here. The first tenet is (1) race and racism are ever present, timeless, and endemic, (2) CRT seeks to challenge constructed ideologies of objectivity and racial neutrality, (3) CRT is committed to social justice and the eradication of racial inequities, and (4) CRT aims to promote the experiential knowledge of Black people and other marginalized racialized groups as legitimate and central to the understanding of subjugated people through their own voices (Dei 2005; Hylton 2010). The exploration of identifiable Black Muslim sportswomen will be utilized through the adoption of a CRT approach to investigate race, sporting cultures, and religion. Capturing the nuances of the Muslim sportswomen must centre race to complicate understandings of critical discourses and examine systemic anti-Black racism within sport studies and sporting cultures.

Black Sportswomen

Satou Sabally is a Women's National Basketball Association (WNBA) player with the Dallas Wings. Sabally entered into the draft after completing three years on a full basketball scholarship at the University of Oregon, where she earned her degree in general social sciences with a focus on criminal law and society and a minor in legal studies. Her mixed-race identity is often a point of inquiry among reporters and interactions with people. Sabally's mother is White, and her father is Black and is a descendant from Gambia (Ayala 2020; Gentry 2020; McGregor 2020). Sabally was born in New York City, New York. When she was two years old, her family moved back to Gambia, located in West Africa. Another relocation to her mother's homeland of Germany coincided with Sabally's entry into the school system. Sabally lived there until she returned to the United States on a full scholarship to play basketball at the University of Oregon. Sabally self-identifies as Muslim and chooses not to wear the hijab. The complexities presented in Sabally's diasporic identity demarcate a departure from the traditional Muslim sportswoman. The University of Oregon Ducks women's basketball team received unprecedented media coverage owing to their reigning success on the court and superstar roster. The 2020 pandemic prevented their path to glory and potentially winning the NCAA title (ESPN 2020). Sabally's decision to enter the WNBA launched participation in a professional league with a bigger platform that she effectively embraced to speak to anti-Blackness and Islam (Ayala 2020; Gentry 2020; McGregor 2020).

This chapter is not an exhaustive account of Black Muslim sportswomen. The limited data presented aims to demonstrate the misogynoir[3] experienced in/outside of Muslim diasporic communities. The mosque, similar to other places of worship, operates as a centrepiece that facilitates religious expression, creation of valuable networks, and execution of various programs in Muslim cultures. In the United States and Canada, the organization of mosques is primarily by national origin and race. The various sects of Muslim, as previously stated, can be labelled "ummah" (Karim 2006; McMurray 2020). Karim (2006) found that most US mosque worshippers align with ethnocultural or racial classification such as African American, South Asian, or Arab. The data revealed that mosques do not appear to culturally mix:

> Most African American Muslims worship at mosques in which over 90% of the population is African American. When two ethnic groups are equally represented in a mosque, they tend to be a combination of two immigrant

groups, Arabs and South Asians, but rarely an African American and immigrant combination. (Karim 2006, 227)

The quote clearly demonstrates how communities "choose" to separate on the basis of racial–ethnocultural markers that also operate to uphold systems that practice anti-Blackness.

Racial Reckoning

The racial awakening consequently sparked conversations surrounding anti-Black racism not only in White communities but among several other racial identity groups (Ojo 2020). South Asians, Southeast Asians, and Arabs were forced to answer questions related to how anti-Blackness served to benefit their existence in the Global North[4] (Sultan 2020). Answering the recent trending question "how do I benefit from anti-Black racism?" critical South Asian academics, community leaders, and religious pundits reignited discourses of how model minority myths align to support White supremacy that ostensibly functions to uphold anti-Blackness (Sultan 2020). Immigrants and people of colour establish a recognizable distance from Blacks who operate to create immeasurable value from placing themselves above Blacks in the racial hierarchy (Ojo 2020; Sultan 2020; Zenquis and Mwaniki 2019). In addition, anti-Blackness is further propagated when non-Black communities fail to acknowledge the pervasiveness of racism (Ojo 2020; Sultan 2020). Several examples are ubiquitous in the current climate of polarizing views. The 2020 US presidential election revealed support for racist ideologies and an outright rejection of antiracism operatives (Byler 2020; Paul 2020; Ray 2020). When Canadian hockey commentator Don Cherry was fired from Rogers Sportsnet two years ago for xenophobic comments, many South Asians, in Canada, participated in protests in rallying cries of support and were subsequently quoted in news articles, radio shows and television appearances as opposing his termination (Robertson 2019). Prominent South Asians have also been hired in powerful positions, including directors of education boards, to be eventually fired for their mishandling and denial of anti-Blackness and systemic racism. Community activists and the media's coverage served to publicly expose the mishandlings of several racial incidents. The intense scrutiny and pressure to terminate leadership positions resulted in the firings (*CBC News* 2020; Javed and Rushowy 2017). Dominant narratives of neoliberalism and meritocracy are often cited among South Asians and other Muslim diasporic communities. For example, "we made it and work hard, why can't they" or "I also experienced racism and I was able to not let it determine my fate" work to absolve their role in the reproduction of oppressive practices that remain unscrutinized and uncomplicated (Ojo 2020; Sultan 2020). The "tangible" by-product of attempts to dismantle systemic racist policies and practices is masked with "comprehensive" diversity policies fulfilled with representation quotas of non-Blacks and/or people of colour ill-equipped or hardly motivated to redress anti-Black racism (Ahmed 2012; Ojo 2020; Sultan 2020).

Therefore, in the Global North a "Muslim privilege" (Karim 2006) by Muslim diasporic communities function to render the Black Muslim invisible. Karim (2006, 227) argues that:

> Immigrants, therefore, do benefit from race-based power structures by distancing themselves from blacks. They perpetuate racism especially when they fail to "acknowledge its existence." The way in which immigrant Muslims speak less about racial discrimination compared to African American Muslims, and in certain cases refuse to acknowledge racism, indicates immigrant Muslim privilege.

There is a lack of analyses of the implication of race and racial hierarchies within popular discourses of Muslim women. Alternatively, new representations of the Muslim sportswomen were buttressed through corporatization efforts by Nike, one of the most powerful, recognizable brands in the world (Bahrainwala and O'Connor 2019). The absence of race and racial hierarchies, as well as representation of "traditional" Muslim sportswomen discourses, were seen as a rightful opportunity for Nike to unquestionably extract capital gain. The next section attempts to explain how athletic industries co-opted Muslim sportswomen global social movements to produce highly visible marketing campaigns that obfuscated the identity of Black Muslim sportswomen.

Corporatization

The rise of the Muslim women in popular discourses and mainstream media was accelerated by sportswomen and their pursuit of being treated equally on the field (Bahrainwala and O'Connor 2019; Rush 2019). Bilqis Abdul-Qaadir achieved international fame after a three-year campaign, #FIBAAllowHijab, that proved to successfully change the rules in the game of basketball.[5] Once FIBA[6] struck down the antiquated policy, behind the FIFA[7] 2014 decision, making head coverings permissible (Aljazeera 2017), a surge in studies of veiled Muslim women in sports followed (Samie 2017). The rule change in sport was simultaneously met with legislation that banned wearing of the hijab in workplaces (Quebec, Canada) and public spaces (France) (Montpetit 2020; Silverstein 2020). Olympic athlete Ibtihaj Mohammed and international basketball player Bilqis Abdul-Qaadir became the US poster women that symbolized that wearing the hijab can also embody Americanness (Wheeler 2019; Safronova 2017; Toffoletti et al. 2018; Ziegler 2020).

Nike quickly realized that the combination of controversy and athlete activism equated a genius marketing campaign that sold a postfeminist sensibility (Cole and Hribar 1995) and created a dominant narrative that Muslim women were in control of their own body by purchasing the athletic fitted Nike branded hijab. The media framing of the Muslim sportswomen narrative was arguably initially controlled by Nike and mainstream media (Bahrainwala and O'Connor, 2019). Nike, however, did not design the "first athletic hijabs" (Bahrainwala and O'Connor, 2019) and Bahrainwala and

O'Connor (2019) further claim that Nike is ultimately responsible for the early narrative framing of the 'Muslim sportswomen.' The framing, however, was not inclusive of a Black Muslim identity. Commercials filmed in Dubai and the United States immediately received notoriety and millions of views. The first Nike commercial filmed in the Middle East, internationally praised for a focus on Muslim women, noticeably had no Afro-Arab representation (Ahmed 2017). Critical sport studies examined the corporatization of the hijab but failed to address the anti-Blackness perpetuated in the corporatization of the Muslim sportswomen identity.

'Oppressed veiled Muslim women' seeking 'freedom' by wearing Nike branded hijab are therefore uncomplicated by race hierarchies and race logic. African American Muslims or the Muslim Black diasporic identities are excluded despite the fact that some of the prominent models of Nike's athletic hijab marketing campaign, were Black Muslims (Ibtijah Muhammed and Bilqis Abdul-Qaadir). Nike's strategic marketing techniques align with familiar discourses of Muslim women's liberation that falsely assert that permitting, demanding, and insisting that hijabs be worn during sport competitions or athletic pursuits is the singular marker of "freedom" for Muslim women (Johnson 2018; Samie 2017; Spalek 2005). Ibtihaj and Abdul-Qaadir typically avoided and/or rarely were given opportunities to discuss race that operated to maintain the hierarchal position that valorized a Muslim identity. The recent racial reckoning, however, has forced Bilqis to reimagine her Blackness:

> Embrace your and our blackness. Embrace our existence, and then at the same time, embrace the rights that we have as Islamic women that make us great. As I mentioned, I just recently embraced my blackness. I used to feel it was cool to feel like you look mixed or whatever. That was not a healthy mindset. So, do not try to change who we are, who you are, your nature, our nature because we are gorgeous and people want to be like us. (Dixon, n.d., para. 19)

Abdul-Qaadir alluded to her disidentification of a Black or African American identity (Dixon, n.d.) A religious hierarchy also exists in the Global North among Blacks; Christianity is privileged and purported in/outside of Black communities (Karim 2006). Therefore, embodying Islam is not favoured in the colonial order, but embodying an identity of Muslim women provides a cultural currency and privilege not afforded to Black women (Dixon, n.d.; Karim 2006; McMurray 2007; Spalek 2005). Abdul-Qaadir's unprecedented media coverage also supports Western feminist ideologies that pathologize, "others" and frames the veiled women as the "desirable Muslim femininity" that is oppressed and needs saving by liberal White women (Toffoletti et al. 2018, 117). Conversely, Muslim women who choose not to cover often receive less media coverage with a few exceptions (Samie 2017). Mainstream media do not often showcase Black Muslim women who cover, and even rarer are depictions of uncovered Black Muslim women (McMurray 2007). Recently, Nike released another commercial featuring Fitriya Mohamed, a Black Muslim sportswoman that runs a basketball summer league for Muslim women. Although Mohamed proudly states her Blackness, all but one are Hijabi Muslims, once again privileging the veiled women (Hagi 2020; Nike 2020). A critical review of Black women in the (sport) media is helpful to understand the discourses of Black Muslim sportswomen.

Black Women and Media

Black women in the media have been critically examined by a host of prominent scholars (Collins 1990; Crenshaw, 2006, 2018; hooks 1990, 2012; Sharpe 2016). The findings are similar yet distinct in sport media (Douglas 2005, 2012, 2014; Douglas and Jamieson 2006; Wensing and Bruce 2003; Ifekwunigwe 2018; Razack and Joseph 2021; Zenquis and Mwaniki 2019). Carter-Francique and Richardson (2016, 13) argue that "media sport cultural complex works to maintain dominant notions and reaffirm societal categorizations" and further argue that "Black women in sport represent the antithesis of the White male—heterosexual—protestant imagery that dominates society; and their 'Othered' status has rendered them invisible and silenced in research, literature, and media (Bruening 2005)" (as cited in Carter-Francique and Richardson 2016, 14). The Global North's preoccupation with the hijab further functions to eliminate critical engagements with varying racial identities of Muslim women.

European standards of beauty are upheld within the Western Islamic fashion space and the media, more broadly, the most dominant representations of Muslim women being thin, middle-class, fair-skinned, and veiled (Lewis 2019; Peterson 2020). Black and plus-sized bodies are often excluded from definitions of modesty because women who exist outside of these categories are made invisible or the targets of scrutiny. Muslim lifestyle blogger Minara el Rahman states that:

> You're dealing with kind of a double discrimination [that] reinforces racial stereotypes if you're a plus size woman of colour stereotypes of laziness, lack of self-control. Ironically, even if you're a hijabi, even [stereotypes of] sexuality; that you're more easy because you're a woman of colo[u]r who's plus size, that you're more willing to take sexual advances even. (Lewis 2019, 252)

Black Muslim woman Miski Muse faced similar issues when a photo she uploaded to Instagram was removed after being flagged as inappropriate (Lewis 2019). The censorship of this image became controversial because Muse was fully dressed, donning a black hijab and long-sleeved shirt tucked into a pair of jeans. Muse criticized the platform in an Instagram post stating that "Curvy is tacitly seen as immodest—sexualized by default—so my photos as a curvy hijabi are consumed and seen as obscene" (Gouda 2017). The story gained traction within modest fashion spaces, and Muse became the target of harassment from predominantly Arab Muslim online communities (Lewis 2019). Many claimed that Muse was not following correct hijab guidelines as she failed to conceal the shape of her body (Lewis 2019). For many Black Muslim women, both their knowledge and authenticity as Muslims are often called into question. It is evident that while many Black Muslim women are fighting against sexualization, erasure, and misrepresentation, they continue to be targeted by members of their community rather than uplifted. Muslim diasporic women simultaneously receive support and scrutiny within sport spaces yet remain extremely vulnerable to harassment and discrimination (Samie 2017). As mentioned earlier, studies lack attention to the "sameness of their oppression" in women's long-standing fight to achieve gender equity in sports (Mohanty 2003, p.22). As noted in critical Muslim sport studies, some women prefer to have no media at practices and games and choose to veil and struggle to balance family life with active participation (Samie 2017). These decisions are ubiquitous social issues common to all cultures and exist within a patriarchal world order but similarly align to the grievances of third-wave feminists that convincingly posited that previous women's movements centred around whiteness and White women aligned with heteronormative values (Collins 1990). More of an intersectional approach in Muslim sport studies is required to adequately investigate race and racial identities. A closer examination of racial hierarchies and race logic that are compounded by gender and class as well as other axes of oppression are necessary to more adequately contribute to Muslim sportswomen scholarship. Current prominent Black Muslim sportswomen are disrupting dominant narratives of the Muslim sportswomen. The next section discusses the complex identity of how Satou Sabally amplifies her voice to speak about anti-Black racism.

Resistance

Many athletes of mixed race often represent complex diasporic identities and often resist speaking about their cultural identity or are unable to contextualize their social position (Razack and Joseph 2021). Sabally is the third youngest of seven children. In several interviews and personal social media platforms, Sabally displays knowledge of CRT and social justice movements: "Black men [and women] being murdered? I can't just forget that. I'm always going to pick that as my priority and speak out and do what's right, and I feel like anyone else should, too" (Gentry 2020). Sabally's off-court involvement in various activism efforts has engendered critical dialogues around anti-Black racism in sport (Ayala 2020; Gentry 2020). Conversely, Batouly Camara, former University of Connecticut Women's basketball player, recent winner of the Billie Jean King Youth Leadership award and *Forbes* 30 under-30 recipient (Philppou 2020), states that "[s]omeone once said that to be Black and to be Muslim at the moment is a place of culture, of activism, of a strong history of education, of innovation and art and creativity, a strong history of survival" (Burn It All Down Podcast: Hot Take June 5, 2020). Centring race and religion is a physical risk, as witnessed by the vitriol experienced by prominent US congresswomen Ilhan Omar (Stewart 2019). The examples demonstrate the fierce dedication of Sabally, Camara, and Omar to acknowledging the moral imperative and work required to dismantle anti-Black racism globally and in/outside of Muslim sporting cultures.

Political figures such as Ilhan also contribute to disrupting hegemonic discourses of Black Muslim women. The repeated Islamophobia and racially motivated attacks faced by veiled Black Muslim women demonstrate a motivation to cling to a particular

Muslim identity (Stewart 2019). Sabally, however, encompasses a different modality, similar to Barack Obama, as they can negotiate their belonging and align with whiteness owing to their parental lineage. The shade of your skin also precludes or inhibits your ability to navigate through spaces and also various forms of acceptance. Black women bear the brunt of shadeism discrimination in sports (Carter-Francique and Richardson 2016), whereas lighter-skinned athletes are glorified and dark-skinned athletes are rarely the receiver of unwavering adoration from the media and/or the public.

Several feature stories capture quotes that express Sabally's recognition of the media's inability to align her identity with colonial binary classifications. The anti-Blackness that she experienced is illustrated through the order of questioning when people are unable to locate her accent and place her within existing racial and religious hierarchies. Often asked about her social location, she expresses:

> If you have lived in so many places as I have, I would really say that I'm kind of from everywhere . . . I'm strongly proud that I'm African and German, well, Gambian and German, which is also a distinction. A lot of people in Germany would always be like, "Oh, Africa!" In my head, it's like saying you're from America and exclude Canada and Mexico. But people really want to know why you're Black, and not where you're from. (Ayala 2020, para. 8)

Sabally has intuitively realized that people who inquire about her identity are most often attempting to locate her Blackness to then place her within a racial hierarchy (Ayala 2020; Gentry 2020; McGregor 2020). Sabally embraces her Blackness yet recognizes the "double consciousness" of internal conflict whereby dominant racial meanings attached to an identity is juxtaposed to an understanding and tensions of your own personal defined identity (Du Bois 1994). Her identity is often determined by geography: "[W]hen I am in Germany I am the Black girl, then when I go to Gambia I'm the white girl" (McGregor 2020, para. 2). Carter-Francique and Richardson (2016, 17) argue that "Black women's way of knowing, or the 'outsider within status'"(p.11), also serves as a method to analyze Black women's experiences." Several other high-profile Black Muslim athletes: Batouly Camara (Guinea, UCONN basketball), Jamad Fiin (D-III basketball), Asisat Oshoala (Nigerian professional soccer-Barcelona), Samia Yusuf Omar, Zeainab Alema (United Kingdom, rugby), Bridget Pettis (former WNBA basketball player, former assistant coach Chicago Sky WNBA team) (Burn It All Down Podcast 2020b) receive(d) moderate media attention that focuses primarily on cultural and religious tenets (Shireen Ahmed, personal communication, November 30, 2020). Each of the athletes has their own unique journey toward acceptance in sporting cultures. Achieving acceptance within sport and respective Muslim communities appears to be an ongoing struggle with most of the athletes.[8]

Dalilah Muhammad is another example that signifies the nuances of race, religion, and gender expression in sport. Muhammad became an Olympic hurdler gold medalist in the 2016 Rio games, representing the United States alongside fencer Ibtihaj

Muhammad. Dalilah proudly identifies as an African American Muslim woman, and her parents attribute her discipline as an athlete to her Islamic teachings (Levine 2016). As an uncovered Black Muslim woman, Dalilah received less media coverage than Muhammed, with several sources failing to mention her faith at all. When questioned about the lack of attention from the media as a Muslim sportswoman, Muhammed told *Teen Vogue*:

> Wearing a hijab may be desirable in the Muslim community but it is not required. In my faith it's most important to have a conscious awareness of God and that can be done with or without a hijab. It's my personal choice to go uncovered. (Webster 2016)

Muhammed went on to state that she "hope[s] to at least break the stereotype of what a Muslim woman looks like" (Webster 2016). Toffoletti et al. (2018) notes that media were reluctant to highlight Muhammed disrupting essentialist representations of the Muslim sportswomen that centre the hijab and omit other aspects of Muslim femininity. A closer examination of Black female athlete ideologies consequently functions to also render the Black Muslim sportswomen invisible.

Black Female Athletes

The Black female athlete is typically conflated with an understanding of "the Black athlete" that supports a "narrow definition that centre Black cisgender men" (Adjepong 2020, 870). The Black female athlete is lumped with Black male athletes that are connected to masculine ideologies subsequently attached to Black women's bodies. In the Global North, White feminine ideologies operate to support discourses that "reify blackness as aggressive masculinity erase [B]lack butches, bulldaggers and masculine women while delimiting access to femininity for [B]lack people of all genders" (Adjepong 2020, 871). Therefore, how "[B]lack women's masculinity is legitimized by contrasting it as less masculine than Black men's, and always in the context of heterosexuality" (Adjepong 2020, 871). Several scholars note that the masculine framing of Black sportswomen is mostly a Eurocentric practice (Bailey 2016; Douglas 2012; Carter-Francique and Richardson 2016; Adjepong 2020). In some Black diasporic communities, Black women are associated by the media with nationalism, athleticism, and femininity and are depicted in a relatively positive light (Carter-Francique and Richardson 2016; Adjepong 2020). An abundance of scholarship on the misogynoir offers discourses that frame Black women as antithetical to acceptable (White) femininity (Bailey 2016; Carter-Francique and Richardson 2016; Douglas 2012; Ifekwunigwe 2018). Mainstream media representations of Black female athletes focus predominantly on "natural" athletic prowess, obfuscating their femininity that operates to fuel dominant ideologies (Carter-Francique and Richardson 2016; Douglas 2012). The veiled Black Muslim sportswoman is attached to notions of femininity, whereas the uncovered remains vulnerable to familiar tropes of Black sportswomen. Batouly Camara and Bridgette Perris have recently chosen to cover, demonstrating the fluidity and complexity of Muslim women discourses (Shireen Ahmed, personal communication, November 30, 2020). Black men are more easily accepted as athletes, and Black Muslim men are rarely, if ever, surveilled or policed for their wardrobe on or off the field (Adjepong and Carrington 2012; Samie 2017). The policing of Black Muslim sportswomen adds constant pressure to align with respectability politics that require endless negotiation and navigation. Any transgressions or "deviant" behaviour cement an ideology that Black Muslim sportswomen are "somehow out of place, even when they win" (Adjepong and Carrington 2012, 4).

CONCLUDING REMARKS

Sport culture is not welcoming for women, and even less so for Black Muslim women. For anyone whose appearance disrupts normative ideologies of aesthetics and sport contributes to the tension of balancing commitments to, for example, Islam. The tension of balancing an outward commitment to the Muslim faith can, at times, outweigh the need to publicly pronounce an alignment with a Black identity. Critical sport scholars need to better integrate religion, race, and racial discourses to interrogate "the exclusion of [B]lack people from the narrative of the imagined community" (Adjepong and Carrington 2012, 7). A Muslim privilege enables a disidentification with Blackness; however, the recent global racial injustice political movements have created new spaces for Black Muslim sportswomen to speak more safely about their intersecting identities (Zirin 2017). The ruptures "biologically, culturally and symbolically (Yuval-Davis 1997), [offered by Black Muslim] sportswomen ... can produce powerful counter-narratives to mono-culturalist political movements" (Adjepong and Carrington 2012, 7). An important consideration is how athletes of mixed race, with a White parental lineage often carry more social capital and an accrued ability to negotiate their identities and belonging owing to a heritage that connects to a racial colonial hierarchy. The tensions within Muslim diasporic communities are impacted by a race logic that functions to privilege a White heteronormative patriarchal order. Resistance is legitimized by contesting representations in the media, and counter-narratives strengthened by the participatory web (Razack and Joseph 2021). Adjepong and Carrington (2012, 7) claim that "tracing the new and varied layers of meaning produced by the very presence and success of [B]lack female athletes will help us to better understand the changing dynamics of gender and sexuality both in sport and wider society." Intersectional Muslim sport studies must attempt to make sense of sporting cultures that continue to be implicated by race and anti-Black racism.

CHAPTER NOTES

[1] Ummah is an Arabic word meaning "community."
[2] Arabic Ḥadīth ("News" or "Story"), also spelled Hadīth, record of the traditions or sayings of the Prophet Muhammad, revered and received as a major source of religious

law and moral guidance, second only to the authority of the Qurān, the holy book of Islam.

[3] Misogynoir is a portmanteau developed by Dr. Moya Bailey to describe the racial discrimination experienced specifically by Black women in the media and everyday life.

[4] The terms Global North/South are used to separate how the world was geographically split into richer and poorer nations. Almost all richer countries are located in the Northern Hemisphere (with the exception of Australia and New Zealand), whereas poor countries are mostly located in tropical regions in the Southern Hemisphere.

[5] Note that Indira Kaljo is also attached to globally lobbying for the rule change in FIBA.

[6] The International Basketball Federation, more commonly known by the French acronym FIBA (Fédération Internationale de Basketball), is an association of national organizations that governs international competition in basketball.

[7] FIFA stands for "Fédération Internationale de Football Association" and is the international federation governing association football (to distinguish it from "union football," i.e., rugby).

[8] Shireen Ahmed, personal communication, November 30, 2020.

REFERENCES

Adjepong, Anima. 2020. "Voetsek! Get[Ting] Lost: African Sportswomen in 'the Sporting Black Diaspora.' " *International Review for the Sociology of Sport* 55 (7): 868–83. https://doi.org/10.1177/1012690219834486.

Adjepong, L. Anima, and Ben Carrington. 2012. "Black Female Athletes as Space Invaders." In *Routledge Handbook of Sport, Gender and Sexuality*. Routledge. https://doi.org/10.4324/9780203121375.ch18.

Ahmad, Nida, and Holly Thorpe. "Muslim sportswomen as digital space invaders: Hashtag politics and everyday visibilities." *Communication & Sport* 8, no. 4-5 (2020): 668-91.

Ahmad, Nida, Holly Thorpe, Justin Richards, and Amy Marfell. 2020. "Building Cultural Diversity in Sport: A Critical Dialogue with Muslim Women and Sports Facilitators." *International Journal of Sport Policy and Politics* 12 (4): 1–17. https://doi.org/10.1080/19406940.2020.1827006.

Ahmed, Sara. 2012. *On Being Included: Racism and Diversity in Institutional Life*. London: Duke University Press.

Ahmed, Shireen. 2017. " 'What Will They Say about Me?': Nike Middle East's New Ad." *Muslim Media Watch*, March 7, 2017. http://www.muslimahmediawatch.org/2017/03/07/what-will-they-say-about-me-nike-middle-easts-new-ad/.

———. 2020. "Personal Communication." November 30, 2020. http://www.shireenahmed.com/.

"FIBA allows hijab in professional basketball." *Al Jazeera*. May 4, 2017

Almila, Anna-Mari. 2016. "Fashion, Anti-Fashion, Non-Fashion and Symbolic Capital: The Uses of Dress among Muslim Minorities in Finland." *Fashion Theory* 20 (1): 81–102. https://doi.org/10.1080/1362704X.2015.1078136.

Ayala, Erica. 2020. "Satou Sabally: Dallas Wings Forward Is a WNBA Unicorn." *Sports Illustrated*, August 27, 2020. https://www.si.com/wnba/2020/08/27/satou-sabally-dallas-wings-oregon-rookie-year

Bahrainwala, Lamiyah, and Erin O'Connor. 2019. "Nike Unveils Muslim Women Athletes." *Feminist Media Studies*, May 28, 2019: 1–16. https://doi.org/10.1080/14680777.2019.1620822.

Bailey, Moya. 2016. "Misogynoir in Medical Media: On Caster Semenya and R. Kelly." *Catalyst: Feminism, Theory, Technoscience* 20 (2): 1–31. https://doi.org/10.28968/cftt.v2i2.28800

Burn It All Down Podcast. 2020a. "Black Women Athletes Speak Out." June 5, 2020. Audio 1:11:08. https://www.burnitalldownpod.com/episodes/black-women-athletes-speak-out?rq=batouly%20camara.

———. 2020b. "Hot Take: Interview with Bridget Pettis, Veteran WNBA Player and Coach." Audio, 16:25. August 20, 2020. https://www.burnitalldownpod.com/episodes/hot-take-interview-with-bridget-pettis-veteran-wnba-player-and-coach?rq=bridget%20pettis.

Byler, David. 2020. "Opinion: Trump Shocked the World with His Latino Support. Here's How It Happened." *The Washington Post*, November 12, 2020. https://www.washingtonpost.com/opinions/2020/11/12/trump-shocked-world-with-his-latino-support-heres-how-it-happened/.

Carter-Francique, Akilah R., and F. Michelle Richardson. 2016. "Controlling Media, Controlling Access: The Role of Sport Media on Black Women's Sport Participation." *Race, Gender & Class* 23 (1/2): 7–33. http://www.jstor.org/stable/26529186

CBC News. 2020. "Ontario Fires Peel School Board's Director of Education in Bid to Confront Systemic Racism." June 23, 2020. https://www.cbc.ca/news/canada/toronto/peel-school-board-peter-joshua-1.5623916.

Cole, Cheryl L., and Amy Hribar. 1995. "Celebrity Feminism: Nike Style Post-Fordism, Transcendence, and Consumer Power." *Sociology of Sport Journal* 12 (4): 347–69. https://doi.org/10.1123/ssj.12.4.347.

Collins, Patricia. 1990. *Black Feminist Thought: Knowledge, Consciousness, and the Politics of Empowerment*. London: Routledge.

Crenshaw, Kimberlé Williams. 2006. "Mapping the Margins: Intersectionality, Identity Politics and Violence against Women of Color." *Kvinder, Køn & Forskning* 2–3 (June): 7–20. https://doi.org/10.7146/kkf.v0i2-3.28090.

———. 2018. "Demarginalizing the Intersection of Race and Sex: A Black Feminist Critique of Antidiscrimination Doctrine, Feminist Theory, and Antiracist Politics [1989]." In *Feminist Legal Theory*. 1st ed., edited by Katharine T. Bartlett and Rosanne Kennedy, 57–80. London: Routledge. https://doi.org/10.4324/9780429500480-5.

Dei, George J. Sefa. 2005. "Chapter One: Critical Issues in Anti-Racist Research Methodologies: An Introduction." *Counterpoints* 252: 1–27. https://www.jstor.org/stable/i40115790

Dixon, Nia Malaika. n.d. "Bilqis Abdul-Qaadir." *#BlackMuslimGirlFly*. https://blackmuslimgirlfly.wordpress.com/portfolio/bilqis-abdul-qaadir/.

Douglas, Delia D. 2005. "Venus, Serena, and the Women's Tennis Association: When and Where 'Race' Enters." *Sociology of Sport Journal* 22 (3): 255–81. https://doi.org/10.1123/ssj.22.3.255.

———. 2012. "Venus, Serena, and the Inconspicuous Consumption of Blackness: A Commentary on Surveillance, Race Talk, and New Racism(s)." *Journal of Black Studies* 43 (2): 127–45. https://doi.org/10.1177/0021934711410880.

———. 2014. "Forget Me . . . Not: Marion Jones and the Politics of Punishment." *Journal of Sport and Social Issues* 38 (1): 3–22. https://doi.org/10.1177/0193723513515892.

Douglas, Delia D., and Katherine M. Jamieson. "A farewell to remember: Interrogating the Nancy Lopez farewell tour." *Sociology of Sport Journal* 23, no. 2 (2006): 117-41.

DuBois, W. EB. *Criteria of Negro Art*. Duke University Press, 1994.

ESPN. 2020. "Why Sabrina Ionescu and Oregon Would Have Won the 2020 NCAA Women's Basketball Championship." *ESPN.com*, April 2, 2020. https://www.espn.com/womens-college-basketball/story/_/id/28983467/why-sabrina-ionescu-oregon-won-2020-ncaa-women-basketball-championship.

Gentry, Dorothy. 2020. " 'I'm Here for a Reason': Satou Sabally Captures WNBA with Her Game and Her Voice." *The Athletic*, July 29, 2020. https://theathletic.co.uk/1959820/2020/07/29/im-here-for-a-reason-satou-sabally-captures-wnba-with-her-game-and-her-voice/.

Gouda, Sarah. 2017. "Instagram Censored This Curvy Muslim Woman's Selfie for No Apparent Reason." *Teen Vogue*, March 7, 2017. https://www.teenvogue.com/story/instagram-curvy-muslim-woman.

Hagi, Sarah. 2020. "Fitriya Mohamed Is Changing the Game—and the Conversation—around Muslim Women in Sports." *Toronto Star*, January 10, 2021. https://www.thestar.com/life/together/people/2021/01/10/fitriya-mohamed-is-changing-the-game-and-the-conversation-around-muslim-women-in-sports.html.

hooks, bell. 1990. *Yearning: Race, Gender, and Cultural Politics*. London: Routledge.

———. 2012. "Eating the Other: Desire and Resistance." In *Media and Cultural Studies: Keyworks*, edited by Meenakshi Gigi Durham and Douglas M. Kellner, 308. Malden, MA: Wiley-Blackwell.

Hylton, Kevin. 2010. "How a Turn to Critical Race Theory Can Contribute to Our Understanding of 'Race', Racism and Anti-Racism in Sport." *International Review for the Sociology of Sport* 45 (3): 335–54. https://doi.org/10.1177/1012690210371045.

Ifekwunigwe, Jayne O. 2018. " 'And Still Serena Rises': Celebrating the Cross-Generational Continuities of Black Feminisms and Black Female Excellence in Sport." In *The Palgrave Handbook of Feminism and Sport, Leisure and Physical Education*, edited by Louise Mansfield, Jayne Caudwell, Belinda Wheaton, and Beccy Watson, 111–31. London: Palgrave Macmillan. https://doi.org/10.1057/978-1-137-53318-0_8.

Ifteqar, Naheed. 2019. "Banana Republic Is Now Selling Hijabs, but Not Everyone Is Happy about It—Here's Why." *Vogue Arabia*, July 31, 2019. https://en.vogue.me/culture/banana-republic-hijabs/.

Javed, Noor, and Kristen Rushowy. 2017. "York School Board Ousts Controversial Director." *Toronto Star*, April 19, 2017, https://www.thestar.com/yourtoronto/education/2017/04/19/york-school-board-ousts-controversial-director.html.

Johnson, Azeezat. 2018. "Centring Black Muslim Women in Britain: A Black Feminist Project." *Gender, Place & Culture* 25 (11): 1676–80. https://doi.org/10.1080/0966369X.2018.1551785.

Karim, Jamillah A. 2006. "To Be Black, Female, and Muslim: A Candid Conversation about Race in the American *Ummah*." *Journal of Muslim Minority Affairs* 26 (2): 225–33. https://doi.org/10.1080/13602000600937655.

Levine, Daniel. 2016. "Dalilah Muhammad: 5 Fast Facts You Need to Know." *Heavy*, August 19, 2016. https://heavy.com/sports/2016/08/dalilah-muhammad-400-meter-hurdles-who-is-bio-favorite-stats-team-usa-rio-olympics-track-family-religion/.

Lewis, Reina. 2019. "Modest Body Politics: The Commercial and Ideological Intersect of Fat, Black, and Muslim in the Modest Fashion Market and Media." *Fashion Theory* 23 (2): 243–73. https://doi.org/10.1080/1362704X.2019.1567063.

McGregor, Nesta. 2020. "Satou Sabally: Dallas Wings Player on Internal Conflict and 'Using Her Platform.' " *BBC Sport*, August 21, 2020. https://www.bbc.com/sport/basketball/53854221

McMurray, Anaya. 2007. "Hotep and Hip-Hop: Can Black Muslim Women Be Doum with Hip-Hop?" *Meridians* 8 (1): 74–92. https://doi.org/10.2979/MER.2007.8.1.74.

Mohanty, Chandra Talpade. 2003. *Feminism without Borders: Decolonizing Theory, Practicing Solidarity.* London: Duke University Press. https://doi.org/10.1215/9780822384649.

Montpetit, Jonathan. 2020. "Uphold Religious Symbol Ban to Spare Children from Being Influenced by Hijab, Quebec Parents Plead." *CBC News*, November 9, 2020. https://www.cbc.ca/news/canada/montreal/bill-21-court-case-quebec-religious-symbols-ban-1.5795610.

Muslim Census. 2020. "A Study into Anti-Blackness amongst Young Muslims within the UK." Muslim Census, July 2020. https://muslimcensus.co.uk/anti-blackness-amongst-young-muslims/.

Nike. 2020. "Fitriya Pushes for Representation—You Can Stop Our Voice—Nike." December 7, 2020. https://www.youtube.com/watch?v=20H8IBv8dKo.

Ojo, Kike. 2020. "Daring to Do: Equity Practice to Change Education Now." September 17, 2020. https://kojoinstitute.com/daring-to-do/

Paul, Sonia. 2020. " 'A Political Awakening': How South Asians Could Tilt Key US Elections." *The Guardian*, September 3, 2020. https://www.theguardian.com/us-news/2020/sep/03/south-asians-us-election-2020.

Peterson, Kristin. 2020. "The Unruly, Loud, and Intersectional Muslim Woman: Interrupting the Aesthetic Styles of Islamic Fashion Images on Instagram." *International Journal of Communication* 14 (20): 1194–213. https://ijoc.org/index.php/ijoc/article/view/12715

Philppou, Alexa. 2020. "Through Starting a Nonprofit, Writing a Children's Book and More, UConn's Batouly Camara Working to Provide Opportunities for Girls through Sports." *Hartford Courant*, April 27, 2020. https://www.courant.com/sports/uconn-womens-basketball/hc-sp-uconn-women-batouly-camara-podcast-20200425-20200427-cyrstzgvyzbifexb4pgxi2xgju-story.html.

Ratna, Aarti. "Not just merely different: Travelling theories, post-feminism and the racialized politics of women of color." *Sociology of Sport Journal* 35, no. 3 (2018): 197-206.

Ratna, Aarti, and Samaya F. Samie, eds. *Race, Gender and Sport: The Politics of Ethnic' Other' Girls and Women.* Routledge, 2017.

Ray, Victor. 2020. "Trump Calls Critical Race Theory 'un-American.' Let's Review." *The Washington Post*, October 2, 2020. https://www.washingtonpost.com/nation/2020/10/02/critical-race-theory-101/

Razack, Sabrina, and Janelle Joseph. 2021. "Misogynoir in Women's Sport Media: Race, Nation, and Diaspora in the Representation of Naomi Osaka." *Media, Culture & Society* 43 (2): 291–308. https://doi.org/10.1177/0163443720960919.

Robertson, Becky. 2019. "There's Now a Rally Planned in Toronto to Support Don Cherry." *blogTO* (blog), November 13, 2019. https://www.blogto.com/sports_play/2019/11/rally-planned-toronto-support-don-cherry/.

Rush, Curtis. 2019. "In Diverse Toronto, the Raptors' Sports Hijab Is Hailed as a Win for Inclusivity." *The Washington Post*, September 19, 2019. https://www.washingtonpost.com/sports/2019/09/19/diverse-toronto-raptors-sports-hijab-is-hailed-win-inclusivity/.

Safronova, Valeriya. 2017. "Nike Reveals the 'Pro Hijab' for Muslim Athletes." *The New York Times*, March 8, 2017, sec. Fashion. https://www.nytimes.com/2017/03/08/fashion/nike-pro-hijab-muslim-athlete.html.

Samie, Samaya Farooq. 2017. "De/Colonising 'Sporting Muslim Women': Post-Colonial Feminist Reflections on the Dominant Portrayal of Sporting Muslim Women in Academic Research, Public Forums and Mediated Representations." In *Race, Gender and Sport: The Politics of Ethnic 'Other' Girls and Women*, 1st ed., edited by Aarti Ratna and Samaya Farooq Samie. New York: Routledge, pp. 35-62. https://doi.org/10.4324/9781315637051.

Samie, Sumaya Farooq, and Sertaç Sehlikoglu. 2015. "Strange, Incompetent and Out-of-Place: Media, Muslim Sportswomen and London 2012." *Feminist Media Studies* 15 (3): 363–81. https://doi.org/10.1080/14680777.2014.947522.

Samie, Sumaya Farooq, and Kim Toffoletti. 2018. "Postfeminist Paradoxes and Cultural Difference: Unpacking Media Representations of American Muslim Sportswomen Ibtihaj and Dalilah Muhammad." In *New Sporting Femininities*, edited by Kim Toffoletti, Holly Thorpe, and Jessica Francombe-Webb, 87–109. New Femininities in Digital, Physical and Sporting Cultures. Cham: Springer International Publishing. https://doi.org/10.1007/978-3-319-72481-2_5.

Sehlikoglu, Sertaç. n.d. "Portrayal of Muslim Female Athletes in the Media: Diversity in Sport." *LSE Equity, Diversity and Inclusion* (blog), August 7, 2012. https://blogs.lse.ac.uk/equityDiversityInclusion/2012/08/portrayal-of-muslim-female-athletes-in-the-media-diversity-in-sport/.

Sharp, David. 2017. "Sporty Hijabs Help Muslim Girls Keep Up Pace in Athletics at Maine High School." *Boston.com*, June 8, 2017. https://www.boston.com/sports/high-school-sports/2017/06/08/sports-hijabs-help-muslim-girls-maine-high-school.

Sharpe, Christina. 2016. *In the Wake: On Blackness and Being*. London: Duke University Press.

Silverstein, Jason. 2020. "France Will Still Ban Islamic Face Coverings Even after Making Masks Mandatory." *CBS News*, May 12, 2020. https://www.cbsnews.com/news/france-burqa-ban-islamic-face-coverings-masks-mandatory/.

Spalek, Basia. 2005. "A Critical Reflection on Researching Black Muslim Women's Lives Post-September 11th." *International Journal of Social Research Methodology* 8 (5): 405–18. https://doi.org/10.1080/1364557032000232862.

Stewart, Emily. 2019. "The Attacks on Ilhan Omar Reveal a Disturbing Truth about Racism in America." *Vox*, December 4, 2019. https://www.vox.com/policy-and-politics/2019/12/4/20995589/ilhan-omar-racism-attacks-twitter-danielle-stella-minnesota.

Sultan, Rana. 2020. "Brown Complicity in White Supremacy towards Solidarity for Black Lives." June 20, 2020. https://www.youtube.com/watch?v=LmaVUiEjb0o&feature=youtu.be.

Tarlo, Emma. 2010. "Hijab Online." *Interventions* 12 (2): 209–25. https://doi.org/10.1080/1369801X.2010.489695.

Taylor, Vanessa. 2019. "Police Took My Hijab. Here's Why It's So Hard to Stop Them from Doing It Again." Talk Poverty, May 13, 2019. https://talkpoverty.org/2019/05/13/police-hijab-stop-again/.

Toffoletti, Kim, Holly Thorpe, and Jessica Francombe-Webb, eds. 2018. *New Sporting Femininities: Embodied Politics in Postfeminist Times*. New Femininities in Digital, Physical and Sporting Cultures. Cham: Springer International Publishing. https://doi.org/10.1007/978-3-319-72481-2.

Webster, Emma Sarran. 2016. "2016 Rio Olympic Gold Medalist Dalilah Muhammad on Making History." *Teen Vogue*, October 7, 2016. https://www.teenvogue.com/story/2016-rio-olympic-gold-medalist-dalilah-muhammad-on-making-history.

59

Wensing, Emma H., and Toni Bruce. 2003. "Bending the Rules: Media Representations of Gender during an International Sporting Event." *International Review for the Sociology of Sport* 38 (4): 387–96. https://doi.org/10.1177/1012690203384001.

Wheeler, Kayla. 2020. "On Centering Black Muslim Women in Critical Race Theory." *Maydan* (blog), September 12, 2020. https://themaydan.com/2020/02/on-centering-black-muslim-women-in-critical-race-theory/.

Yuval-Davis, Nira. 1997. "Women, Citizenship and Difference." *Feminist Review* 57 (1): 4–27. https://doi.org/10.1080/014177897339632.

Zenquis, Manuel R., and Munene F. Mwaniki. 2019. "The Intersection of Race, Gender, and Nationality in Sport: Media Representation of the Ogwumike Sisters." *Journal of Sport and Social Issues* 43 (1): 23–43. https://doi.org/10.1177/0193723518823338.

Ziegler, Hannah. 2020. "Olympic Medalist Ibtihaj Muhammad Talks Inclusivity in Sports." *Elle Canada*, October 15, 2020. https://www.ellecanada.com/culture/society/olympic-medalist-ibtihaj-muhammad-on-inclusivity-in-sports.

Zirin, Dave. 2017. "3 Generations of Athlete Activists All in 1 Place." *The Nation*, October 24, 2017. https://www.thenation.com/article/archive/three-generations-of-athlete-activists-all-in-one-place/.

Chapter 4

Muslim Women's Experiences of Sport and Sport Culture in Toronto

Laurel Walzak and Danica Vidotto, Ph.D.

Introduction

Toronto has a rich and diverse sporting culture. From grassroots organizations like Canadian Girls Baseball (Lebel and Vidotto 2021) to one female professional sports team, Toronto Six, and seven male professional sports teams featuring sports like hockey, basketball, baseball, soccer, football, and rugby (i.e., Leafs, Raptors, Jays, Argos, Arrows, Toronto Rock, Toronto Football Club). Sports are a vibrant part of the city. Toronto's sportswomen, in particular, have emerged in the spotlight in recent years. In 2019, Greater Toronto Area (GTA) native Bianca Andreescu was Canada's highest ranked female tennis player in the Women's Tennis Association (WTA) after placing first at the 2019 US Open, a Grand Slam designated tournament, and first at the Roger's Cup hosted in Toronto, Canada. Rosie MacLennan won bronze at the 2019 Trampoline Gymnastics World Championships, where she also guaranteed Canada a spot for the Tokyo Olympics in 2021. In para swimming, Toronto's Aly Van Wyck-Smart set a world record at the 2019 Canadian Swimming Trials in Toronto in the SM2 150-m individual medley. In sport media, a new Toronto-born startup, called *The Gist,* is producing sports news by women, for women. And the Hijabi Ballers has been created to "recognize and celebrate the athleticism of Muslim girls and women. [HB] work to increase representation, and consequently participation, of Muslim females in sport spaces and sports programs" (Hijabi Ballers, n.d.).

With all the excitement of athletics in the city, there is a need to understand how people of diverse perspectives engage with and experience Toronto's sports culture. This article turns to a Toronto local sports organization, Hijabi Ballers [HB], to investigate the unique perspectives of Muslim sportswomen.

The Hijabi Ballers

The HB is a local community sports organization in Toronto, founded by Amreen Kadwa, offering sports programs and sports participation opportunities, community events, and conferences (Hijabi Ballers, n.d.). The HB works toward four main goals:

1. Increased representation of Muslim females in Toronto's sport spaces and sport media
2. Further opportunities for Muslim females to participate in sport, try new ones, and hone their skills
3. Recognition and celebration of the accomplishments of Muslim female athletes
4. Integration of allies (i.e., coaches, parents, community mentors) in the growth of Muslim females in the sport space (Hijabi Ballers, n.d.).

HB has created space in Toronto's sports culture to bring Muslim sportswomen into the conversation about who belongs in sports and who is celebrated for participating. Since their founding, HB has made waves. In 2019, National Basketball Association (NBA) franchise Toronto Raptors partnered with HB to launch the first professionally branded sports hijab (Rush 2019), close on the heels of the announcement by Nike, in 2017, "[of] the launch of a new product, a pro hijab" (Moore 2018, 1). The visibility and representation of a team as popular as the Raptors supporting the Muslim community, as an audience, in Toronto's sports landscape demonstrate the need to understand how Muslim sportswomen engage with and experience sports culture in Canada and to determine whether factors associated with their experiences support relationships that affect their experiences in sports and sports culture in Toronto.

Muslim Women and Sports

Early research about Muslim women and sports has identified barriers, challenges, and solutions to Muslim women's participation in sports and physical activity (Carrington, Chivers, and Williams 1989; Kay 2006), a focus on the hijab (Jiwani and Rail 2010), and female Muslim representation in media at the Olympic level (Samie and Toffoletti 2018). Often in sporting research, Muslims, especially Muslim sportswomen, have been portrayed as "Other," underrepresented, and/or constructed in a colonial and racialized manner (Abdel-Fattah and Carland 2010; Thorpe, Hayhurst, and Chawansky 2018). Consistently low participation rates of Muslim women in sports and physical activity is apparent in even Islamic countries (Hamzeh and Oliver 2012). Additionally, veiled Muslim women have been typecast to have low socioeconomic status and/or the lack of freedom to exercise (Alwi and Melewar 2017); Summers et al. 2018).

Study Aims

In this study, we explore the experiences and engagements of HB within sports culture in Toronto. This article aims to further understand Muslim women and their negotiations of sports and sports culture. We intend to answer the following two questions: How do Muslim women come to engage with and experience sports and sports culture in Toronto? Are there factors associated with their experiences that support relationships that affect their experiences in sports culture in Toronto? These questions recognize a multidimensional approach to studying sportswomen that include accounting for the "holistic experiences" (Toffoletti and Palmer 2017, 159) of Muslim sportswomen. Answering these questions will provide new insights into the experiences and factors that affect the experiences of Muslim sportswomen. Furthermore, this study heeds the call by Toffoletti and Palmer (2017, 146), who urge researchers to consider "how Muslim women are constructed within sport discourses." Thus, a key objective of this study is to offer a unique perspective on feminist discourses in the sporting landscape. This article produces knowledge on the experiences of Muslim women born in Canada and of those who immigrated to Canada in sports and sports culture in Toronto. In addition, this study will aim to provide the HB organization key insights to possibly inform programming, education, and enhancement of relationships between Muslim sportswomen in sport cultures in Toronto and beyond.

Theoretical Framework

This study employs an intersectional approach (Crenshaw 1991; Hill-Collins 1990). It uses intersectional thinking to untangle and understand the experiences and challenges around what it means to be a Muslim woman engaged in sports and sports culture in Toronto. Studying Muslim women adds another vantage point to discussions of sportswomen. Barak et al. (2018) identify being a female athlete as an intersectional identity. Unique to this study, then, is that we consider the intersecting identities of participants as Muslim, female, and sportswomen. Looking at these intersecting points, we attempt to unearth patterns, contrasts, characteristics, and relationships to make sense of the picture and perspective of participants' lives and autobiographical experiences. Using an intersectional approach expands discourses on women in sports and sporting cultures to facilitate a more inclusive and holistic lens.

METHODOLOGY

We approached the HB organization to gather data and evidence from a convenient sample. This study, however, for any avoidance of doubt, was not commissioned by the HB; rather, they agreed to provide us with access to their organization in order to study their membership. Our original intention to adopt a mixed methodology approach, using a qualitative and quantitative research design, was to conduct internet-based surveys and semistructured interviews with participants. Unfortunately, the initial response rate for this study was low, most likely, if not solely, because of the concern, fear, and priority of the surge of the global pandemic COVID-19, including an Ontario government declaration of a "state of emergency" (Nielsen 2020), which included the GTA. Months later, once the Ontario government started to "propose a recovery plan and start to reopen the province and loosen restrictions" (Nielsen 2020), we decided that it may be an appropriate time to send out the survey again via e-mail to the HB membership to increase the number of respondents for the study. We did this in September 2020 and saw an increase in the number of respondents. This increase provided a sufficient data set to analyze and continue our research. However, in the second stage of our study, semi structured interviews were cancelled because of continued restrictions in place at both the governmental and university levels owing to COVID-19. Thus, this article presents the preliminary findings of our study.

In April 2020, our online digital survey link and instructions were emailed to our HB representative, who then sent this information to their entire membership e-mail list. We relied on the HB membership to receive and read the e-mail and decide whether or not they would like to actively volunteer in the study. If they did participate, they did so by using the internet-based survey, which made it convenient and relatively easy for them to respond and privileged the health and safety requirements resulting from the COVID-19 pandemic. Digital surveys privilege anonymity, flexibility with completion time, access to more significant geographic regions and settings, and alleviation of tensions between interviewer and interviewee (Robinson 2001; Shields 2003) Challenges to using an internet-based survey include technological issues (such as backing-up survey data or connectivity issues), none of which we experienced, cognitive challenges for participants (e.g., literacy and demand), quality of responses issues, and accuracy of data (Blasius and Thiessen 2012; Suzuki et al. 2007; Weisburg 2005). The survey data was collected virtually via Google forms and subsequently transferred into a Microsoft Excel spreadsheet. The data was then examined for patterns, in a more qualitative approach. We also administered an empirical approach using correlation analysis and statistical modelling to determine whether there are factors associated with their experiences that support relationships that affect their experiences.

In total, we had 66 participants, who met the criteria we set out for HB to participate in this study and to complete the survey. To satisfy the research agenda, participants met four criteria: (1) identify as female, (2) identify as Muslim, (3) identify as an HB, and (4) be 18 years of age. The purpose of this survey was three-fold: (1) to inform and contextualize the research questions, (2) to get a basic understanding of current happenings within the participant group, and (3) to examine associations and relationships between various factors, outlined herein. Additionally, we considered participants' intersectional identities (Hill-Collins 1990) in our analysis.

Limitations

This study was largely impacted by the COVID-19 crisis. As mentioned, this survey was first during a provincewide lockdown in April 2020. At this time, all sports facilities were closed, as were "nonessential" businesses, and citizens were told to "stay home." The second distribution was in September 2020, when access to businesses and sporting facilities were restricted, and the scale of social gathering limited. As a result of the pandemic, survey results may be altered. First, we do not have clarity on whether participants were thinking about their pre-pandemic sporting experiences or whether they were thinking "at present." Nor is it clear whether participants' social media habits increased during COVID-19 as screen-time usage seems to have increased dramatically.

Additionally, we consider our reflexivity and positionality in this study to ensure a multiplicity of perspectives. Reflexivity will be an ongoing disruptive narrative as we question our biases, thinking, and presumptions in knowledge and language (Creswell 2013; Hesse-Biber 2007). To this end, we also engage in critical research practices that address *"how* sports knowledges are constructed, *by whom and why"* (Mohanty 2003, as cited in Toffoletti and Palmer 2017, 157). In addition, our study attends to several research and knowledge gaps, including how feminist scholars research sports, how Muslim women are portrayed and depicted in sports scholarship, and how we may shape and reshape sports and sports culture in Toronto to be more reflective and inclusive of the city's diverse population.

Limitations Continued—A Special Note from the Authors

A difficulty with this study arises from our role as researchers, whereby we identify as White, nonreligious, female athletes, and emerging scholars. In this case, we will need to be sensitive to our insider–outsider position as female athletes born in Canada experiencing sport culture, a sport culture that was constructed by the influence of hegemonic masculinity (Burton 2015) but not as Muslim women. Nor do we intend to "assume a position of superiority about the belief systems and values of Muslim women judged against (our) experience" (Abdel-Fattah and Carland 2010).

One of the authors, Laurel Walzak, met Amreen Kadwa, founder, Hijabi Ballers, at the Sport Information Research Centre (SIRC) conference held in Ottawa, Canada, in October 2019. Kadwa was a plenary speaker, who gave an elaborate account of the HB organization. Learning more about the HB's vision and mission spurred Walzak, an advocate of gender equity in sport, to approach Kadwa to explore the possibility of a tie-up between her organization and Walzak's research lab, the Global Experiential Sport Lab (GXSLab) at X University. Kadwa and Walzak immediately determined there was a fit and identified how they could support one another for mutual benefit in their goals of achieving greater equity for women in sport. This meeting of their minds led them to a formal collaborative partnership between the HB and the GXSLab. One was to secure funding for a mutually relevant research project, one of which funded this study. Second, the GXSLab and the HB partnership included bringing the Hijabi Ballers Annual Community Conference (Hijabi Ballers, n.d.) to X University, where GXSLab physically resides, to support the integration of Muslim females in sport spaces, to galvanize our collective audiences, and to educate and advocate for Muslim women in sport. Owing to the pandemic of 2020, the annual conference that was to take place at X University in April 2020, was postponed to Fall 2020 and took the new format of a virtual community conference. Throughout the virtual conference, the HB launched, for its membership and the public, in general, a resource referred to as the "Toolkit, a resource designed to provide tips for coaches, sports clubs and athletes on how to include Muslim Females in the athletic space." Toolkit included tips on clothing and hijab, food and drink, Ramadan, prayer, and physical contact and was distributed on the HB website and HB and GXSLab social media platforms as part of the 2020 Hijabi Ballers Virtual Community Conference #IAM2020 in Fall 2020. This tool kit

Figures 4.1–4.5, respectively was co-developed by GXSLab's student team, led by Ruqayah Rahaman, second-year student in RTA Sport Media program at X University. She shared her experience thus:

> Hijabi Ballers is truly an organization that helps empower Muslim girls to compete and be involved in sports. As a person that is a part of the Muslim community and the visible minority, I was extremely grateful to be a part of the virtual conference and spread inspiration. (Ruqayah Rahaman 2020)

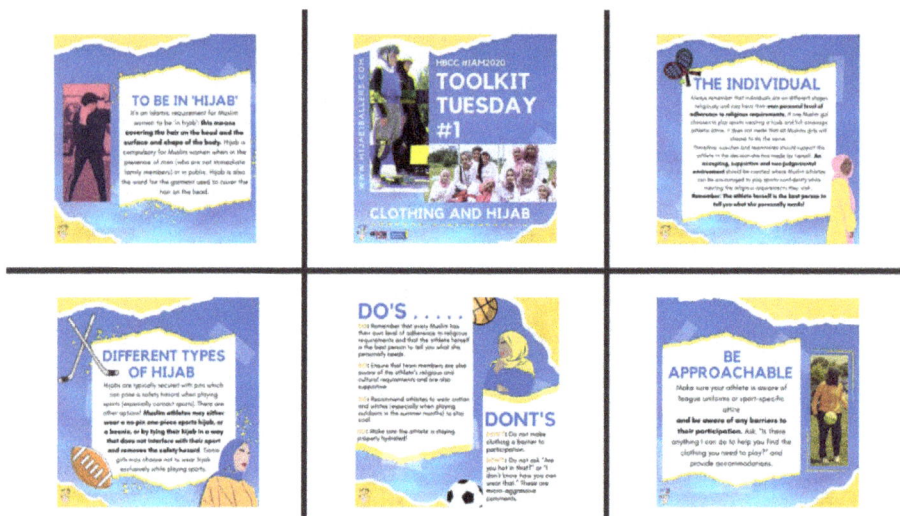

Figure 4.1: Examples of HB Toolkit—Clothing and Hijab
Source: Toolkit for Coaches, 2020. Accessed June 10, 2021. hijabiballers.com

Overview of Participants

The data collected represented a specific subset of the membership, essentially a sample of the HB population. Seventy-nine women and one man responded to this study. The respondents were born in a variety of countries around the world, including Canada, lived in the GTA, and were aged between 14 and 47. Note that we removed the 14- to 17-year-olds from the data analysis because we were unclear about how this age group took the survey, our instructions in the e-mail to the HB membership being that one must be 18 years of age to be eligible for this study. We also refrained from making any assumptions about their participation and elected to remove this age group from the data altogether. We also removed the one person who identified as being male, because, again, anyone identifying as male did not qualify for participation. Therefore, we removed 13 of the 79 respondents and analyzed the data from the remaining 66. Overall, participants varied in age, languages spoken, and country of origin, demonstrating the ethnically, culturally, and racially diverse nature of Toronto's sporting communities. Some of the shared characteristics observed between the respondents were not unexpected: 100 percent of the participants identified as HB, female, and Muslim (religion is Islam). Additionally, the respondent group identified as heterosexual (100%), 97 percent identified as not having a disability, and respondents spoke a range of languages where every participant spoke English. The respondents also spoke French, Spanish, Farsi, Arabic, and Amharic (0.79%). Tamil was spoken by 1.6 percent of the participants. Hindi, Punjabi, and Bengali were spoken by 4 percent of the participants. 39.3% of the participants spoke Urdu. 20.5% of the participants spoke Gujarati. 56.6% of the respondents were born in Canada, whereas 40.91 percent identified as not being born in Canada. The birthplace breakdown is as follows: (America 3.0%, Pakistan 1.5%, Saudi Arabia 1.5%, South Africa 1.5%, Trinidad and Tobago >1%, Pakistan 17.9%, UAE 7.5%, Zambia 1.5%, India 1.5%, Mozambique 3.0%, Malawi 1.5%, Iran 1.5%, and 3.03% Unknown). 42.7% of participants were aged 18–29. 3.16% of participants were 30–39 and even less, 1.6 percent of participants were aged 40–49. Thus, the primary age group for our survey findings was the 18–29 age group.

SOME FINDINGS

Recall the research questions: How do Muslim women come to, engage with, and experience sport and sport culture in Toronto, and do the factors associated with their experiences support any relationship/s that affect their experiences in sport and sport culture in Toronto. Overall findings reveal that participants are varied in their engagements with Toronto's sports culture both in-person and online.

Participants were asked about the frequency of attending live sporting events and watching sports events by professionals, both on TV and on the internet. Participants were evenly split between never engaging and engaging all the time. Subsequently, participants were asked about which athletes, teams, or leagues they follow on social media. Open-ended responses highlighted examples such as Muslim female basketball player Bilqis Abdul-Qaadir. Overwhelmingly, however, Muslim female US Olympic fencer Ibtihaj Muhammad was the most noted athlete. Other examples of athletes followed were Muslim male boxer Sonny Bill Williams, Muslim female fitness influencer Saman Munir, and Muslim retired male basketball player Kareem Abdul-Jabbar.

If participants did follow Muslim athletes, teams, or leagues on social media, participants were asked to provide a brief reason why they follow them. Reasons varied from inspiration to acceptance and welcome in sports. For instance, one participant wrote, "They motivate me to do sports." Another participant responded, "Following Muslim Athletes makes me feel accepted for who I am and for what I believe in." Further reasons for following these athletes include one such participant response,

> I follow [the athletes] because I like to learn both how they dress for exercise and their techniques. I love to see Muslim athletes thriving and pushing themselves to a limit. It helps me create a personal goal for myself . . .

Interestingly and overwhelmingly, 96.2 percent of the participants agreed that Muslim athletes are not adequately showcased in media. And so perhaps further research should investigate the inspiration and motivation behind representation of Muslim athletes in media.

Participants were also asked about the frequency of sports conversations with friends. 7.6% of participants stated they talked about sports "all the time," whereas 17.7 percent stated they never speak about sports. Most participants, however, said they "sometimes" (36.7%) or "often" (39.2%) speak about sports with friends. Interestingly, when asked if these discussions take place on social media these conversations were had less frequently. Only 2.5 percent of participants said they discussed sports on social media "all the time," and, overwhelmingly, 59.5 percent of participants stated they never discussed sports on social media. 10.1% and 28% said "often" and "sometimes," respectively.

When asked about whether participants were interested in learning about their favourite athlete's personal lives, 57% of respondents said "no" 43% of respondents said "yes." Previous research findings suggest that sporting audiences are more engaged with a sports performer's athletic life and less interested in their personal lives online (Lebel and Danylchuk 2014). Our research contests Lebel's and Danylchuk's (2014) findings and suggests Muslim female athletes may be interested in a more holistic experience of their favourite athlete's lives. This is important as celebrity athletes, teams, and leagues continue to brand themselves online to connect with sports fans.

Following Barak et al. (2018), we recognize "athlete" as an intersecting identity. 13.4% of respondents identified as "athletes," and 31.2% identified as athletes "sometimes." Most of our participants, 55.2%, Figure 4.2, did not identify as athletes. It is unclear what the term "athlete" means to the respondents because this was intended to be discussed during the interview stage of data collection. However, this percentage, 55.2%, not identifying as an athlete was somewhat surprising because 100 percent of respondents identified as being a HB. As a reminder, the HB organization:

> celebrates the athleticism of Muslim girls and women. Through our programs, we also work to increase participation, and consequently representation, of Muslim females in sport spaces and sports programs around the city. (Hijabi Ballers, n.d.)

Perhaps the interpretation of the word athlete was problematic and more importance was given to being an HB rather than merely being an athlete, and more emphasis on being an HB is also placed on representation, participation, and allyship. This supports the work of Toffoletti and Palmer, who state that much research in this realm

> examines Muslim women who partake in physical activity. In this context, participation is assumed to mean *active* participation—that is, the physical activity of playing sport or exercising. Other forms of participation in sport as

consumers of sport experiences and sport media have thus far been left out of the discussion about Muslim women's relationship to sport. (Toffoletti and Palmer 2017)

Unfortunately, we did not have the second stage of the study, where we hoped to conduct interviews to understand this answer, and so we cannot make any conclusions or implicit assumptions at this time. Perhaps in the next iteration of this study, we will plan to investigate this variable further.

Do You Consider Yourself An Athlete

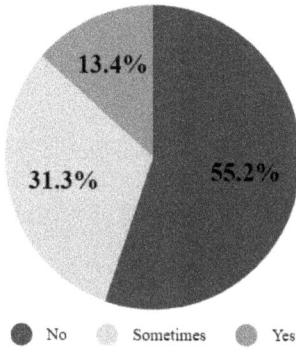

Figure 4.2: Percentage Breakdown of Respondents' Answers to "Do You Consider Yourself an Athlete"
Source: Data from Muslim Sportswomen Muslim Women's Experiences of Sports and Sports Culture in Toronto Survey, October 2020

Some Additional Patterns to the Findings

When empirically analyzing the data via means and comparative and correlation analysis in Microsoft Excel to determine whether there are factors associated with HB experiences that support relationships that affect their experiences in sport and sport culture in Toronto, patterns emerged versus conclusive relationships. Patterns specifically related to the multiple independent variables within the groups, such as "where respondents were born" and associations between the variables (Scholten 2008) of birthplace, sport played, and challenges to being a Muslim female athlete in Canada.

Challenges to Being a Muslim Female Athlete

Participants were asked about some of their challenges to being a Muslim female athlete in sport and sport culture in Toronto. Respondents could select any of the following challenges listed: Not enough women-only sports, not easy access, cost, clothing apparel options, and racism, and they were given the option to include a short written paragraph or sentence about their personal challenge(s). Percentages of the respondents showed that 75.7% of the respondents experienced two or more challenges listed, and 44% of the respondents experienced a minimum of four out of the five challenges listed in the survey. 85% of the respondents identified clothing apparel options as a challenge. This was an interesting finding for a few reasons: First, this study does not examine Muslim women who wear hijab or not; nor does it examine Muslim women who,

> express varying degrees of religiosity through the type of veiling they choose, from partial to full covering of their bodies, including *hijab* (many varieties of headscarves to cover the hair, neck, and ears completely but leaving the entire face exposed) and *niqab* (veils that cloak the hair, neck, shoulders, and face entirely, except the eyes). (Hwang and Kim 2020, 131, and Benhabib 2002)

> Remember that every Muslim has their own level of adherence to religious requirements and that the athlete herself is the best person to tell you what she personally needs. For example, if one Muslim girl chooses to play sports wearing a hijab and full-coverage athletic attire, it does not mean that all Muslim girls will choose to do the same (Figure 4.3: Hijabi Ballers ToolKit: Do's and Don'ts and The Individual 2020).

Second, recall the respondents' overwhelming open-ended responses to the question of which athletes, teams, or leagues they follow on social media: Muslim US Olympic fencer Ibtihaj Muhammad turned out to be the most noted athlete. Also, one respondent mentioned she "follows [the athletes] because she likes to learn both how they dress for exercise" . . . Assuming the respondents are aware that Olympian and medalist Ibtihaj Muhammad was not safe from religious or racial discrimination, this awareness plausibly explains why 85 percent of respondents selected clothing apparel options as a challenge because, again, it is the individual who chooses her approach to modesty and level of veiling (Hwang and Kim 2020) and the HB most noted athlete Ibtihaj Muhammed was not immune to such discrimination.

> Muslim American champions like Ibtihaj Muhammad, best known for being the first Muslim American woman to wear hijab while competing for the United States in the Olympics was not safe from misogyny and violent commentary. (Acim 2019, 37)

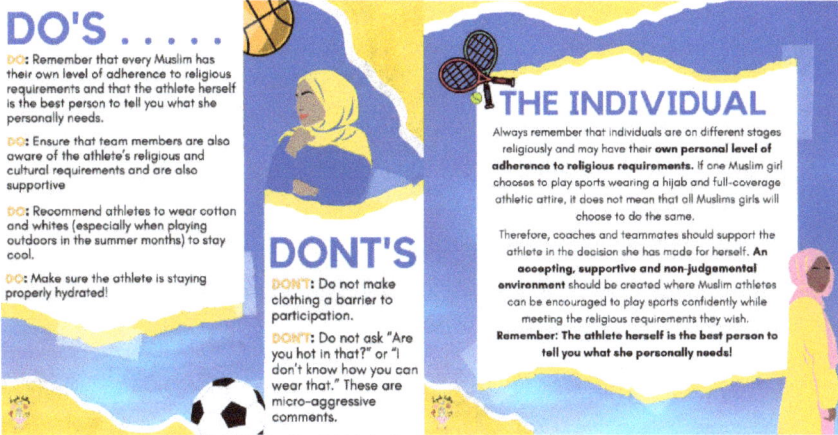

DO'S . . . . .

DO: Remember that every Muslim has their own level of adherence to religious requirements and that the athlete herself is the best person to tell you what she personally needs.

DO: Ensure that team members are also aware of the athlete's religious and cultural requirements and are also supportive

DO: Recommend athletes to wear cotton and whites (especially when playing outdoors in the summer months) to stay cool.

DO: Make sure the athlete is staying properly hydrated!

DONT'S

DON'T: Do not make clothing a barrier to participation.

DON'T: Do not ask "Are you hot in that?" or "I don't know how you can wear that." These are micro-aggressive comments.

THE INDIVIDUAL

Always remember that individuals are on different stages religiously and may have their **own personal level of adherence to religious requirements.** If one Muslim girl chooses to play sports wearing a hijab and full-coverage athletic attire, it does not mean that all Muslims girls will choose to do the same.

Therefore, coaches and teammates should support the athlete in the decision she has made for herself. **An accepting, supportive and non-judgemental environment** should be created where Muslim athletes can be encouraged to play sports confidently while meeting the religious requirements they wish.

Remember: The athlete herself is the best person to tell you what she personally needs!

Figure 4.3: Hijabi Baller Toolkit Do's, Don'ts, and the Individual—Clothing and Hijab
Source: Toolkit for Coaches, 2020. Accessed June 10, 2021. hijabiballers.com

Third, the study did not address the challenge of clothing apparel options as functional or aesthetic for the women wearing the clothing (Hwang and Kim 2020) or whether the clothing apparel options were a challenge because they "compromised their modesty" (Ahmad et al. 2020, 643). This can be investigated in future research.

65.2% of respondents selected racism as a challenge. As stated earlier, we were unable to conduct the second portion of this study, the semi structured interviews, and so we do not know the extent of the racism the HBs faced. However, we can reasonably assume, on the basis of several researchers' work, that the racial discrimination they experienced could have also included various levels of Islamophobia, meaning discrimination intersecting religion and race.

> Islamophobia: [It] is a form of religious and cultural intolerance of Islam and Muslims and Islamophobia or anti-Muslim racism is clearly not a new phenomenon. (Acim 2019, 27, 29)

Additionally, the 65.2 percent, the highest level of racism reported, breaks down into the following categories: 19 percent of those who selected racism as a challenge play badminton, 22.5 percent play soccer, 12.9 percent play volleyball, and 29 percent play basketball. Note that team sports report a higher selection of women-only sports and racism as a challenge.

Next, 85 percent of the respondents selected not enough women-only sports as a challenge. This finding was not surprising and is consistent with the work of Ahmad et al. in 2020 titled "Building Cultural Diversity in Sport: A Critical Dialogue with Muslim Women and Sports Facilitators" and where their article commented on other scholars that addressed the importance of women-only spaces for Muslim women in sport as follows:

Research on Muslim women in sport, active recreation and physical education is the importance of women-only spaces. Other research has also expressed the importance of women-only spaces because they are "essential to maximising participation for many Muslim" girls and women (Dagkas et al. 2011, 236; Amara and Henry 2010; Benn 1996; Benn and Dagkas 2006; Kahan 2003; Kuppinger 2015; Rana 2018; Zaman 1997). (Ahmad et al. 2020, 640)

72.3% of the respondents responded that not having easy access was a challenge, and just over 50 percent of the respondents selected costs as a challenge. Four women added their personal challenges to the survey:

> Women don't often receive or have access to the same level of training as men do.

> I am the only girl who plays ice hockey at my age, I have no one to play with, there are no role models to look up to, I want more people to play with and support.

> Cultural barriers (are challenges).

> Islamophobia (is a challenge).

Although this study does not "address the cultural difference of Muslim sportswomen such as Islamic states and in the West" (Toffoletti and Palmer 2017, 149), it is acknowledged that Muslim sportswomen's challenges in sport and sport culture in Toronto may differ pending their cultural experiences by country of birth, race, religious diversity, and where they experienced sport culture globally, and inform associations with the challenges they experienced in Toronto (Nakamura 2002). It is worth noting that this study did not ask those respondents who were not born in Canada where they experienced sport culture, nor did it ask about intersections between race and religious diversity related to their experiences.

Next, we analyzed what "sport do you play," and the most common sports played among all respondents were identified as basketball, soccer, badminton, volleyball, other (which included rugby, Frisbee, and fencing), and grouped were running, hiking, and biking. Further, we analyzed the sports HB played and identified a pattern in which certain sports such as volleyball, soccer, badminton, and basketball presented more of the challenges such as *not enough women-only sports, not easy access, clothing apparel options, and racism* than other sports like running, Frisbee, or rugby. This suggests that certain sports such as baseball, biking, running, hiking, CrossFit, rugby, and Frisbee presented fewer challenges to being a Muslim female athlete, as there were fewer challenges such as cost, ease of access, and racism selected by the respondents.

This caused us to look further at one more variable, birthplace. We analyzed whether an HB was born in Canada or not, and findings showed a pattern between "birthplace" and a "sport one plays." Three sports were of significance; soccer, badminton, and "other" ("other" included—Frisbee, rugby, and fencing), see Table 4.1. When we measured where an HB was born: Canada or other, the "sport they play," and analyzed it with the "challenges to being a Muslim female athlete," we found that Canadian-born HBs overall play different sports than HBs not born in Canada, except basketball, and it is fair to suggest that those who play basketball, soccer, badminton, and volleyball and who are born in Canada face greater challenges than those who play rugby, Frisbee, fencing (which tends to be those respondents who were not born in Canada). Cross-examining these patterns with the sport they play and birthplace using correlation analysis, we found evidence to indicate an association (Figures 4.4 and 4.5). Hence, it is fair to suggest that age and where you were born show a pattern of association. The data shows that the younger the HB, the more likely they were born in Canada versus immigrating to Canada. This suggests an association between the younger demographic and the different challenges they experience compared with those who immigrated to Canada. This is worth investigating further in future research in order to understand these patterns more conclusively.

Table 4.1: Sport Played by Birthplace

Sport	Canadian Born (%)	Non-Canadian Born (%)
Basketball	26	28
Soccer	26	9
Badminton	20	3
Volleyball	13	19
Running/Hiking/Biking	12	16
Other (i.e., Frisbee, Rugby, Fencing, etc.)	9	19
Softball	7	3
Swimming	6	9
Ice Hockey	2	0
Field/Floor Hockey	2	6

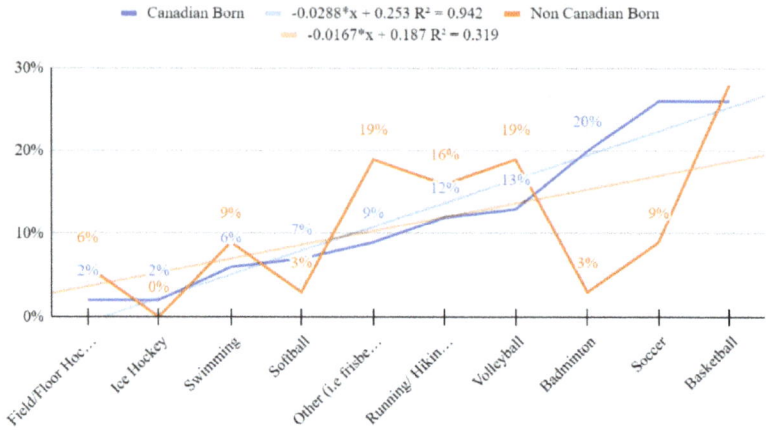

Source: Data from Muslim Sportswomen Muslim Women's Experiences of Sports and Sports. Culture in Toronto Survey, October 2020

Figure 4.4: Sport Played and Place of Birth via Empirical Data Analysis
Source: Data analyzed from Muslim Women's Experiences of Sports and Sports Culture in Toronto Survey, October 2020

BIRTH: CANADIAN BORN/ NON-CANADIAN BORN

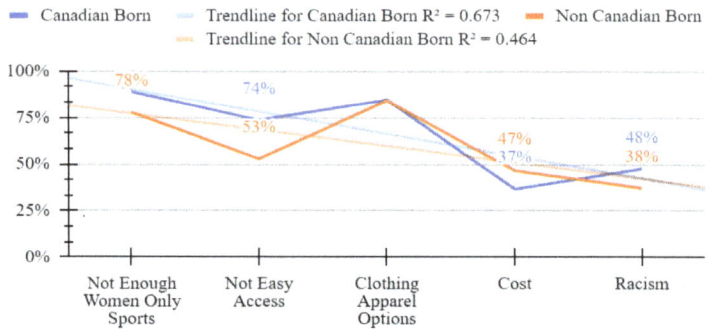

CHALLENGES TO BEING A FEMALE MUSLIM ATHLETE

Figure 4.5: Challenges and Place of Birth Empirical Data Analysis
Source: Data from Muslim Sportswomen Muslim Women's Experiences of Sports and Sports Culture in Toronto Survey, October 2020

As for cost, the cost was selected more often as a challenge by the younger HB demographic. And the younger the demographic, the more likely an HB was born in Canada. An implicit assumption can suggest and even explain that the younger demographic is at a different stage of life and that the likelihood of having disposable income for sports is lower than in the case of an older HB. Additional rationale supports that if you are a younger HB, female, and of a racialized population you have had little to no income growth in Canada both recently and over the last 35 years, providing more reasons to explain cost as a challenge for the respondents, according to the Toronto Foundation Income and Wealth Vital Signs Report 2019/2020:

> Over the last 35 years, racialized populations, newcomers, and young people have had no income growth, whereas the rest of the population has often had greater than

> 50% income growth

> Lower-income challenges are even more concentrated among women. (Ayer and Foster 2019–2020, 25, 31)

DISCUSSION AND CONCLUSION

The diversity of the HB participants in this study varied in age, languages spoken, and country of origin, demonstrating the ethnically, culturally, and racially diverse nature of Toronto's sporting communities. By unravelling and revealing how Muslim women who identify as HB come to engage with and experience sport and sport culture in Toronto, which is known to have a rich and diverse sporting culture, this study contributes to new insights and discussions into their experiences and supports Toffoletti and Palmer's work, suggesting a reconsideration of how Muslim women in sport are constructed.

The findings also evidence that HB's overall experiences within the constructs of Toronto sport culture presented positive experiences yet, unfortunately and not surprisingly, many challenges. Specifically, these overall findings suggest that athlete representation, such as from role models like Ibtihaj Muhammad, can positively shape the HB's experiences. Yet the fact that Muslim athletes are considered by HB's as not adequately showcased in media should be further investigated to understand the inspiration and motivation of representation these athletes in media can have on HB's experiences, because this is a positive insight that could be useful in eventually and ideally improving experiences. More investigation is required into the significance of the findings related to the role of clothing apparel options and the perceptions, stigmas, and relevance of these options to their experiences; the impact on varied intersections between religion and religious practices, culture, place of birth, and race; the higher rates of racism within certain sports, the importance of women-only spaces (Ahmad et al. 2020) and who constructs sport and sport culture in Toronto,.

Overall, these findings are consistent with other studies that have shown that sport and sport organizations tended to be "expressed in terms relating to the broader agenda of 'sport (and health) for all' (Ahmad et al. 2020, 640) (Amara and Henry 2010, 440), versus taking into consideration 'multicultural practices' (Ahmad et al. 2020, 640) that exist within the diverse populations wishing to participate in sport culture, and that based on the HB" experiences described herein, that sport and sport culture in Toronto, as rich and diverse as it is perceived to be, does not meet the needs and interests of the HB. Despite this, it is encouraging to witness the HB women who have created and "offer sports programs and sports participation opportunities, community events, and conferences for fellow Muslim females" (Hijabi Ballers, n.d).

FUTURE DIRECTION

The next stage of our research, ideally, will be to conduct the semistructured interviews with the HB to resolve many of our questions and validate our assumptions. Additionally, several other questions we aim to explore came up as a result of those related to these findings, such as, but not limited to, the following:

1. Does the sport you play in Canada depend on where you were born and where you originally had or first experienced sport culture?
2. Do the challenges to being a Muslim female athlete and your sport experiences depend on the sport you play, your age, your race, where you were born, your economic status, or your religious beliefs and that of your family and community?
3. If we eliminated one or more of their challenges listed in the original survey, for example, if we took cost away, would the other challenges still remain, and if so which ones, or are they dependent on one another?
4. And/or do the athletes the HB follow on social media influence the sport they play.

Clearly, further iterations of this study and additional studies would be of interest.

ACKNOWLEDGEMENTS

We would like to thank Amreen Kadwa, founder of Hijabi Ballers, and the Hijabi Ballers for their participation in this research.

FUNDING

Funding for this research was awarded by the then Faculty of Communication and Design, now named The Creative School, X University, Seed Grant.

REFERENCES

Abdel-Fattah, Randa, and Susan Carland. 2010, Jan 28. "Muslim Feminists Deserve to Be Heard." *Sydney Morning Herald*. Accessed June 5, 2021. http://www.theage.com.au/it-pro/muslim-feminists-deserve-to-be-heard-20100127-mywf.html

Acim, Rachid. 2019. "Islamophobia, Racism and the Vilification of the Muslim Diaspora." *Islamophobia Studies Journal* 5 (1): 27–44. https://doi.org/10.13169/islastudj.5.1.0026.

Ahmad, Nida, Holly Thorpe, Justin Richards, and Amy Marfell. 2020. "Building Cultural Diversity in Sport: A Critical Dialogue with Muslim Women and Sports Facilitators." *International Journal of Sport Policy and Politics* 12 (4): 637–53. https://doi.org/10.1080/19406940.2020.1827006.

Alwi, Sharifah Faridah Syed, and T. C. Melewar. 2018. *Islamic Marketing and Branding: Theory and Practice*. 1st ed. New York: Routledge. https://doi.org/10.4324/9781315590035.

Ayer, Steven, and Jennifer D. Foster. 2019–2020. "Report 2019/20—Toronto's Vital Signs—01 Income and Wealth." torontofoundation.ca. https://torontofoundation.ca/wp-content/uploads/2019/10/VitalSigns2019_01_IncomeAndWealth.pdf.

Barak, Katie Sullivan, Vikki Krane, Sally R. Ross, Mallory E. Mann, and Chelsea A. Kaunert. 2018. "Visual Negotiation: How Female Athletes Present Intersectional Identities in Photographic Self-Representations." *Quest* 70 (4): 471–91. https://doi.org/10.1080/00336297.2018.1461661.

Benhabib, Seyla. 2002. *The Claims of Culture: Equality and Diversity in the Global Era*. Princeton, NJ: Princeton University Press.

Blasius, Jörg, and Victor Thiessen. 2012. *Assessing the Quality of Survey Data*. London: Sage.

Burton, Laura J. 2015. "Underrepresentation of Women in Sport Leadership: A Review of Research." *Sport Management Review* 18 (2): 155–65. https://doi.org/10.1016/j.smr.2014.02.004.

Carrington, Ben, Terry Chivers, and Trevor Williams. 1989. "Gender, Leisure and Sport: A Case Study of Young People of South Asian Descent—A Response." *Leisure Studies* 8 (3): 237–40. https://doi.org/10.1080/02614368900390241.

Crenshaw, Kimberlé. 1991. "Mapping the Margins: Intersectionality, Identity Politics, and Violence against Women of Color." *Stanford Law Review* 43 (6): 1241–99. https://doi.org/10.2307/1229039.

Creswell, John W.. 2007. Qualitative Inquiry & Research Design : Choosing Among Five Approaches 2nd ed. Thousand Oaks: Sage Publications.

Hamzeh, Manal, and Kimberly L. Oliver. 2012. " 'Because I Am Muslim, I Cannot Wear a Swimsuit': Muslim Girls Negotiate Participation Opportunities for Physical Activity." *Research Quarterly for Exercise and Sport* 83 (2): 330–39. https://doi.org/10.1080/02701367.2012.10599864.

Hesse-Biber, Sharlene Nagy. 2012. Handbook of Feminist Research : Theory and Praxis Second edition. Thousand Oaks, California: Sage.

Hijabiballers, 2020. https://www.Hijabiballers.com. Access April to June 2021.

Hill-Collins, Patricia. 1990. *Black Feminist Thought: Knowledge, Consciousness, and the Politics of Empowerment*. New York: Routledge.

Hwang, Chanmi, and Tae Ho Kim. 2020. "Religiosity and Modesty: How Veiled Muslim Women in the United States Define Modest Activewear." *International Journal of Fashion Design, Technology and Education* 13 (2): 131–39. https://doi.org/10.1080/17543266.2020.1753246.

Jiwani, Nisara, and Geneviève Rail. 2010. "Islam, Hijab and Young Shia Muslim Canadian Women's Discursive Constructions of Physical Activity." *Sociology of Sport Journal* 27 (3): 251–67. https://doi.org/10.1123/ssj.27.3.251.

Kay, Tess. 2006. "Daughters of Islam: Family Influences on Muslim Young Women's Participation in Sport." *International Review for the Sociology of Sport* 41 (3–4): 357–73. https://doi.org/10.1177/1012690207077705.

Lebel, Katie, and Karen Danylchuk. 2014. "An Audience Interpretation of Professional Athlete Self-Presentation on Twitter." *Journal of Applied Sport Management* 6, (2).

Lebel, Katie, and Danica Vidotto. 2021. "Chapter 9: Stepping Up to the Plate: Why an Investment in Girls' Athletic Apparel Is Good for the Game." In *Sportswomen's Apparel around the World:*

Uniformly Discussed, edited by Linda K. Fuller, 151–63. Cham: Palgrave Macmillan. https://doi.org/10.1007/978-3-030-46843-9_10.

Moore, Rick Clifton. 2018. "Islamophobia, Patriarchy, or Corporate Hegemony?: News Coverage of Nike's Pro Sport Hijab." *Journal of Media and Religion* 17 (3–4): 106–16. https://doi.org/10.1080/15348423.2019.1595840.

Nakamura, Yuka. 2002. "Beyond the Hijab: Female Muslims and Physical Activity." *Women in Sport and Physical Activity Journal* 11 (2): 21–48. https://doi.org/10.1123/wspaj.11.2.21.

Nielsen, Kevin. 2020. "A Timeline of Covid-19 in Ontario." *Global News*, April 24, 2020. Accessed May 30, 2021. https://globalnews.ca/news/6859636/ontario-coronavirus-timeline/.

Rahaman, Ruqayah. 2020. TOOLKIT FOR COACHES (https:// www.hijabiballers.com/toolkit.html). Accessed June 1, 2021.

Robinson, Katherine Morton. 2001. "Unsolicited Narratives from the Internet: A Rich Source of Qualitative Data." *Qualitative Health Research* 11 (5): 706–14. https://doi.org/10.1177/104973201129119398.

Rush, Curtis. 2019. "In Diverse Toronto, the Raptors' Sports Hijab Is Hailed as a Win for Inclusivity." *The Washington Post*, September 19, 2019. https://www.washingtonpost.com/sports/2019/09/19/diverse-toronto-raptors-sports-hijab-is-hailed-win-inclusivity/.

Samie, Sumaya, and Kim Toffoletti. 2018. "Postfeminist Paradoxes and Cultural Difference: Unpacking Media Representations of American Muslim Sportswomen Ibtihaj and Dalilah Muhammad." In *New Sporting Femininities: New Femininities in Digital, Physical and Sporting Cultures*, edited by Kim Toffoletti, Holly Thorpe, and Jessica Francombe-Webb, 89–107. Cham: Palgrave MacMillan. https://doi. org/10.1007/978-3-319-72481-2_15

Shields, Carolyn. (2003). "Giving voice" to students: Using the Internet for data collection. *Qualitative Research*, 3, 397-41

Scholten, Annemarie Zand. 2021a. "Methods and Statistics in Social Sciences Specialization." Coursera, University of Amsterdam, Netherlands, https://coursera.org/specializations/socialsciences. Accessed May 2021.

———. 2021b. "Quantitative Methods." Coursera, University of Amsterdam, Netherlands, via Accessed June 2021. https://www.coursera.org/learn/quantitative-methods, Access May 2021.

Summers, Jane, Rumman Hassan, Derek Ong, and Munir Hossain. 2018. "Australian Muslim Women and Fitness Choices—Myths Debunked." *Journal of Services Marketing* 32 (5): 605–15. https://doi.org/10.1108/JSM-07-2017-0261.

Thorpe, Holly, Lyndsay Hayhurst, and Megan Chawansky. 2018. " 'Once My Relatives See Me on Social Media … It Will Be Something Very Bad for My Family': The Ethics and Risks of Organizational Representations of Sporting Girls from the Global South." *Sociology of Sport Journal* 35 (3): 226–37. https://doi.org/10.1123/ssj.2017-0020.

Toffoletti, Kim, and Catherine Palmer. 2017. "New Approaches for Studies of Muslim Women and Sport." *International Review for the Sociology of Sport* 52 (2): 146–63. https://doi.org/10.1177/1012690215589326.

Weisberg, Herbert F. 2005. The Total Survey Error Approach a Guide to the New Science of Survey Research Chicago: University of Chicago Press. https://doi.org/10.7208/9780226891293.

CHAPTER 5

"We Are the Movement"

Shireen Ahmed

INTRODUCTION

Mainstream sport media arguably has the least racial and gender diversity in the sport media industry. Sport media has traditionally been lacking in intersectional perspectives while framing complex discussions on Muslim women and their clothing without nuance (Samie and Sehlikoglu 2015; Abu-Lughod 2013). Communities of Muslim women have used social networking sites such as YouTube, Twitter, Instagram, Facebook, and TikTok to not only amplify their ongoing roles as participants in sport, but also to simultaneously advocate for themselves (see Ahmad and Thorpe 2020; Olow 2020). Acting as media makers, Muslim women in sport media demonstrate the inclusion of a very specific community that maintains authenticity in the storytelling. Mainstream sport media is famously practicing culturally defined gender boundaries that certainly have limitations on race and religion, by ignoring, trivializing, and sexualizing women in sports (Bruce 2016).

As a hijab-wearing and racialized Muslim woman and athlete, I have been a part of the sports landscape for over 40 years. Professionally, I have written and researched Muslim women in sports from a journalistic perspective for over a decade. My expertise is rooted in lived experience in sports, and the work I have done on Muslim women in sports is scaffolded by researchers and academics. It is important for the industry that I make my mark in this space as well and to disseminate knowledge about the community I am a part of and the identity that I hold. I have experienced significant abuse online that is rooted in gendered Islamophobia and manifests in abusive tweets, angry e-mails and violent direct messages on Instagram and Tumblr. Although my experience has not always been easy, it has not deterred me from continuing the work.

This chapter examines the ways in which three Muslim female athletes and one local sports organization use Instagram and Twitter to represent themselves, their interactions, and their relationships to sports spaces. Specifically, I look to athletes Jamad Fiin, Nadia Nadim, Fadumo Olow, and the Toronto-based organization Hijabi Ballers. The primary question I sought to answer was, what narratives are Muslim female athletes perpetuating or promoting on social media? How, if at all, do participants use their social media agency to debunk myths and crush tropes often used in mainstream media about Muslim women and their identities?

The Muslim women's profiles I examine are all racialized but not all may wear hijab (religious headscarf), and that is specifically why I wish to include them. Not including non-hijab wearing athletes is problematic and fails to address the challenges of Muslim women who cover in an alternate style or not at all (Ahmed 2013).

I take the position that despite its limitations, social media and new forms of media have not only amplified Muslim sportswomen and Muslim women in sports spaces, but have also helped change the narrative around their identities. When Muslim women create content for social media, it leads the discussion.

METHODOLOGY

Using the examples and social media accounts of three Muslim women, I examined two social media accounts, Twitter and Instagram, of three Muslim women, one of whom is a journalist, and one that is a community-based organization advocating for the creation of space for Muslim women in sports. I looked at the impressions on Twitter and the engagement on Instagram to gauge their interactions with their followers, as well as how they were curating their content and presenting it to audiences. Although social media spaces can be chaotic cesspools of racist, Islamophobic, and misogynistic abuse (Awan 2014), it can also provide space for Muslim women to share details of their own lives in a manner suitable to them. It is this storytelling, dissemination of knowledge with the community that interests me and the way in which their images, anecdotes, and posts are created. All the accounts are handled by the women themselves. This is relevant to maintain a level of authenticity for this research.

In Our Own Voices

Instagram, Snapchat, TikTok, and Twitter platforms are key in the analysis of curated content by athletes. My chapter focuses on two of the mediums: Instagram and Twitter. But along with new media comes a path to self-representation and user-generated storytelling through a lens infrequently offered by mainstream sport media and that can influence wider society. Conversations can be started and people who may never have interacted with Muslim women before may get an opportunity to observe and engage with Muslim sportswomen. A position or opinion can be stated with a call to action, and this platform allows for it. People can read and reflect, bookmark by liking, and ruminate over what they have read. The discussion can shift when Muslim women share their own experiences and address topics firsthand on a digital platform (Ahmad 2020).

The increased use of social media handles and self-promotion is not only storytelling but a view of different elements of religious observation and involvement in sport. The known risks (Noble 2018) of online abuse experienced by racialized women do not seem to be preventing racialized Muslim women in sport from sharing on social media. Muslim sportswomen do not all choose to dress in the same manner, nor are their preferences about engaging in physical activity the same; and some may want all-women's spaces while some are comfortable exercising in public (Abu-Lughod 2013). Irrespective of their choices, they may choose to share their stories and experiences online. The burgeoning social media accounts of Muslim women in the sports sphere are also creating a community of support for one another that helps combat trolls and offers support to the sisterhood (Ahmad 2020).

The importance of making media by Muslim women in sports as athletes, officials, fans, and those in sport-adjacent roles cannot be overstated (Rezak 2018). Mainstream media in North America and the UK has very few Muslim women in mainstream sport media, and even fewer hijab-wearing sports reporters, columnists, or contributors. Therefore, Muslim women amplifying the challenges, lives, and contributions of other Muslim women are critical to changing the narrative and creating a representative change in sport media.

Since Muslim women media makers have begun creating their own content (Ahmed 2013), there has been a more relevant examination and representation of the lives of Muslim women in society (Ahmad 2020). In their seminal work on Muslim women creating and taking up space by digital platforms, Nida Ahmad and Holly Thorpe (2020) examined the ways in which Muslim sportswomen used different social media platforms to challenge stereotypical representations of Muslim women in sports. According to their study, Ahmad and Thorpe note that sportswomen have increasingly used sport and their lived experiences to share information and to tell stories in their own words. Whether or not self-branding is helpful or effective remains one of the key questions posed by feminist media scholars (Toffoletti and Thorpe 2018). But although there is a gap in scholarship where those questions may apply specifically to racialized Muslim women in sport, there is no doubt that Muslim women have a right to communicate effectively and authentically (Dakroury 2016).

As one of the very few Muslim women sports journalists in North America, I know that content creation and the ways that stories are curated are critical to the narratives that will be played out. Mainstream sport media do not realize that Muslim women are not a monolith. It is imperative to understand that the complexities regarding culture and assumptions around Muslim women vary according to community, immigrant experience, age, socioeconomic strata and ethnic background. The ways that stories are written of Muslim women are often appalling and misleading (Ahmed 2015a, 2015b), leading to their individual and intersectional circumstances being misunderstood or not considered. As social media becomes more readily available and as platforms like Facebook or Instagram provide an opportunity to share one's own experience, it can be utilized in a manner that the Muslim woman feels is best.

FINDINGS AND DISCUSSION

Using the examples and the social voice of Muslim women in sports is essential in the sports sphere. A stunning example of how to take to social media to share ones' skill but also help reframe discussions and broaden the reach to different sports communities is Jamad Fiin. Fiin is a former Division III basketball player from Boston, Massachusetts, whose online presence as an influencer skyrocketed over the last two years. She features in TikTok videos that have gone viral many times. Fiin's verified Instagram account has 368,000 followers, whereas her Twitter boasts 32,400 followers. Her short videos and commentary, including a YouTube channel, feature Fiin speaking often of Somalia, her home country. Her videos feature her playing street ball in a hijab and an abaya (a long, loose, robelike dress that is often worn over pants and a shirt to cover the shape of a woman's body).

Big Up the "Handles" and Platforms

Her basketball dribbling technique, known as "handles," was enhanced by her nontraditional Muslim clothing. From my observations, the visual of her playing basketball while in a flowing robe and hijab is not only a juxtaposition of traditional media representation, but also a very apt clapback at the naysayers who believe that uniform accommodations should not be made and that Muslim women in religious garb should not grace a court, a pitch, or a pool. The reality is that instead of waiting for a broadcast network to feature her, although many have, Fiin created her own media to share her own experiences. She stars in a powerful video, set in a public park in Boston that she co-created, in which she speaks of her childhood and how she came to love basketball. The catchy video has Fiin describing how "Muslim women can ball- and break ankles" (Fiin 2019), a reference to how they can fake out opponents and simultaneously embarrass on the court.

Another way in which Muslim women media creating content affects mainstream sport media is by generating so much attention that mainstream media spaces need to catch up and join the conversation or run the risk of being out of touch with the eager public. Fiin has been remarkably successful at "going viral," and that has forced traditional basketball social media accounts and sites to jump on the bandwagon because there is an audience ready to watch her play basketball. Fiin shared a video to her TikTok, Twitter, and Instagram accounts that showed off her dribbling skills set to the tune of Megan Thee Stallion's popular song "Sex Talk." Finn was wearing a long black dress, a hijab and ballet flats. She choreographed her movements to the song, and the effect is incredible from a digital perspective. According to an article in *Newsweek*, the video was shared by Overtime and Bleacher Report—two of the biggest sports accounts on social media—and "has been viewed over 2.3 million times, retweeted nearly 10,000 times and liked by over 57,800 people as of 9:33 a.m. EST" (Crowley 2020).

Fiin crafted and curated the content using her expertise and knowledge of what is current in social media pop culture and sport. In my observation, her crossovers between proudly showing off her identity as a Black Muslim woman and also being able to impress with her obvious skill is a part of new media in sport that few might have predicted. Muslim women are certainly changing the way their bodies are discussed and shared. Muslim women as producers and content creators are a critical part of this evolving path in digital storytelling.

Representation in the Discussion

Fadumo Olow is a sports journalist with the *Women's Telegraph* in London, England. She is a Black Muslim woman in a space that is undiverse in racial or religious makeup. In a podcast interview hosted by another young, Black Muslim woman, Olow explains that she started a podcast to have "underrepresented discussions" in sport with another Muslim woman of South Asian descent (Olow 2020). Her efforts to not only be a part of mainstream sport media discussions on soccer and soccer culture are not mutually exclusive to her discussions on Islam, race, or gender. The reality is that Olow cannot remove herself from her lived experiences but that those experiences can enhance and deepen her contributions to sport media. Like Fiin, Olow is incredibly proud of her Somalian heritage and speaks of it publicly and with pride.

Not only are Fiin and Olow in very different realms of sport—one as an athlete-influencer and the other working in a journalistic capacity—but both are sharing their views and talents in the media they create themselves. As a sports journalist and a social media manager of *Telegraph Women's Sport* Twitter account, Olow can select headlines that are shared. There is a different power of social media in that role that affords her the ability to craft a message that is not reductive or sexist.

Fiin and Olow's choices to be public-facing and to take on roles involving social media engagement are part of taking up space as digital invaders, as described by Ahmad and Thorpe (2020). As sport media continues to evolve with society and requires dynamic changes, there is a place for nontraditional storytelling in the sports vertical. Digital platforms are a huge part of the industry, and when Muslim women decide to take on roles as advocates while engaging in sport, the results can often exceed expectations by increasing public awareness of the various hows and whys of Muslim women engaging in sport. And as Fiin stated in the aforementioned video, "We are the movement!" (Fiin 2019).

There is no doubt that Muslim women face an abundance of vitriol online and on their choices of engaging physically in sport. Internalized misogyny from within the community is something that Muslim women experience all the time as well as external criticism and unwanted feedback. Islamophobic and sexist abuse is common on the internet. According to the Canadian Council of Muslim Women (CCMW) (2019), hate crime in Canada has increased 47 percent, which includes online hate speech and extremism. In fact, gendered Islamophobia has become so pervasive online that the organization initiated community and organizational Digital Anti-Racism Education (D.A.R.E.) training from May until July 2021 (Figure 5.1).

More About the D.A.R.E. Project

In Canada, there has been a substantial increase in police-reported hate crimes.

Learn More

20%

OF CANADIANS EXPERIENCE DISCRIMINATION

According to Race Relations Canada, 1 in 5 Canadians (20%) experience discrimination regularly or from time to time. Among Black and Indigenous peoples, the rate of discrimination recorded was 38%.

253%

INCREASE IN HATE CRIMES AGAINST MUSLIMS

According to Statistics Canada, between 2012 and 2015, police-reported hate crimes increased against Muslims in Canada.

73%

OF WOMEN ARE ABUSED ONLINE WORLDWIDE

Women ages 18–24 are the most likely to experience severe forms of online abuse, such as stalking, sexual harassment and physical threats.

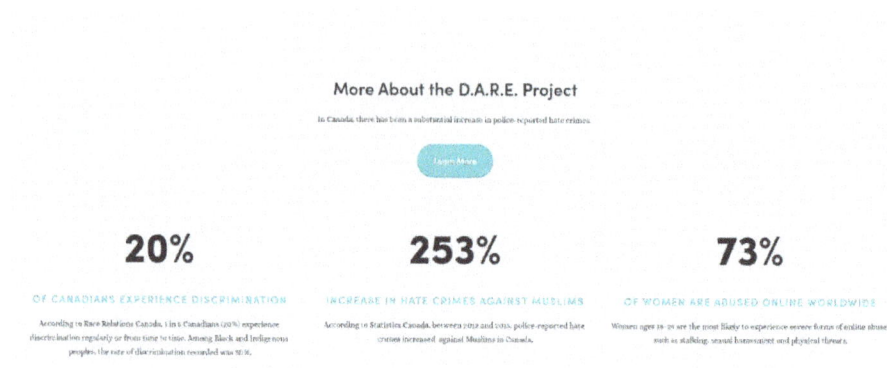

Figure 5.1: Screen Grab, Canadian Council of Muslim Women (CCMW) and D.A.R.E. Programming
Source: CCMW webpage, May 2021, from the D.A.R.E. programming beginning

Muslim women often received misogynistic abuse with added layers of racist and xenophobic vitriol—and in fields of play, facilities, in policies and discourses, and with regard to moving bodies and emotion (Thorpe et al. 2020). But the need to continue with the work supersedes the concern of online abuse, which can be upsetting and distracting. I have been on the receiving end of a targeted campaign, and it is frustrating and very exhausting. British sportswriter detailed some experiences I had endured in an article for the soccer website *Daily Cannon*:

> Social media abuse goes much further than entitlement too. Women are judged on their race, appearance and almost everything except their opinion on a relevant topic. Shireen revealed how bad it can get when so many launch unprovoked attacks for her being a Muslim journalist. "I get called every cuss word possible as well as generous sprinkles of gendered Islamophobic and xenophobic slurs. The most painful comments are ones about my children. Bar none. I will be sent racist and sexist tweets. I block people regularly. I also get emails via my website that are usually after I have published something." (Cooke 2018)

Racialized women will receive disproportionate amounts of online abuse (Noble 2018). But one way to combat this is the deep relationships and camaraderie between communities of Muslim women who amplify each other.

Creating and Taking Up Space

Another example of Muslim women in sports taking up space and using ingenuity, creativity, and community support is Hijabi Ballers. The community-based organization was born in East End, Toronto, Canada, and was the brainchild of a young woman named Amreen Kadwa. I am an advisory board member of Hijabi Ballers and have been associated with the organization since its inception. Kadwa approached me in 2017 and explained her vision for a group that would advocate and promote the inclusion of Muslim women in sports in Toronto. I had no idea that it would become one of the biggest organizations in the country to create conversations and opportunities for Muslim women and girls to be so visible in sports (Cazmi 2019).

Kadwa worked with volunteers—racialized Muslim women—and grew steadily. They started with local programming initiatives and hosted a sports festival in Flemingdon Park in Toronto's East End. They offer sports programming and hold community events and conferences to engage in discussions with young women and girls. According to their website, Hijabi Ballers has the following four main goals:

1. Increase representation of Muslim females in Toronto's sport spaces and sport media.
2. Provide opportunities for Muslim females to participate in sport, try new sports, and hone their skills.
3. Recognize the accomplishments of and celebrate Muslim female athletes.
4. Integrate allies (i.e., coaches, parents, community mentors) in the growth of Muslim females in the sport space ("Hijabi Ballers," n.d.).

From these goals, outcomes are possible and plausible. Because Hijabi Ballers began as a very small organization, the connection to supporters and possible participants relied heavily on communication and outreach. This has been facilitated and propelled by social media engagement (Ahmad and Thorpe 2020). Hijabi Ballers is not for the non-Muslim gaze. It seeks to fill gaps in sports society and provide opportunity and amplification for marginalized women.

Young Muslims are taking to digital platforms and new media in order to share authentically (Ahmad 2020). This creates more spaces for Muslim women in sports, be it as an athlete, a community member, a seasonal fan, or a recreational participant, to engage in sports in a way that is not intimidating or exclusionary. In Ontario, Muslim women have experienced exclusion in sports spaces and have felt alienated owing to political and ideological discourses that frame them and their identities as "other" or "alien" (Khalil 2018). Hijabi Ballers cannot address systems of oppression that are deeply embedded in sports culture, but it can certainly create opportunities for exchange and dialogue using sports as a vehicle for connection.

Hijabi Ballers have connected with and supported other initiatives through their own organization, including the Muslim Women Summer Basketball League (MWSBL), that will launch in the summer of 2021 (Hagi 2021). Hijabi Ballers continue to grow and have made impactful contributions through community engagement and word of mouth, which is extremely important in racialized communities. The needs of the participants are considered by the organizers; whether it may be a place to perform prayers, play without the presence of men, or employ women referees, these specific needs will not only be addressed but will also be accommodated. These needs are essential to the participation of Muslim women. They also seek to engage in discussions about anti-Black racism and sexism in sport. Hijabi Ballers use their Instagram account primarily to connect with followers and share information about their upcoming events and any media.

Hijabi Ballers has been in charge of the narratives around the organization. Two years ago, they shot a video (using a local filmmaker) with athletes, including mothers and younger girls from the Toronto area, and shared it on social media. It is a captivating spot that showcases hijab-wearing women engaging in all sorts of sporting activities including running, swimming, golf, fitness training, rugby, basketball, and soccer.

This form of media is undoubtedly compelling; when shared on their Instagram account, which has over 5,700 followers, the video, which premiered on March 8, 2019, garnered over 2,000 impressions, Kadwa told me. It was their first major Instagram post, and the effect was important because it made an impact and drew attention. The effects of this kind of social media influence may also affect the ways that Muslim women participate in sport; by encouraging, by the sheer representation, and by the ways in which Muslim women were portrayed in the post.

As we see more stories about Muslim sportswomen in not only Olympic athlete positions but also recreational, fan-based as well as interloping participation, we notice a rise in the number of women who not only engage in sport but who also then share their own experiences. This can not only help communities of Muslim women engage holistically with sport, but can also possibly affect the way that women in sport are covered and portrayed in mass media where traditional sport media has failed (Ahmad 2020).

Learn more about the video here. Download the video here.

Figure 5.2: Screengrab from Hijabi Ballers Webpage of the Hijabi Ballers Video

Hijabi Ballers has also been the catalyst for some unprecedented developments of the visibility of Muslim women in professional sports as nonathletes. During the 2019 NBA playoffs, the *Toronto Star* national newspaper ran an article coauthored by Evelyn Kwong and Sahar Fatima. The article detailed various Toronto Raptors fan groups and basketball lovers in a city as racially diverse as Toronto (Kwong and Fatima 2019). One of the groups featured in the piece was the Hijabi Ballers. The organization has undoubtedly caught the attention of mainstream media such as the *Toronto Star* and some global organizations like Nike, in Toronto, with whom Kadwa had done a collaboration for the 2019 FIFA Women's World Cup and featured her wearing the Canadian women's national team kit and a matching Nike sports hijab.

In the fall of 2019, the Toronto Raptors, NBA franchise, went one step further and decided to launch the first-ever professional team-branded sports hijab. This may not seem important to many people out there who are aware of the long-standing existence of sports hijabs (Ahmed 2017a) or to those who are not impacted by hijab bans in sport. Arguably, this has had a tremendous impact on Muslim communities from a perspective of inclusion. Merchandise is a part of the sports fan experience, and for Muslim women to be included in that realm is fulfilling in a most visceral manner. Of how the idea came, Jerry Ferguson, director of marketing at Maple Leaf Sports and Entertainment (MLSE), said: "There was a story about them that came out during the playoffs in the Star talking about how we connect with our diverse group of fans, and that's where the idea came from. We were very inspired by them" (Fraser 2019). Sport organizations have a goal of increasing their audiences. If they interact and include the untapped audiences, they do not run the risk of alienating or ignoring them.

As a woman who has often felt, on the margins of sport and sport culture, that there is a team that even after a World Championship thought to look to the wider community and say "we see you" is an experience that I have never had before. It is one thing to sell jerseys or toques or tracksuits that can obviously be worn by Muslim women, but to take a piece of cloth like a hijab, one that has been ideologically and politically challenged—even in basketball—is affirming and important.

The Nike Pro-Sport Toronto Raptors Hijab may not have been an attempt to reconcile the ways in which Muslim women were organizationally barred from professional basketball by the highest echelons of governance and exclusionary policy (Ahmed 2017a). But the result is that an established team and front office has very publicly stated that Muslim women are a part of the basketball family. Hijabi Ballers was a partner in the discussions with MLSE and also in the rollout of the product. This type of involvement shapes the way Muslim women are included in sports and can potentially broaden the inclusion and participation of Muslim women in sports (Cook 2018). Hijabi Ballers drew attention with their social media platforms, which is how the *Toronto Star's* reporters sought them out to be featured. There is a direct correlation between the changes in the inclusion of Muslim women in sport and the social media they use.

Most recently, on World Hijab Day, celebrated on February 1, 2020, Nike partnered with Hijabi Ballers in a series of photos and video clips using the #MadeToPlay hashtag featuring notable Muslim women athletes who are Nike hijab-wearing athletes, including Ibtihaj Muhammad (fencing, USA), Manal Rostom (fitness, UEA), and Jawahir Roble (soccer, UK). One can argue that although Nike is currently at the top of the modest sportswear game, its intentions can be challenged. Nike is not a nonprofit or an advocacy group for Muslim women (Bahrainwala and O'Connor 2019). It is a corporation that has come under fire for a questionable track record of injustice toward Black mothers, in particular, of which former USA Nike athlete Alysia Montano wrote for the *New York Times* in 2019. And then there is the case of sweatshop labour in the Global South that Nike has allegedly used to produce its garments (Katebi 2017).

Has Nike used hijab to redeem itself? Should we be wary of the corporate attempts to engage with racialized Muslim women? The hijabs are a product being sold, and there is a market for them. Is this simply a business arrangement? All of this is complex and cannot be easily dissected without understanding all the moving parts. There is a way to critique unjust and racist policies while understanding that amplification of racialized Muslim women in the world of sports is important and necessary; perhaps future research and discussion are required to answer these questions. In the meantime, Muslim women should be at the design tables, strategizing with companies to provide the most authentic products for Muslim sportswomen.

As long as Muslim women have an opportunity to make use of the resources offered by Nike and also to craft their own narrative while steering conversations about Muslim women and their portrayals, it is possible. We live in a capitalist system, and it would be naive to suggest that we can ignore or navigate Nike in a world where their influence is paramount.

According to a press release from Nike, the original design was created and then offered to several Nike athletes, including weightlifter Amna Al Haddad, figure skater Zahra Lari, runner Manal Rostom, and Zeina Nassar, a German boxer (Nike News, 2017). The women, all Middle-Eastern hijab-wearing athletes, gave feedback and offered suggestions. Nike was explicit in explaining the process, but, from my previous research, Nike failed to include para athletes and Afro-Arabs from their Middle Eastern launch of the Pro-Hijab (Ahmed 2017a). The process by which the hijab was designed and then marketed included Muslim women, which satisfied the most basic tenets of inclusion.

Representation to Others

When one's social media use is so profound and sincere while maintaining a large following, is it possible to remain authentic and partner with a major company? Another Muslim woman athlete who has managed to remain outspoken on issues such as being a refugee and being a woman with multiple identities and partake in a campaign of equal pay in women's sport is Nadia Nadim. The Afghan-born soccer superstar now plays for the Danish national team and French professional team Paris St. Germain. When Nadim is not playing professional sports, she is a medical student. She has over 100K Instagram followers, and her feed is a mix of beautifully natural poses and candid shots of her playing or training in Nike gear. She also posts photos of herself in traditional Afghan clothes and in class at medical school. Nadim's Snapchat account, which I follow and enjoy, is far more personal and shows her singing Bollywood songs, which she admits she enjoys. Even as she shares the required posts owing to her contractual obligations with Nike, Nadim is uniquely embracing all parts of her identity, which makes her more powerful. In a June 2020 piece that she penned for The Players' Tribune, Nadim wrote about her feelings on displaced people from war-torn countries and refugees. Her father was killed by the Taliban in Afghanistan, and her mother took her and her young siblings and fled to Denmark.

> I know some people will criticise me for talking about this. They'll say that athletes should stick to sports' cause we're not politicians or whatever. But I think that's bullshit. Everyone—everyone—has a responsibility to try to improve the lives of other people. (Agergaard 2020)

By writing about the displacement of vulnerable persons, emotional and social distress, and adaptation into a new country and all the economic and emotional struggles that many athletes may not be able to speak to, but that are common in Muslim-majority societies, Nadim crosses into activism. The lines of this are being blurred by her existence and continued conversations on issues that are not specifically revolving around her sport.

Nadim turns the dial on the negative narratives in which Afghan women are frequently presented in the media as oppressed and lacking agency (Abu-Lughod 2013). Nadim is very generous with interviews and is featured not only by mainstream football media but also in smaller outlets, including platforms for those of an immigrant experience. Nadim's identity is also intertwined with discussions in Europe about nationalism and how transnationalism creeps into discussions about athletes and how and where they represent themselves along team lines (Agergaard 2019). Although both Nadim and Fiin are unapologetic about embracing their identities, they also identify as Muslim women. Although Nadim does not choose to cover or wear hijab and plays in shorts and a short-sleeved uniform, it does not cause a disturbance in how she views herself as part of the Afghan or Muslim community. Whether it causes disruption in other spaces is not what Nadim concerns herself with: she focuses on her family, her studies, and her sport. What Nadim does in sharing her lived experiences with the world and connecting to her family and religious and ethnic community offers another perspective, one that is not hijab-centred. It is important to remember that mainstream media has fixated on hijab-wearing athletes in the past and has often overlooked nonhijab wearing athletes such as Ibtihaj Muhammad, who wears the hijab, and Dalilah Muhammad (no relation), who does not wear one (Figure 5.3).

Figure 5.3: Ibtihaj Muhammad and Dalilah Muhammad
Source: Ibtihaj Muhammad Facebook Account, 2016

Sertaç Sehlikoglu is a cultural anthropologist who has studied Muslim women in sport and media portrayals. Sehlikoglu observes that nonstereotypical images of Muslim women confuse the male colonial gaze and that mainstream sport media still caters to those audiences (Sehlikoglu 2012; Ahmed 2013). In addition to retooling antiquated ideas about Muslim women, Nadim is very much in control of how her image is used within the football or activist circles. She has control of her agency and uses her platforms casually as well as professionally.

CONCLUSION

The Muslim women mentioned in this chapter are truly exemplary in regard to the use of social media to influence public interest, media narratives, steer conversations about

Muslim women, and have a real impact on the lives of Muslim women in the sport sphere. Whether it is the careful crafting of media content, strategic sharing to different communities, or ownership of ideas and creativity, Muslim women in sports are affecting their representation at every conceivable level: consumers, content creators, and creatives. As aptly stated, "We Are the Movement" (Fiin 2019).

Even with multiple roles as athletes, fans, or advocates, Muslim women using new media forms and social media are weighing in on scores and the discussions—both are critical to the inclusion and longevity of racialized Muslim women in sports. Muslim women's increasing representation in sports has been thrilling to watch for someone like myself, who has been in the industry for over a decade. The impact of Muslim women making media has impacted me as a Muslim woman, an athlete, an observer, and a chronicler of Muslim women in sports.

By using new media and social media, Muslim women in sport (as athletes and as part of sport media) establish and affirm that they are in control of their bodies and, their stories, and refuse to be written off as oppressed women who are monolithic. There are different ways to observe faith and different ways of (un)covering religiously. By sharing personal messages and lived experiences and engaging with audiences, Muslim women are decimating ideas that they are inarticulate or that they cannot participate in sport.

The sport media landscape is not a diverse space (Harrison 2019), and the power from the voices of Muslim women in sports, the depth of their shared experiences, and the richness of their honesty online are impactful. It is not only about representation, it is about the possibility. The possibility was not intended to be an unattainable concept, but for too long were Muslim women spoken at instead of with. Media has empowered and enabled Muslim women in sports to encourage other Muslims to understand that we are in this space—for good.

REFERENCES

Abu-Lughod, Lila. 2013. *Do Muslim Women Need Saving?* 19–22. Cambridge, MA: Harvard University Press.

Agergaard, Sine. 2019. "Nationalising Minority Ethnic Athletes: Danish Media Representations of Nadia Nadim around the UEFA Women's Euro 2017." *Sport in History* 39 (2): 130–46. https://doi.org/10.1080/17460263.2019.1608849.

Ahmad, Nida. 2020. "Muslim Women, Sport, and Social Media." *The International Encyclopedia of Gender, Media, and Communication,* 1–4. Hoboken, NJ: Wiley. https://doi.org/10.1002/9781119429128.iegmc222.

Ahmad, Nida, and Holly Thorpe. 2020. "Muslim Sportswomen as Digital Space Invaders: Hashtag Politics and Everyday Visibilities." *Communication & Sport* 8 (4–5): 668–91. https://doi.org/10.1177/2167479519898447.

Ahmed, Shireen. 2013. "Hijab in Sport and Unhelpful Media Biases." *Muslimah Media Watch,* March 19, 2013. https://www.patheos.com/blogs/mmw/2013/03/hijab-in-sport-and-unhelpful-media-biases/.

———. 2015a. "British Footballer or ISIS Bride." *Muslimah Media Watch,* September 22, 2015. https://www.patheos.com/blogs/mmw/2015/09/british-footballer-or-isis-bride/.

———. 2015b. "Ignorant Solidarity with Muslim Sportswomen." *Muslimah Media Watch*, May 26, 2015. https://www.patheos.com/blogs/mmw/2015/05/ignorant-solidarity-with-muslim-sportswomen/.

———. 2017a. "Nike's Pro Hijab: A Great Leap into Modest Sportswear, But They're Not the First." *The Guardian*, March 8, 2017. https://www.theguardian.com/sport/blog/2017/mar/08/nike-performance-hijab-female-muslim-athletes.

———. 2017b. " 'What Will They Say About Me?': Nike Middle East's New Ad." *Muslimah Media Watch*, March 7, 2017. http://www.muslimahmediawatch.org/2017/03/07/what-will-they-say-about-me-nike-middle-easts-new-ad/.

Awan, Imran. 2014. "Islamophobia and Twitter: A Typology of Online Hate Against Muslims on Social Media." *Policy & Internet* 6 (2): 133–50. https://doi.org/10.1002/1944-2866.poi364.

Bahrainwala, Lamiyah, and Erin O'Connor. "Nike unveils Muslim women athletes." *Feminist Media Studies* (2019): 1-16.

Bruce, Toni. 2016. "New Rules for New Times: Sportswomen and Media Representation in the Third Wave." *Sex Roles* 74 (7): 361–76. https://doi.org/10.1007/s11199-015-0497-6.

Cazmi, Mishal. 2019. "This Woman Is Breaking Barriers for Hijab-Wearing Girls in Sports." *FLARE*, November 19, 2019. https://www.flare.com/how-i-made-it/amreen-kadwa/.

CCMW (Canadian Council of Muslim Women). 2019. "Digital Anti-Racism Education (D.A.R.E.) Project." *Dare to Be Aware!.* https://www.daretobeaware.ca/.

Cook, Kristen. 2018. "Uncovering the Evolution of Hijabs in Women's Sports." *The Graduate Review* 3: 62–67. https://vc.bridgew.edu/cgi/viewcontent.cgi?referer=https://scholar.google.ca/&httpsredir=1&article=1064&context=grad_rev.

Cooke, Crippy. 2018. " 'Gendered Islamophobic & Xenophobic Slurs,' 'Racist & Sexist Tweets': Being a Woman on Social Media." *Daily Cannon*, January 21, 2018. https://dailycannon.com/2018/01/gendered-islamophobic-xenophobic-slurs-racist-sexist-tweets-woman-social-media/.

Crowley, James. 2020. "Muslim Somali Basketball Player Breaks the Internet with Incredible Dribbling Skills." *Newsweek*, February 19, 2020. https://www.newsweek.com/viral-video-muslim-somali-basketball-player-dribbling-1488016.

Dakroury, Aliaa. 2016. "Muslim Resilience and the Right to Communicate." *Media Development*, February 2016: 5-1. https://new.waccglobal.org/wp-content/uploads/wacc-global/resources/md-2016-2/2-2016.06.Muslim%20resilience%20and%20the%20right%20to%20communicate.pdf.

Fiin, Jamad. 2019. " 'I've Been Told My Whole Life What Muslims Girls CAN'T DO.' Meet Jamad!" Overtime, January 13, 2019. https://www.youtube.com/watch?v=IYEE9_aanU0.

Fraser, Ted. 2019. "Hijabi Ballers Inspire Raptors to Sell Branded Sports Hijab, the First of Its Kind in NBA." https://www.*Thestar.com*, September 13, 2019, accessed March, 2021. https://www.thestar.com/news/gta/2019/09/13/hijabi-ballers-inspire-raptors-to-sell-branded-sports-hijab-the-first-of-its-kind-in-nba.html.

Hagi, Sarah. 2021. "Fitriya Mohamed Is Changing the Game—and the Conversation—around Muslim Women in Sports." https://www.*Thestar.com*, January 10, 2021, Accessed March 2021, https://www.thestar.com/life/together/people/2021/01/10/fitriya-mohamed-is-changing-the-game-and-the-conversation-around-muslim-women-in-sports.html.

Harrison, Guy. 2019. " 'We Want to See You Sex It Up and Be Slutty:' Post-Feminism and Sports Media's Appearance Double Standard." *Critical Studies in Media Communication* 36 (2): 140–55. https://doi.org/10.1080/15295036.2019.1566628.

HijabiBallers. 2017. "hijabiballers." [Mobile app]. Instagram, https://www.instagram.com/hijabiballers/, accessed February 2021.

Katebi, H. "No Representation in Sweatshops: Ethical & Muslim-Owned Alternatives to Nike's 'pro-Hijab' (Joojoo Azad: جوجو آزاد)." Bloglovin', March 10, 2017. https://www.bloglovin.com/blogs/joojoo-azad-12853397/no-representation-in-sweatshops-ethical-muslim-5501338381.

Khalil, Asma Ahmed Abdin. 2018. "In and Out: Exploring Inclusion and Alienation within the Sport Experiences of Hijabi Athletes in Ontario." Master of Science thesis, University of Toronto.

Kwong, Evelyn, and Sahar Fatima. 2019. "Represented by Raptors: How One Team Connects the Most Diverse City in the World." https://www.*Thestar.com*, accessed May 10, 2019. https://www.thestar.com/news/gta/2019/05/10/represented-by-the-raptors.html.

Noble, Safiya Umoja. *Algorithms of Oppression: How Search Engines Reinforce Racism*. New York, USA: New York University Press, 2018. https://doi.org/10.18574/9781479833641

Olow, Fadumo. 2020. "Start Your Dream Career & Make Your Voice Heard w/ Fadumo Olow—Shared Diversity with Sina Port." Listen Notes, May 11, 2020. https://www.listennotes.com/podcasts/shared-diversity/start-your-dream-career-make-dfuO0yi2roe/.

Rezak, Tanya. 2018. "Voices of the Game: Shireen Ahmed Is a Powerful Advocate for Women of Color in Sports." *SB Nation Raw Charge*, July 20, 2018. https://www.rawcharge.com/2018/7/20/17590076/voices-of-the-game-shireen-ahmed-is-an-powerful-voice-for-women-in-sports.

Samie, Sumaya Farooq, and Sertaç Sehlikoglu. 2015. "Strange, Incompetent and Out-of-Place: Media, Muslim Sportswomen and London 2012." *Feminist Media Studies* 15 (3): 363–81. https://doi.org/10.1080/14680777.2014.947522.

Sehlikoglu, Sertaç. 2012. Review of *Portrayal of Muslim Female Athletes in the Media: Diversity in Sport*. Equity, Diversity and Inclusion. LSE. August 7, 2012. https://blogs.lse.ac.uk/equityDiversityInclusion/2012/08/portrayal-of-muslim-female-athletes-in-the-media-diversity-in-sport/.

Thorpe, Holly, Nida Ahmad, Amy Marfell, and Justin Richards. 2020. "Muslim Women's Sporting Spatialities: Navigating Culture, Religion and Moving Bodies in Aotearoa New Zealand." *Gender, Place & Culture*, December 7, 2020: 1–39. https://doi.org/10.1080/0966369x.2020.1855123.

Toffoletti, Kim, and Holly Thorpe. 2018. "Female Athletes' Self-Representation on Social Media: A Feminist Analysis of Neoliberal Marketing Strategies in 'Economies of Visibility.' " *Feminism & Psychology* 28 (1): 359–83. https://doi.org/ezproxy.lib.ryerson.ca/10.1177/0959353517726705.

93

An Investigation on How Women's Basketball in North America Has Been Silenced by the NBA and Men in the Sports Industry

Dana Daschuk

INTRODUCTION

Chimamanda Ngozi Adichie said in her 2009 Ted Talk that the creation of a single story happens when people are shown "as one thing, as only one thing, over and over again, and that is what they become" (Adichie 2009). The story of North American basketball is no different. Basketball across the United States and Canada is powered by a Euro-Western, middle-upper-class, White, cis-male media industry. The single-story perpetuated across broadcast platforms is that basketball, specifically the National Basketball Association (NBA), is male dominated, starring majority Black athletes, such as LeBron James, Michael Jordan, Kobe Bryant, and Stephen Curry. Most important, the single story that continues to saturate and perpetuate through North America's media is that men's basketball is generating gross amounts of revenue per year, and therefore players are earning millions of dollars per season and are essentially more worthy than women's basketball in funding, coverage, airtime, and resources. As a result, the women's game remains in the shadows.

Year 2020, however, has brought new heights for the Women's National Basketball Association (WNBA). With the COVID-19 pandemic forever altering the way sports are conducted, and ever since the reemergence of the Black Lives Matter (BLM) movement, specifically after the death of George Floyd in May 2020, the WNBA has begun to occupy more mainstream media coverage. WNBA commissioner Cathy Engelbert said, "the league has seen a 68% increase in average television ratings for its national games" (Megdal 2020). The WNBA and NBA, respectively, decided to commit their seasons to fight racial injustices. The women of the WNBA have long been on the front lines of "protests, speaking out against police brutality and gun violence" (Perry 2020). Specifically, at the restart of the 2020 season in the "Wubble" (women's bubble), set up to keep players safe during the COVID-19 pandemic, the WNBA continued their advocacy. The WNBA dedicated its season to Breonna Taylor, who was shot and killed by Kentucky police in 2020 (Cwik 2020a). Support for Taylor and her family was shown through imagery printed on the court and on WNBA player jerseys. Two BLM signs were placed on the court near the centre WNBA logo, one in the top left and the other in the bottom right (Cwik 2020b). Taylor's name was placed on the back of the WNBA player's jerseys with outcries for justice and awareness on both the WNBA and WNBA players' social media platforms (Minutaglio 2020). Many players also knelt on the court during the national anthem in solidarity with former NFL superstar and activist, Colin Kapernick, in his efforts to bring awareness to inequalities.

As leaders of change, activism, and athleticism, it is time we got to know the women of the WNBA substantially. This chapter explores women's basketball in the WNBA by unpacking the single story of basketball told through North American sport media. Through a comparative analysis, I look to understand the differences in how the NBA and WNBA's stories get told through mainstream media. Analyzing mainstream television coverage of NBA games versus WNBA games during finals, I investigate the narratives around the women's game. This research adds to the current literature in sport media scholarship focusing on the intersection of mainstream media narratives of men's and women's basketball. With an effort to understand the one-sided narrative of North American basketball, this chapter argues that it is time to create a more inclusive basketball story and that the women of the WNBA are single-handedly driving a (mediated) basketball evolution. The WNBA is beginning to take back the narrative showcasing a side of women's professional basketball that was once hidden.

THE HER-STORY OF WOMEN'S BASKETBALL

The history of professional women's basketball in the United States started with the Women's Professional Basketball League (WBL). The WBL started to play in 1978, trying to capture attention after the United States' women's basketball team won silver at the Montreal Summer Olympic Games in 1976. The victory was especially notable because it was the first time women's basketball was included in the Olympic Games (USA Basketball 2020).

The WBL was created by Bill Bryne, starting with eight teams across the United States. The eight teams were The Iowa Cornets, New Jersey Gems, Milwaukee Does, Chicago Hustle, Minnesota Fillies, Dayton Rockettes, New York Stars, and the Houston Angels. Organizationally, the WBL centred its focus on gaining an audience and corporate sponsorships and held its inaugural game in Milwaukee on December 9, 1978. The game featured the Milwaukee Does and the Chicago Hustle and initiated a promising start—due to on-air mentions and notable coverage from a Chicago TV channel that played ten of Hustle's games and doubling the anticipated viewership (Grundy and Shackelford 2005). The WBL quickly expanded with six more teams in Washington, DC, Philadelphia, Dallas, Anaheim, San Francisco, and New Orleans (Grundy and Shackelford 2005). In addition, during this time, women's college basketball had a growing audience (Grundy and Shackelford 2005). Considering the success and skill of athletes in college basketball at the time, many of the women that were drafted to play in the WBL were recruited from college basketball teams. Outside of physical play, much of the success of women's college basketball in the United States and the WBL was credited not solely to a player's athleticism but to the "formula of combining athletic prowess with strict adherence to ladylike convention" (Grundy and Shackelford 2005, 187).

Women's sports have long been intertwined with feminine mandates and the sex appeal of players. Considering basketball prioritized player value and capability around traditional masculine traits, such as height and strength, the introduction of women was a splash in the masculine-gendered nature of the basketball world. The ideal image of a basketball player was tall, to reach the basket, delivering layups and dunks, and one who was strong and agile, to face tall opponents. With preexisting notions of basketball thriving on traditionally masculine traits, the public and media drew connections between female basketball players' height and masculinity. The idea of female athletes being tall, strong, and powerful players correlated with their being masculine, further supporting skeptics' thoughts that athletic women were unnatural (Grundy and Shackelford 2005). The idea that women could not be tall, powerful, strong, and skillful players, while also being feminine, created controversy among basketball fans and leaders in women's basketball that female athletes are unnatural. The controversy created the need for women's leagues to highlight femininity in players, sexualize female athletes, and hide the fact that some players were lesbian (Grundy and Shackelford 2005).

This femininity in women's sports was so important that the owners of the WBL decided that they were not just selling women's basketball but sex appeal. The WBL began to oversexualize the league and the players, with makeup mandates, and some team's sending players to charm school, such as the "John Robert Powers Charm School in Los Angeles" (Pinchevsky 2018). Players were taught etiquette and social graces, such as how to dress and move more femininely off the court, while also learning how to interact with the opposite sex (Pinchevsky 2018).

These feminine mandates are similar to those imposed upon the All American Girls Professional Baseball League (AAGPBL). In 1943, the AAGPBL was created in fear that the Major League Baseball (MLB) season would get cancelled when men were deployed to fight in WWII (Kenow 2010). As a consequence of having an all-female team, there was a strong focus on femininity and sexualization, to counter the "rampant suspicions of homosexuality prevalent in softball leagues of the time" (Kenow 2010, 65). This included a strict dress code forbidding AAGPBL players to be dressed in pants or shorts in public and prohibiting short haircuts. The AAGPBL made mandatory rules requiring players to always be dressed in feminine clothing and lipstick (AAGPBL, n.d.). Their uniforms consisted of skirts to further emphasize the idea of femininity among these athletes. At the time, both the sport industry and teams, specifically baseball and basketball, were almost entirely run by men. This masculine, male-dominated management strongly influenced the sexualization of female athletes.

Further efforts were made to hide masculine appearances and sexual identities of WBL players, such as players who were lesbian, because the WBL was concerned that such information and appearances might be controversial or against the ideal image of what a woman was at this time (Grundy and Shackelford 2005). The WBL chose to hide these women's athletic accomplishments, in accordance with their idea that it would support skeptics' thoughts that athletic women were unnatural (Grundy and

Shackelford 2005). Despite the fact that much of the foundations and frameworks for women's basketball institutions were predominantly built by single and lesbian women, early years of professional basketball institutions failed to recognize their contributions. It was common for teams and the league to not give credit to the work players had done, often omitting players from promotional campaigns and interviews if teams thought they may be lesbian or supported the image of masculine female athletes. Teams were quick to release players that were suspected or rumoured to be lesbian in further hopes of distancing themselves from the masculine female athlete portrayal (Grundy and Shackelford 2005).

After a quick expansion of the league from 8 to 14 teams, the WBL was much closer to failure than success. With surmounting financial issues and a failure to make payments to players on time, the league folded after its third season (Grundy and Shackelford 2005). The official end to the WBL was in February 1982.

After the WBL folded, the NBA considered sponsoring a professional women's league (Grundy and Shackelford 2005). However, before the NBA could bring a women's league to fruition, a new WBL was created by a collective of independent owners from California in the fall of 1996 (Grundy and Shackelford 2005). The new league was The American Basketball League (ABL), which consisted of eight teams across the United States. The ABL was the first independent basketball league for women in America, with values focused on players, such as, "player salaries averag[ing at] $80,000 per year, and . . . . year-round medical insurance and stock purchase options" that were included in contracts (Grundy and Shackelford 2005, 225). Just a year later, in 1997, the NBA's sponsored women's league, the WNBA, joined the professional women's basketball scene and opened its first season with eight teams across the United States. Led by former NBA commissioner, David Stern, the NBA created the women's league to capitalize on the excitement circulating women's basketball at the time following the 1996 Olympic Games.

The WNBA's games commenced just seven months after the inauguration of the ABL. Thus began the battle between the two leagues (Grundy and Shackelford 2005). The WNBA and the ABL had two very different approaches and values to the game and their athletes. The ABL focused on small arenas, college audiences, saving money on rent, paying players more, and focusing on player benefits (Grundy and Shackelford 2005). The ABL also scheduled its games to play through the "traditional basketball season" during the fall and winter months (Grundy and Shackelford 2005, 225). However, the WNBA took a very different approach. The WNBA capitalized on the NBA's offseason, scheduling the women's games during the summer, taking advantage of TV time, and the lack of men's sports in North America, specifically basketball (Grundy and Shackelford 2005). During the summer months, the notable "Big Four" in men's sports—basketball, hockey, football, and baseball—are in low supply as only the MLB plays through the summer months. The WNBA initially offered much lower contracts and lacked extensive benefits in comparison with the ABL. It was apparent that only one league was going to survive (Grundy and Shackelford 2005). The WNBA lacked the talent that the ABL had, which made the league struggle at first. In spite of the WNBA's slow start as a league, they had something the ABL did not have, which was the monetary support from the NBA sponsors and broadcast deals, ultimately giving them an advantage compared with the ABL (Grundy and Shackelford 2005).

Thanks to the WNBA being an NBA-sponsored league, the WNBA was able to leverage the NBA's broadcast deals and secure some of the largest American networks including NBC and ESPN. Monetary support from the NBA also helped secure large corporate sponsorships for the WNBA as well as the use of NBA arenas. Although there is a dearth of broadcast data available for the WNBA's inaugural season in 1997, *The Washington Post* detailed a partial list of the National TV Schedule for channels and game times of the 1998 WNBA season, from June 19, 1998, to August 17, 1998. Out of the 26 games listed on the 1998 National TV Schedule for the WNBA, 18 of the 26 games were broadcasted during "prime time" (Shapiro 1998). "Prime time" for sports broadcasting has been defined as, "8 to 11 o'clock at night, Monday through Friday" (Nielsen 2011). The remainder of the eight WNBA games fell in the afternoon time slot of either a Saturday or a Sunday (Shapiro 1998). Between three networks, NBC, ESPN, and Lifetime Television, the WNBA had "more than 50 million viewers" watch the games over the span of their inaugural season in 1997 (WNBA 2016). Additional promotions worked as the first WNBA game brought more than three times the fans compared with the ABL's first tip-off (Grundy and Shackelford 2005). Even though the WNBA had a promising first season, the league struggled to maintain a considerable and consistent fan base, which became a factor in the league's struggle to generate revenue (Zhang et al. 2011).

Due to the great success of the WNBA's launch, the ABL's investors were nervous about the future of the league (Grundy and Shackelford 2005). Hopes of landing larger sponsorships and broadcast deals were virtually none because the NBA-sponsored league began to dominate the basketball industry and the mainstream sport media. Although the ABL was facing possible extinction, they still held better talent than the WNBA, although the ABL players were not receiving the same exposure (Grundy and Shackelford 2005). This led to future talent favouring WNBA contracts and the ABL losing their monopoly on top-tier college athletes. Eventually, the ABL lost large broadcast deals, dropping their games on-air from 36 to 16 and making them unable to continue or sign more sponsorships. During the 1998–99 season, the ABL folded, filing for bankruptcy on New Year's Eve. The talent from the ABL joined the WNBA in the following draft, leading to a league that had both talent and promotion (Grundy and Shackelford 2005). Yet, the WNBA was being held in their place by the very league that founded it.

NBA AND WNBA—A MESSY AFFAIR

The WNBA has become one of the most successful women's sports leagues in basketball history, surpassing the longevity of women's professional leagues in the past (Zhang et al. 2003). When the WNBA was created, the NBA was involved with the operations, finances, ownership, broadcast rights, sponsorships, and marketing

(McDonald 2000; Zhang et al. 2011). The unique relationship of "the WNBA as a brand extension of the NBA provides an opportunity to examine the strategic leveraging opportunities that exist for league stakeholders" (Walker, Sartore, and MacIntosh 2012, 1). The WNBA was, and still is, significantly reliant on the NBA for monetary support (Brown 2020; Jope 2019). Although it remains unknown how long the NBA plans to financially back the WNBA, the women's league is far from becoming financially independent (Jope 2019; Zhang et al. 2003). However, the connection to the NBA may be a factor in the WNBA's instability.

One of the most notable and important involvements between the leagues is their integrated promotions. When the WNBA was first created, the NBA created an aligning marketing strategy to be played during games to promote the new women's league. This promotion was called "We Got Next," which ran in the 1997 season. "We Got Next" was soon replaced by "Join In" in 1998 and later changed to "We Got Game" from 1999 to 2001. The promotional name has changed titles a few times, but the same narrative that was promoted is present in current advertisements and continues today. "We Got Next" is a popular saying in street-corner pick-up basketball. It was something that was said to claim the court for playing next after a team currently playing. "We Got Next," quickly became the marketing slogan for the WNBA, as the WNBA's season ran through the summer months. The slogan complimented the fact that the NBA season was ending, and it was time to showcase the women, exemplifying this idea that they are "up next" to play. During the inaugural season of the WNBA, the NBA spent $15 million on marketing and promotional efforts on the women's league (Zhang et al. 2003). The undeniable success and excitement surrounding the WNBA's first season would not have been possible without the reputation and monetary support produced by the NBA (Zhang et al. 2003).

The WNBA is reliant on growing media coverage and changing public perception of women's sports, showcasing that women's sports are just as valuable and worthy as men's to achieve sustainability as a league, generating income, and support from the public (Zhang et al. 2011). Additional media coverage of the WNBA would not only help develop awareness and interest in the women's league but also likely lead to a larger consumer fan base. Yet, the NBA is benefiting from a "symbiotic relationship" with the WNBA, in which the women's league is a component of the NBA's global conglomerate growth (McDonald 2012, 213). The NBA presents a more "entertaining" league through promotion—highlighting the large percentage of players able to dunk—presenting themselves as a basketball entertainment monopoly, generating high television ratings. Sport media often produces women's sports segments with poor production techniques, often highlighting only the most extraordinary women's sports accomplishments. However, SportsCenter can create a segment of an NBA team losing a game with "production techniques such as holiday-themed music, green lights, and special effects," turning an insignificant piece into a "'must watch' event designed to entertain viewers" (Musto, Cooky, and Messner 2017, 582). As a result, the public is led to believe that the WNBA is not as valuable or entertaining in comparison. This leads to poor public perception of the women's league, undervaluing the capability and skillfulness of its athletes (Garcia 2020).

Adam Silver, the fifth and current commissioner of the NBA, is on record stating more ESPN coverage for the WNBA "isn't a top priority" (Fader 2018). Silver minimized the WNBA's need for exposure expressing "that he felt ESPN had been generous with its airing" of the women's league (Garcia 2020, 44). Although Silver has talked openly about the financial decisions the NBA has made regarding control over the women's league, past, current, and future decisions governing the WNBA have exemplified the NBA's interests of benefiting from patriarchal capitalist growth (Garcia 2020). It seems as though the NBA is much more focused on its monetary gain than helping the WNBA succeed, and eventually becoming independent.

The NBA and WNBA remain in close quarters, collaborating on broadcast times, promotions, marketing, and sponsorships. In addition, both of the league's offices are located in the same New York City building (Ettienne 2019). The NBA franchise owns half of the 12 WNBA teams, with six out of the 12 WNBA owners also being an NBA owner (Fader 2018). Silver has said that the NBA is "doubling down" on the WNBA (Ettienne 2019; Fader 2018). However, the NBA's interests and growth plans seem focused on anywhere but the WNBA.

MONETARY DISPARITY

The NBA's focus centres on the growth of men's basketball, minimizing the women's league and perpetuating unfair treatment, scarce benefits, and minimal pay for athletes in the WNBA. Yet, the WNBA is limited on how far they can separate from the NBA and its "profit-oriented motivations" because of their financial dependency on the NBA (Garcia 2020, 49).

Through studies of monetary disparity of men's and women's basketball, Berri and Krautmann (2013) found an extreme lack of parity. Their research details the WNBA's reported $12 million in annual losses. As previously mentioned, the success and failure of previous women's basketball leagues depended greatly on their ability to generate revenue and the possibilities of sponsorships and partnerships. The WNBA also struggles in comparison with the NBA with audiences, despite lower ticket prices (Berri and Krautmann 2013). The NBA generates the majority of its revenue through ticket sales, television, sponsorships, and merchandising (Reiff 2020). The WNBA does not even generate a fraction of what the NBA brings in. The NBA reportedly generated more than 100 times what the WNBA made in the 2016/17 season, bringing in close to $7.4 billion (Berri 2018).

As the WNBA seeks to generate more revenue, sponsorship deals are made. The WNBA is one of few leagues, in regard to the "Big Four" sports in North America, with large sponsorships taking up primary real estate on their jerseys. In 2019, a partnership with a mobile brand was the largest in WNBA history and can be seen on many of the WNBA jerseys (Berri and Krautmann 2020). In comparison, NBA jerseys are minimal—with team logo, player number, and name taking up the majority of the jersey, with only a small area dedicated to sponsors in the top left or right. Although it is uncommon for sponsorships to take over large areas of jerseys in North America, this is common in professional soccer or even seen in professional European basketball, such as the Euroleague (Glass 2019). The WNBA's sponsored jerseys provide financial stability and advancement opportunities as a league (Glass 2019). The WNBA made new logo placements to its sponsored jerseys to ensure the team logo is visible and significantly larger than the sponsor's logo. This was in a plan to improve long-term merchandise opportunities, to increase sales and have more of the public wear WNBA jerseys, to further boost revenue (Glass 2019). Despite the NBA and WNBA's close connection, with six out of 12 WNBA teams owned by their corresponding NBA team, and numerous joint promotions and partnerships, the difference in player salary is extreme (Ettienne 2019) (Figure 6.1).

NBA vs WNBA Comparison Table

NBA	WNBA
Revenue	
$7.4 billion	$60 million
Average Salaries	
$6.4 million	$71,635
Ticket Price	
$89 USD	$17.42 USD
Highest-Paid Player	
Stephen Curry $40 million	Brittney Griner $113,500
Average Viewership	
2019 NBA Finals 15.14 million	In 2018: 231,000 viewers
Average Attendance	
18,000	6,768
Ratings	
2019 NBA Finals had an 8.8 rating reaching 15.14 million	2019 WNBA season had a 0.6 rating, a 200% increase
	Highest viewed game ~ 18.7 rating, reached 29.04 million viewers

Figure 6.1: NBA versus WNBA Comparison Table
Source: Jope 2019

Beyond the WNBA's need for more media coverage, ticket sales, and merchandising revenue, to become more financially independent from the NBA, WNBA athletes are also seeking higher pay. It is not just the leagues that have substantial monetary differences but also player contracts. By comparing the WNBA and the NBA for the 2019–2020 season, a $7.32-million wage gap was calculated for players' salaries alone. The WNBA's average salary was less than $80,000, in contrast to the average $7.4 million salaries of the NBA (Berri 2020). As of 2019, the WNBA is home to 12 teams, with the average player wage coming in around $116,000 (Delmore 2020). In 2020, the WNBA reached a new Collective Bargaining Agreement (CBA) that will increase the average salary to $130,000 and the maximum salary to $215,000 (Evans 2020;

McCann 2020). Along with these new salary possibilities, offseason development opportunities were expanded, in addition to maternity leave and extended benefits for childcare (Evans 2020; Feldman 2020; McCann 2020). Yet, there is a huge pay gap between top players in both leagues with comparable player statistics.

Lebron James (LA Lakers) and Sue Bird (Seattle Storm) both won championship titles in the 2020 season. James and Bird have both played in their respective leagues for 17 seasons, and each has won four championships. However, their salaries are not even close to comparable. James earned an estimated salary of $37.44 million in his 2020 season compared with Bird's $215,000 salary in the same 2020 season (Cash 2020; Vazquez 2020). Consideration does have to be made for the revenue generated by the prospective leagues because this influences the amount of money that can be distributed among players. As previously mentioned, the WNBA does not stand close to reaching the revenues of the NBA, and there is a huge difference in the way the revenue is shared between players and the league.

The NBA has, and currently shares, 50 percent of shared revenue with its players compared with the roughly 20 percent WNBA players were receiving leading up to 2020 (Berri 2020). When the Women's National Basketball Players Association (WNBPA) was working on a new CBA, the main goal was to accomplish a 50/50 shared revenue agreement, which was written into the new CBA. Yet, this 50/50 split is dependent on the league reaching certain revenue targets (Berri 2020). Within the CBA, it states that 25 percent of revenue will be shared with players, and the other 25 percent will be put toward the WNBA's marketing and promotional agreements, in an effort to grow the game (Berri 2020; Evans 2020). Further breaking down this new CBA, even if the league is able to reach the outlined revenue targets, WNBA players remain unlikely to receive the 50/50 shared revenue (Berri 2020). Further analysis of the new CBA has led to the conclusion that the women of the WNBA will continue to get significantly underpaid in comparison with their male counterparts, and their 50/50 split agreement on shared revenue for the duration of the new CBA may never equate to a 50/50 split (Berri 2020).

Before the WNBA's new CBA, when talks of pay and revenue increases were discussed, Silver had voiced his concerns, reasoning that the league was not profitable and was draining NBA's resources (Berri 2019). Yet, the NBA was not opposed to investing in another of its affiliated leagues, a newer league that was not generating revenue either (Fader 2018). In 2018, the NBA announced that "it would pay elite high school prospects $125,000 . . . . to play in the G League for a year . . . ." (Fader 2018). The G-League is the NBA's official minor league basketball organization founded in 2001. This announcement was significant considering that an 18-year-old with a select contract would be getting paid twice as much as the WNBA's league MVP at the time, and more than the max WNBA contract (Berri 2018). The G-League was recorded with low attendance, low national interest, low revenue, and "less-entertaining gameplay," yet the NBA continued to pour money into this league because they saw it as a good opportunity for developing new players (Flannery and Geelan 2020). Berri (2018) has explained that by the NBA choosing to look past the financial struggles of the G-League, continuing to saturate and pay a minor league instead of the WNBA, means that the NBA sees the WNBA as a cost and the G-League as an investment. "Before the January 2020 agreement, the NBA consistently responded to the WNBA's demands for increased revenue sharing by claiming they were unpopular and unprofitable" (Garcia 2020, 43–44).

The dynamic between the two leagues is particularly unique in the sense that the WNBA needs to become financially independent to diverge from the NBA and its "profit-oriented" motives (Garcia 2020, 49). The WNBA's success is reliant on social and cultural perspectives of women's sports to change in order to grow the women's game of basketball (Walker, Sartore, and MacIntosh 2012). The media needs to highlight and promote the narratives of women, and women in sports, because it is increasingly vital to the acceptance of women's sports, specifically the WNBA. The mainstream media continues to perpetuate the narrative that men's sports are more valued, desired, and worthy of coverage than are women's sports.

IT'S A MAN'S WORLD

The underrepresentation and promotion of women in sport are much due to the people that run the sports industry. A study conducted by Cooky, Messner, and Musto (2015) examined the coverage of women's sports, finding that the sport media industry is primarily flooded by a male workforce, with 95 percent of sports news anchors being male and only a minuscule 3.2 percent of total sports broadcast time being dedicated to women's sports (Cooky, Messner, and Musto 2015). The sport media world has long been powered by a Euro-Western, White cis-male perspective, highlighting that men's sports are more desired, deserve more attention, and are more profitable. The sport media world has been described as one that is run by men, to promote and celebrate the successes of men, in men's sports (Cooky, Messner, and Musto 2015). As a result, the sport media industry has failed to include and promote women's perspectives, narratives, and sports as a whole. Although there was a perception that women's sports were undesired by the public, Nielsen Sports (2018) discovered that 84 percent of sports fans were interested in women's sports.

The sport media industry upholds masculine hegemony, failing to recognize the large viewership of women, who are interested not only in sports but also in many that play. A recent example of the interest in women's sports, via broadcast, can be seen in the 2019 Women's World Cup. Throughout the tournament, the Women's World Cup secured an audience of roughly 1 billion viewers (Fédération Internationale de Football Association [FIFA] 2020). In addition, in the women's 2018 US Open Finals, between Serena Williams and Naomi Osaka, viewership reached roughly 3.1 million, surpassing the men's final match the following day by 50 percent (Bloomberg 2018).

By continuing the exclusion of women in the media, the sport media industry, and the people behind it, the media fails to bring a thoughtful and diverse perspective, continuing inaccurate representation of the women that play sports and women's sports leagues. The underrepresentation of female athletes and women in sport media can be seen through sports broadcasts. A key aspect to a sports broadcast, and the promotion of sports in media, is updates and information found in the "ticker time," which is displayed in the lower third of the screen (highlighting running updates, scores, and game times) (Cooky, Messner, and Musto 2015). A study conducted by Cooky, Messner, and Musto (2015) found that in 2014 only 2 percent of SportsCenter's ticker time was dedicated to women's sports. Cooky, Messner, and Musto (2015) combined the main broadcast coverage and ticker time from local network affiliates and SportsCenter in 2014 and found that men's football, basketball, and baseball received a combined 68 percent of total screen time. During the broadcast, women's sport coverage was found to have fewer replays, less analysis of games, using less descriptions and statistics (Cooky, Messner, and Hextrum 2013; Duncan et al. 2000). It was also found that not only do women's sports receive less coverage than men's, but the quality of coverage is also lower, specifically in regard to camera angles, graphics, audio quality, pregame, half-time, and postgame coverage (Cooky, Messner, and Hextrum 2013; Duncan and Hasbrook 1998; Higgs and Weiller 1994). In addition, coverage of men's basketball, baseball, and football, even out of their regular season, "far exceeded the coverage of all women's sports, whether those women's sports were in season or out of season" (Cooky, Messner, and Hextrum 2013, 212–13).

Although there is an audience that is interested in watching women's sports, it is apparent that there is a lack of women's sports being covered, discussed, and promoted. The exclusion of narratives from female perspectives and inaccurate representation of women and women's sports creates a toxic cycle. This cycle creates an illusion that because there is less and lower quality coverage of women's sports, women's sports are less desired. This illusion is a theory that Janet Fink studied, and it is called the "sport media commercial complex" (Fink 2015). The sport media commercial complex details the negative effects of consuming sport media and how it relates to poor perception of women's sports and female athletes (Fink 2015). When women's sports fail to get the recognition and coverage they deserve, they receive lesser quality media coverage. This starts a phenomenon where the viewer perceives women's sports as less attractive and less desired owing to the poor coverage, thus leading to disinterest and undermining the credibility of women's sports among viewers. Barnett (2013) found that female athletes who participate in more "traditionally" feminine sports such as figure skating and tennis receive more media coverage than women's sports that are viewed as "masculine" or "violent." Women's sports are not given a likely chance to succeed with such a disparity in media coverage and unequal quality of promotion.

LADYLIKE CONVENTION

Central to the idea of women in sports, and the problems they face, is the way in which women are perceived in the sports world. Sports have frequently been referred to as a gendered space. Krane, Barak, and Mann (2012, 15) explained that "the essence of sport is predicated on the assumption that individuals neatly fit into the categories of female and male." Since the beginning of time, men and women have often been separated when competing or playing. This segregation has led to differences in structure, formation, and opportunities between men and women's sports. This segregation has also furthered the idea that female athletes are physically inferior (Kane 1995; Travers 2008).

The sports industry has been designed and maintained by hegemonic masculine culture, bringing forth the idea that being both female and an athlete is a paradox in itself (Clasen 2001). When women are included in sports coverage, their representation is presented as the ideals of society, sometimes hiding their successes, achievements, and confident personas. This image of what society defines as feminism in the western culture is built on the conventional, heteronormative, White middle-class ideals (Ingraham, 1994). Therefore, the common representation of women in sports is that women are often undermined, sexualized, and underrepresented (Cooky, Messner, and Musto 2015). The historical sexualization of female athletes can be rooted back to the entertainment industry that created "a model of femininity that stresse[d] high style sexual appeal, in which female celebrities combine[d] energy and ability with high heels . . . . along with other measures focused on attracting men" (Grundy and Shackelford 2005, 249).

As discussed prior, there has been a history of presenting female athletes as feminine—referring back to strict dress codes and makeup mandates that were enforced in the AAGPBL and, more recently, the makeup mandates and charm schools that WBL teams put in place to increase sex appeal and attract male audiences. Since the beginning of women's sports, there have been efforts to hide masculinity because it was often "met with hate from the public perception of female athletes [for] not being ladylike" (Meân and Kassing 2008, 129). However, when female athletes are sexualized or appear feminine, their athletic capability is often questioned (Meân and Kassing 2008). This perpetuates the female athlete paradox, where a woman who performs hegemonic femininity while also showing that they are a strong and powerful athlete, which is often defined as masculine—due to the gendered sports world—are met with choosing one or the other because this paired identity of femininity and athleticism does not meet the ideal image of "woman" in the western culture (Clasen 2001).

Duncan et al. (2000) found that female athletes were often framed to showcase stereotypical feminine behaviour. A study using objectification theory by Gurung and Chrouser (2007) found that female athletes that were performing hegemonic femininity or were represented in a sexualized manner in the media were seen as less powerful, less driven, less cerebral, and less self-respecting than were female athletes that were showcased in sports attire. Gurung and Chrouser (2007) also found that women who were pictured in sexualized clothing were seen as less skillful athletes. This has become problematic as the history of women's sports has continuously highlighted femininity and sexualized its players, perpetuating a perception of female athletes to be showcased as more feminine than to be showcased as an athlete. Just one example of this can be seen in the early years of the WNBA when the league made efforts to hide that certain players were lesbian lest it reinforce stereotypes of female athletes and unnatural athletic ability, or decrease sex appeal.

When female athletes oppose performing hegemonic femininity and present themselves as powerful, athletic, or strong, the perception from the public is met with labelling the player as either masculine or lesbian (Meân and Kassing 2008). Women's basketball is a sport that often has players above the average height for a woman, as it is beneficial for play. Sue Bird, a point guard for the Seattle Storm, said in an interview with CNN that players are often very tall and muscular, on top of being Black or gay, which might lead to intimidation of viewers or men (CNN 2020; Hendricks 2020). Compared with other women's sports leagues, such as women's soccer, the women of the WNBA face another set of struggles—that of player's minoritarian identities. Bird addressed these inequalities, saying that due to the league having predominantly Black and LGBTQ+ players, "the problem is how society and the outside world is willing to accept 'the cute girl next door,' but not willing to accept and embrace or not judge these basketball players who are tall, black, gay" (CNN 2020; Hendricks 2020). The discrimination and reluctance from society to accept the WNBA, and the women who make up the league, perpetuates a lack of sport media coverage and representation.

Despite scarce research on the lack of coverage in sport media for Black women, Lumpkin and Williams (1991) investigated articles from *Sports Illustrated* magazine from 1954 to 1987. Their research concluded that compared with White female and male counterparts, Black women were neglected in coverage, with only 16 out of 3,723 articles speaking to Black women's involvement (Lumpkin and Williams 1991). According to a 2019 report by Dr. Richard Lapchick, roughly 83 percent of WNBA players were players of colour, with 67 percent of players being Black or African American (Lapchick 2019). As previously mentioned, the ideal image of a woman and femininity in the western society was based on the ideals of the heteronormative, White middle-class female (Ingraham, 1994). Black women have been contrasted with this image and have been discriminated against and stereotyped for not fitting the ideal image. The ways in which Black women are stereotyped is a reminder of the slavery and colorism era of the United States (Zenquis and Mwaniki 2019). At this time, the stereotypes used to represent Black women "encouraged notions that they lacked physical and emotional sensitivity, were hypersexual and possessed 'natural' strength due to their 'closeness' with apes" (Zenquis and Mwaniki 2019, 27 cited Vertinsky and Captain 1998; Withycombe 2011). In correlation with these stereotypes, the physique of Black female athletes has commonly been portrayed as "hypersexual and muscular with manly strength" (Withycombe 2011, 541).

With roughly 67 percent of WNBA players being Black or African American, the weight of discrimination against Black women, particularly Black female athletes, is vital to recognize when addressing the unjust and unequal treatment of the WNBA (Lapchick 2019). The significance of the number of players that identify as people of colour is in the challenges it presents to the WNBA and its players. When one of these women identifies under a combination of racial and social identities that are often labelled as minorities, it creates an overlap of discrimination and disadvantage (Collins and Sirma 2016; UN Women 2020). This idea is defined as intersectionality but can be broken down further into intersectional feminism. United Nations Women defines the use of "Intersectional feminism [as it] centres the voices of those experiencing overlapping, concurrent forms of oppression in order to understand the depths of the inequalities and the relationships among them in any given context" (UN Women 2020). This idea of intersectional feminism is specifically evident in the WNBA because of a high percentage of players being women of colour and a significant number of players identifying as LGBTQ+. The lack of coverage compared with other leagues falls on the discrimination against the WNBA for not being straight, White, and "cute" (CNN 2020). Mass amounts of discrimination and criticism toward the WNBA are generated from the public because of poor perception and representation of the WNBA and female athletes. I would argue that proper representation and promotion of the WNBA and female athletes would change the women's game, resulting in greater acceptance and growth.

METHODOLOGY

To examine narratives of the WNBA as portrayed by the NBA and men in the sport media industry, I performed a qualitative case study. Specifically, I investigated how NBA games depicted and promoted WNBA games during the finals of the 2020 season. Approximately 19,000 hours of data were collected over a one-month period, with the data culmination after the championship game for each league. Data were collected from the NBA and WNBA games broadcasted by American networks on two ESPN channels, through the Canadian network The Sports Network (TSN). Research questions included, How does the NBA depict and promote the WNBA during their prime-time broadcasts? How, if at all, is the single story of North American basketball evolving through the commentary and imagery shown in American broadcasts on ESPN? How, if at all, does the NBA and male broadcasters on ESPN promote the WNBA during the final play-offs?

Once the data were collected, it was inductively and deductively coded on the basis of commentary, imagery, and the off-court promotional agenda for players. Commentary codes included recognition portrayed by broadcasters about the leagues and players and key topics including off-court or game-play moments. Images were coded on the basis of ticker time, recap pre- or postgame, and outside of game-play visuals. The off-court promotional agenda for players were categorized by extending the athlete into other arenas including their fashion sense, social justice activism, and social media activity. Categories were refined until no new categories could be created and a hierarchy of themes could be solidified (Patton 1990). A content analysis was then used to further identify key themes. Themes were then compared across the data.

FINDINGS

Analyzing the single story of basketball being told in North America, findings uncovered the WNBA's failure to receive recognition and support from the public, the sports industry, and the NBA. Historically, female athletes have been sexualized, trivialized, and absent from sport media coverage, further perpetuating the "single story" of hegemonic masculinity in North American basketball. My research demonstrates North American basketball remains stagnant, as the NBA continues to control the women's game. During the NBA and WNBA's 2020 play-off season, the NBA's broadcasts were primarily focused on the promotion of the men's game and other men's sports, before highlighting the WNBA's games, players, or stats. The NBA's broadcasts had minimal coverage of the women's game and showcased the need for independent media produced by the WNBA to change a male-driven narrative that has undermined female athletes and women's basketball. The overarching themes include discrediting WNBA players and their efforts in social activism, undermining their athleticism. The themes also showed the prioritization and worshipping of NBA players and their lives on and off the court, making them larger-than-life celebrities.

The WNBA faces difficulty securing substantial screen time, as most women's sports only receive a fraction of allotted time in the sport media world, as previously mentioned. This low percentage of screen time falls back to the idea that women's sports are not as deserving as men's. In addition, the women of the WNBA are often met with more discrimination and less support from the public, because of the minoritarian composition of the league, compared with other women's sports.

Screen Time during the WNBA and NBA 2020 Play-offs

The NBA and mainstream sport media continue to provide inadequate representation and media coverage of women's basketball, specifically when looking at the play-offs of the WNBA and NBA's 2020 play-off season. Most media coverages had a high concentration of the men's league and promotion, leaving commentary and visuals that were diminutive for the WNBA in comparison. The broadcasters failed to equally promote the WNBA play-offs during NBA broadcasts and games, and, further, the quality of coverage, when available, was low.

Screen Time: Commentary Quality, Promotion, and Agenda

During prime-time sportscasting, the mention and conversations of women's basketball were substandard in comparison with many male sports and that of the NBA.

During NBA play-off broadcasts, commentators quickly mentioned WNBA play-off games, but it was in passing and often lacked details. With both the NBA and WNBA running on a similar timeline and schedule, some games overlapped, and when they did, there was little to no mention of these WNBA games. Commentary lacked updated and detailed information for WNBA player stats, scores, and game times, among other interesting facts or figures that are often given for men's sports and male athletes.

On the evening of October 6, 2020, the WNBA's play-off game three, between Seattle Storm and Los Vegas Aces, was scheduled, and so were the NBA's game four match-ups between Los Angeles Lakers and Miami Heat. The WNBA's play-off game three, of the Storm and Aces final series, started at 3:00 p.m. Pacific Time (PT), and the NBA's play-off game four, of the Lakers versus Heat final series, started at 6:00 p.m. PT. The WNBA's Seattle Storm had won two games already against the Las Vegas Aces. This meant that the October-6th game could be the final game in their play-off series, and Seattle Storm could potentially win the championship. Whereas the NBA's game four between the Lakers and Heat was not a game that could've ended in one team winning the championship. This is because an NBA team needs to win four games in a series, and the Lakers were going into game four with two wins. In spite of this, promotion for the WNBA's possible championship game, via broadcast conversation at prime-time, was minimal and hard to come by, especially in the evening prior. Commentary the night before was flooded with information and stats concerning the NBA's game four of the Lakers versus Heat final series.

During the WNBA's final play-off game three, commentators did make regards and mentions to the Lakers versus Heat game that was to start that same evening. The Seattle Storm won the final play-off series against Las Vegas Aces ending the 2020 season. The Seattle Storm won the championship a few minutes before the Lakers versus Heat 6:00 p.m. PT game start time. Yet, when the Lakers versus Heat game began at 6:00 p.m. PT, there was hardly any conversation about Seattle's championship win. Conversations were centred around game four of the Lakers and Heat series. There was a large focus on Jimmy Butler's diligent efforts in previous games, and the performance of Lebron James and Anthony Davis.

During the NBA game four between Lakers and Heat, no significant commentary was made, nor enthusiastic commentary was made regarding the WNBA championship game or the WNBA play-offs. In my opinion, it was safe to say you would not have known the WNBA championship game had happened at all, let alone minutes before the NBA game, nor would you have known that Seattle Storm won. In contrast to the NBA broadcast, talks and conversations of the NBA's play-off series were included and significantly mentioned during the WNBA championship game and previous games. Commentary regarding the NBA during WNBA broadcasts included stats, scores, game time, starting lineups and information about the men's league and its players.

Screen Time: Tickets, Game Recaps, and Visual Promotion

ESPN's "ticker," which is displayed in the lower third of the screen, designed to show running updates, scores, and game times, had little to no details of WNBA play-offs, stats, information, game times, or scores. This is usually the area that details information that is not covered by regular broadcast conversation. The ticker at the bottom of the screen consistently showed NBA information, and the same cannot be said about the WNBA.

Furthermore, when the WNBA championship game was scheduled, the promotion was sparse and hard to come across during prime-time media coverage. During this time, coverage of the NBA play-off stats, information, game times, scores, starting lineups, and promotion were flooding the broadcast through the ticker. Beyond the ticker, further visual promotion and screen time of the NBA was pushed through via game recaps, infographics, and commercials. Whereas the imagery and visual promotion of WNBA was difficult to find through these broadcasts and oftentimes was not seen at all. In order to find substantial information about the WNBA games, stats, times, and information, third-party resources, outside of the prime-time broadcast, had to be used.

One of the most notable findings regarding the visual promotion and media during the NBA and WNBA play-offs was that of the WNBA championship game between the Seattle Storm and Las Vegas Aces. As previously mentioned, the October-6th-2020 game was game three of the finals and was the possible WNBA's final championship game. However, that same night was game four of the Miami Heat and Los Angeles Lakers finals for the NBA. Visual promotion and screen time surrounding game four of the NBA saturated the broadcasts, pregame, postgame, and for days leading up to it. Emphasis was put on NBA player stats, past game analysis, play-off predictions, and player information. During commercial breaks, there was significant imagery and promotion of the upcoming NBA play-off games, starting lineup, and game times. In addition, between game play there was notable screen time dedicated to the NBA play-offs, whereas the imagery and visual promotion of WNBA's championship win by Seattle Storm was difficult to detect. Game recaps and highlights of past WNBA games and the championship were extremely infrequent, if at all. When highlights, imagery, or visuals of WNBA players or game play was included, it was quick, simple, and oftentimes uneventful.

Screen Time: Recognition of Players Social Activism and Involvement off the Court

Although both the WNBA and NBA, among other leagues, made efforts to fight against systemic racism and police brutality, specifically with their push toward the BLM movement, media coverage did not depict their efforts equally or with the same weight.

The NBA's protest retained significant screen time, and their efforts and support of the BLM movement was heavily promoted and pictured through media coverage. The NBA and its players were the centre of conversation around sports and activism and the BLM movement. The media and broadcasts drew attention to the men's actions, with substantial screen time highlighting what they wore, including apparel that highlighted voter rights, BLM, and even pregame outfits in the bubble, what NBA players tweeted and their activity on social media, and their protests and their kneeling at the games during the national anthem. Imagery was focused not only on the NBA's support of the BLM movement but also on the NBA players, both on and off the court.

Even though the WNBA and its players were making significant strides for the BLM movement, their efforts and actions were depicted less during broadcasts. Coverage and imagery of WNBA's extensive social activism work to inform the public and to make known the importance of the BLM movement and the impacts of systemic racism, police brutality, and social injustices seemed to be dimmed in comparison with its male counterparts. In addition, when WNBA and NBA players advocated for voter rights and awareness, the women of the WNBA were once again overshadowed by

NBA players in the media. Broadcasts frequently featured images and videos of NBA players' tweets, speeches, involvement, and promotion of voter rights. NBA players were shown more during broadcasts when mentioning voter rights and the importance of voting.

It is evident that the broadcasts continued to highlight and promote a male narrative over the women's league, even highlighting other men's sports before the accomplishment and information around the WNBA's players, games, or championship.

DISCUSSION

Although women's sports are slowly catching up to the popularity of men's, it is evident that there is a distorted image of female athletes being represented in the media. This inaccurate representation perpetuates the idea that women's sports are not as important or as worthy of attention as men's sports and therefore continue to receive unfair treatment, pay, and opportunity. As Chimamanda Ngozi Adichie said, the creation of a single story happens when people are shown "as one thing, as only one thing, over and over again, and that is what they become" (Adichie 2009). The findings discussed in this chapter indicate that the WNBA is restricted by financial resources, minimal support from the public—owing to player's social identities—and discrimination against not only women in sports but also specifically basketball and women of colour. In addition, women's professional basketball and the WNBA face more discrimination from the public compared with other women's sports because of a majority Black and LGBTQ+ league (Garcia 2020). This means the WNBA has to overcome more obstacles to change public perception to reach a larger audience and further achieve equal pay, treatment, and opportunity.

Historically, women's sports have been faced with the female athlete paradox. This has resulted in efforts to hide aspects of female athletes that might "suggest" or support ideas of masculinity. Owing to this, sportswomen have been framed in a way that highlights feminine features and behaviours. This long-withstanding tradition to hide a female athletes' strength and power, owing to negative societal views of masculinity in women, has presented female athletes as lesser than their male counterparts. Through evidence showcased in the literature review, it was often players who identified as people of colour or LGBTQ+ that were vulnerable to being silenced or shadowed.

For the WNBA to change the public perception of women's basketball, it needs to take control of the narrative of women's sports and female athletes. The WNBA is in a unique position to highlight a majority minoritarian league of women on a global scale, and in partnership with the NBA. By producing and promoting media and voices produced by the WNBA and its athletes, it can present a narrative powered by women. This female narrative will begin to break the stereotypes that women's sports are less skilled, less respected, and less deserving than men's. These stereotypes are credited to the men that have historically controlled the representation of women's sports and athletes in the sports industry and media. With a concentration on women in power and female voices, the WNBA can break down the female athlete paradox and bring awareness to female empowerment, women's involvement in sports, and new generations of fans.

Evidently, with men running the sports industry, the mainstream media has historically highlighted masculine hegemony in sports. This has pushed sportswomen to the side and advertised their femininity and sexuality when they were included. As mentioned in the literature review, it is not new or uncommon for women's sports to receive low coverage and less screen time than men's sports. However, this continuation of unequal coverage, treatment, and opportunity prolongs an inaccurate portrayal of women's sports, pushing forward the idea that women's sports are less valued and less deserving compared with men's sports.

Mainstream sport media continues to publish and promote the singular story of basketball in North America as male dominated, Black, and profitable. The media continues to be powered and run by majority Euro-Western, White cis-males, perpetuating a cycle of men's sports being the focal point of the sport's industry. This continuation will prolong inaccurate representation of women's sports and unequal treatment. Most important, men will maintain the power to govern decisions regarding women's sports and their representation in the media. The power held by Euro-Western, White cis-males in the sports industry is extremely problematic regarding leagues such as the WNBA that have a majority minoritarian makeup. This is a league that needs to break the stereotypes that have long been promoted and produced by a male-dominated authority. Historically, men in the sports industry have presented idealized, sexualized, and stereotyped female athletes. If men continue to occupy a high percentage of executive positions in the sports industry, such as those that control the image and narrative of women's basketball, women may never achieve fair treatment, pay, or opportunity. The agenda of the sports industry has long been in favour of men's sports to highlight and promote male athletes and discredit and undermine female athletes. Through the findings in this chapter, it is evident that screen time for women's sports fails to increase. Without more women in governing positions of the sports industry, the narrative of women's sports will be controlled and told through a male perspective, maintaining media and a society that highlights and promotes masculine hegemony in sports.

The NBA has long governed much of the WNBA and has made many public comments regarding its efforts to help the WNBA succeed. However, the NBA is doing nothing but holding the WNBA and the women behind the league in their place.

As previously mentioned in the literature review, the offseason timing of the WNBA trivializes women's basketball because it takes them out of the regular basketball season. Because of the pandemic, it is evident that it is not the low screen time or offseason placement that is affecting viewership but the sheer lack of televised games. Owing to the limited WNBA games being broadcast, the WNBA had a partnership with Twitter to stream "10 live regular-season WNBA games" (NBA 2020).

The 2020 season was notable because there was a 68-percent increase in WNBA games over the summer (Megdal 2020). This increase was unusual given that viewership was down across all sports leagues, and women's sports on average do not see this type of increase (Megdal 2020). However, it was found that the increase might have been due to WNBA games being more accessible to preexisting sports fans (Megdal 2020).

One of the reasons the WNBA is not receiving the airtime they deserve is that there is a societal perception that sports fans do not want to watch women's basketball, despite Nielsen Sports' (2018) finding that 84 percent of sports fans were interested in women's sports. It was announced in May 2021 that only 51 percent of WNBA games will broadcast on TV for the 2021 season. From 2019 to the 2020 WNBA season, there was a 68-percent increase in games that were nationally televised, and this raises the question as to why the 2021 season would have fewer broadcasted games despite the proven interest in women's sports (Megdal 2020). This broaches the question whether or not the growth in viewership in 2020 was connected to WNBA games being placed at the same times as men's leagues, deconstructing the idea that women's sports are less worthy of viewership. The simultaneous scheduling of the WNBA and NBA could create an equal experience ultimately building respect toward the WNBA.

Continuing with the WNBA and the NBA's past connections to social justice movements, the WNBA dedicated their season to Breonna Taylor to further their commitment to the BLM movement. The media frequently pictured male athletes in support of the BLM movement whereas the WNBA's efforts seemed to be in the shadows despite its history of social justice involvement. With a majority Black league, could increased viewership be due to society being pushed to focus on diversity and inclusion, in coordination with the BLM movement? Despite the increased viewership of the WNBA's 2020 season, monetary support and investment into the women's league are scarce. With the NBA owning roughly half the league, the WNBA is treated as an expense as opposed to an investment.

Unfortunately, the WNBA is stuck in a loop where it needs more airtime to garner sponsorships, to raise the profits of the league, allowing it to gain respect and notoriety. Coupled with the minoritarian composition of the WNBA, this is a vicious cycle that is hard to break. However, male athletes are continuously praised in the media, being pictured and covered around the clock, creating stardom and demand. Compared with the WNBA, and other women's sports, that seem to be on a media blackout when not playing. The lack of excitement, promotion, and screen time of women's basketball also affects ticket sales, and because people are not fighting for seats for WNBA games, ticket prices remain ridiculously low in comparison with the NBA. All of these factors contribute to the vicious cycle of low screen time, low revenue, and low recognition of players.

David Berri, a sports economist and professor of economics at Southern Utah University, wrote an article regarding the wage gap of the WNBA and the newly funded G-League. This article was published in *Forbes* but was quickly taken down when the NBA reached out expressing concerns (Bogage 2018). There was a *Washington Post* article that detailed the information behind why the article was taken down, explaining that the NBA expressed concerns asking for more information to be added (Bogage 2018). Berri noted in the *Washington Post* article that none of this information went against his thesis and the NBA's request was more PR related; however, he agreed to add the additional context (Bogage 2018). Yet, despite Berri's agreement, *Forbes* took down the article permanently and dismissed Berri. I reached out to Berri for further context. During a Zoom call, Berri mentioned that this was not the first time the NBA had reached out with concerns. Berri said that the NBA often tried to control the narrative and did not want to be pictured in a bad light for not supporting the women's league.

David Berri explained the major inequality of women's sports lies in the enthusiasm of the owners. Owners of men's sports teams and leagues love men. They picture themselves playing as these men, almost as though it is a real-life fantasy team. These owners are living vicariously through their teams and their players, and this is something they cannot do with women's sports. Men will continue to sink money into a team or league despite countless losses and failure to generate revenue because they want to be these players. Berri gave an example of the Pittsburgh Steelers when it was first created by Art Rooney. In Rooney's biography, he said he had continuously put money into a failing league because he loved it. The men that run the sports industry own these teams and power these leagues and are quick to abandon ship when they do not see immediate success in women's sports. Berri talked about the possibility of change, coming to the conclusion that until more women are in power in sports, owning teams and leagues and having their presence in the media, the importance of men's sports will continue to dominate the narrative and women's sports will fail to receive proper funding and recognition.

CONCLUSION

The WNBA is reliant on the NBA to exist as a league. However, it is the men of the sports industry and the NBA that are the very cause of the WNBA's faults and failures. The WNBA is being portrayed as a league that fails to find viewer support, even though we know this is not true. The WNBA is a league that is made up of women who identify under a variety of minority groups, and even when they are presented as athletes, they are met with criticism for failing to meet the ideals of femininity. This single story of basketball in North America perpetuates the silence of the WNBA and the women behind it. Without proper representation and coverage in the media, the league will fail to meet the sponsorship and broadcasting partnerships that are needed to begin generating mass revenue. Yet, the NBA is holding the women and the women's league in its place. The NBA has continuously shown that its values and growth plans are focused on the men in basketball. The NBA has historically silenced the female narrative and the women of the WNBA. They have controlled the women's league and presented an idealized, sexualized, and stereotyped league of female players. NBA commissioner Silver has undermined the need for more coverage and brought forth reasons for low pay to WNBA athletes. At the same time, the NBA has invested significant amounts of money, support, and promotion to its new men's basketball minor league called the G-League. This is a league that has generated no revenue, had little support from the public, low viewership, and consisted of players straight out of high school.

Through this chapter, I have found that the NBA is benefiting from a "symbiotic relationship" with the WNBA, in which the women's league is a component of the NBA's global conglomerate growth. Furthermore, despite the women pushing the agenda forward, the men of the sports industry and the NBA are holding them in their place. The financial decisions the NBA has made regarding its control over the women's league and past, current, and future decisions governing the WNBA have exemplified the NBA's interests of benefiting from patriarchal capitalist growth. The NBA and the men of the sports industry continue to power and control the single story of basketball in North America. Findings of this case study indicate that there is a singular story of hegemonic masculinity in sports being told, in a male-dominated world, perpetuating the idea that basketball is male.

REFERENCES

AAGPBL (All American Girls Professional Baseball League). n.d. "Rules of Conduct." Accessed December 13, 2020. https://www.aagpbl.org/history/rules-of-conduct.

Adichie, Chimamanda Ngozi. 2009. "The Danger of a Single Story." *TED Global*, July 2009. https://www.ted.com/talks/chimamanda_ngozi_adichie_the_danger_of_a_single_story/details?language=e.

Barnett, Barbara. 2013. "The Babe/Baby Factor: Sport, Women, and Mass Media." In *Routledge Handbook of Sport Communication*, edited by P. Pedersen, 544. London: Routledge. March 2013. https://doi.org/10.4324/9780203123485.ch35.

Berri, David. 2018. "Why Is the Michael Jordan of the WNBA Paid Less Than Adonis Jordan in 1999?" *Forbes*, July 9, 2018. https://www.forbes.com/sites/davidberri/2018/07/09/why-isnt-the-michael-jordan-of-the-wnba-paid-at-least-as-well-as-adonis-jordan-was/?sh=4d8b3046dce5.

———. 2019. "The Relative Success Story of the WNBA." In *Routledge Handbook of the Business of Women's Sport*, edited by N. Lough and A. N. Geurin, 186–99. New York: Routledge.

———. 2020. "Basketball's Gender Wage Gap Narrows (but Doesn't Vanish!)." *Winsidr*, February 12, 2020. https://winsidr.com/2020/02/basketballs-gender-wage-gap-narrows-but-doesnt-vanish/.

Berri, David J., and Anthony C. Krautmann. 2013. "Understanding the WNBA On and Off the Court." In *Handbook on the Economics of Women in Sports*, edited by Eva Marikova Leeds and Michael A. Leeds, 132–55. Northampton, MA: Edward Elgar Publishing. https://www.elgaronline.com/view/edcoll/9781849809382/9781849809382.00015.xml.

Bloomberg. 2018. "Serena Williams Match Drew 50% More Viewers Than Men's Finals." *Fortune*, September 11, 2018. https://fortune.com/2018/09/11/serena-williams-carlos-ramos/.

Bogage, Jacob. 2018. "Forbes Cuts Ties With Sports Business Columnist, Deletes Piece About WNBA Player Salaries." *The Washington Post*, November 2, 2018. https://www.washingtonpost.com/sports/2018/11/02/forbes-cuts-ties-with-sports-business-columnist-deletes-piece-about-wnba-player-salaries/

Brown, Josiah. 2020. "Does the WNBA Make Money?" *Self Improvement Base*, December 2, 2020. https://selfimprovementbase.com/does-the-wnba-make-money/.

Cash, Meredith. 2020. "WNBA Legend Sue Bird Says Calls for Equality with the NBA Are Not about Equal Pay." *Insider*, October 30, 2020. https://www.insider.com/sue-bird-wnba-nba-equal-pay-2020-10.

Clasen, Patricia R. W. 2001. "The Female Athlete: Dualisms and Paradox in Practice." *Women and Language* 24 (2): 36–41. https://go.gale.com/ps/i.do?p=LitRC&u=utoronto_main&id=GALE|A82352864&v=2.1&it=r&sid=bookmark-LitRC&asid=d10cd3e8.

CNN. 2020. "Sue Bird: 'We Are Not Cute White Girls Like Soccer Players.'" October 16, 2020. https://www.cnn.com/videos/sports/2020/10/16/sue-bird-seattle-storm-wnba-womens-equality-football-megan-rapinoe-spt-intl.cnn/video/playlists/women-and-sports/.

Collins, Patricia H., and Bilge Sirma. 2016. "What Is Intersectionality." In *Intersectionality*, 11–31. Cambridge: Polity Press, June 13, 2016. https://doi.org/10.1177%2F0268580918791974d.

Cooky, Cheryl, Michael A. Messner, and Robin H. Hextrum. 2013. "Women Play Sport, But Not on TV: A Longitudinal Study of Televised News Media." *Communication & Sport* 1 (3): 203–30. https://doi.org/10.1177/2167479513476947.

Cooky, Cheryl, Michael A. Messner, and Michela Musto. 2015. " 'It's Dude Time!': A Quarter Century of Excluding Women's Sports in Televised News and Highlight Shows." *Communication & Sport* 3 (3): 261–87. https://journals.sagepub.com/doi/pdf/10.1177/2167479515588761.

Cwik, Chris. 2020a. "WNBA Dedicates Season to Breonna Taylor, Holds 26-Second Long Moment of Silence in Her Honor." *Yahoo! Sports*, July 25, 2020. https://ca.news.yahoo.com/wnba-dedicates-season-to-breonna-taylor-holds-26-second-long-moment-of-silence-to-honor-her-162759602.html.

———. 2020b. "WNBA Unveils 2020 Court, Which Features Two Black Lives Matter Signs." *Yahoo! Sports*, July 25, 2020. https://ca.style.yahoo.com/wnba-unveils-2020-court-which-features-two-black-lives-matter-signs-142634533.html.

Delmore, Erin. 2020. " 'We Didn't Back Down': How Women's Basketball Players Scored Major Wins for Equal Pay." *NBC News*, February 6, 2020. https://www.nbcnews.com/know-your-value/feature/we-didn-t-back-down-how-women-s-basketball-players-ncna1131561.

Duncan, M. C., & Hasbrook, C. 1988. "Denial of Power in Televised Women's Sports." *Sociology of Sport Journal*, 5,1–21. https://journals.humankinetics.com/view/journals/ssj/5/1/article-p1.xml.

Duncan, Margaret C., Michael A. Messner, Cheryl Cooky, and Wayne Wilson. 2000. *Gender in Televised Sports: 1989, 1993 and 1999*. Los Angeles: Amateur Athletic Foundation of Los Angeles. https://la84.org/wp-content/uploads/2016/09/tv2000.pdf.

Ettienne, Lerae. 2019. "It's Time to Pay Up, the Justification for Higher Salaries for WNBA Players: An Analysis of the WNBA's Success and Employing Mediation between the WNBA and NBA to Leverage Future Success." *Pepperdine Dispute Resolution Law Journal* 19 (2): 175–200. https://digitalcommons.pepperdine.edu/cgi/viewcontent.cgi?article=1431&context=drlj.

Evans, Ross. 2020. "Demographics and Identity in the New WNBA-WNBPA CBA." *OnLabour*, May 13, 2020. https://www.onlabor.org/demographics-and-identity-in-the-new-wnba-wnbpa-cba/.

Fader, Mirin. 2018. "Inside the WNBA's Fight for Higher Pay." *Bleacher Report*, October 30, 2018. https://bleacherreport.com/articles/2802759-inside-the-wnbas-fight-for-higher-pay.

Feldman, Dan. 2020. "New WNBA CBA Increases Average Salary to Nearly $130K, Maximum Salary above $500K." *NBC Sports*, January 14, 2020. https://nba.nbcsports.com/2020/01/14/new-wnba-cba-increases-average-salary-to-nearly-130k-maximum-salary-above-500k/.

FIFA (Fédération Internationale de Football Association). n.d. "FIFA Women's World Cup France 2019™." Retrieved February 1, 2021. https://img.fifa.com/image/upload/rvgxekduqpeo1ptbgcng.pdf. [The reference "FIFA (Fédération Internationale de Football Association) (n.d.)" is given in the reference list but not cited in the text. Please provide in-text citation or delete the reference from the list.]

Fink, Janet S. 2015. "Female Athletes, Women's Sport, and the Sport Media Commercial Complex: Have We Really 'Come a Long Way, Baby?' " *Sport Management Review* 18 (3): 331–42. https://doi.org/10.1016/j.smr.2014.05.001.

Flannery, Connor, and Conor Geelan. 2020. "Why the NBA G League Will Become Profitable: The Jalen Green Effect." *Medium*, October 21, 2020. https://medium.com/@spacethefloorpodcast/why-the-nba-g-league-will-become-profitable-the-jalen-green-effect-d94984209b39.

Garcia, Christopher. 2020. " 'Betting on Women': A Feminist Political Economic Critique of Ideological Sports Narratives Surrounding the WNBA." *The Political Economy of Communication* 8 (1): 34–56. https://www.polecom.org/index.php/polecom/article/view/119.

Glass, Alana. 2019. "WNBA, Nike Unveil 2019 Uniforms." *Forbes*, April 10, 2019. https://www.forbes.com/sites/alanaglass/2019/04/10/wnba-nike-unveil-2019-uniforms/?sh=3e427b0c444c.

Grundy, Pamela, and Susan Shackelford. 2005. *Shattering the Glass: The Remarkable History of Women's Basketball*. New York: The New Press.

Gurung, Regan A. R., and Carly J. Chrouser. 2007. "Predicting Objectification: Do Provocative Clothing and Observer Characteristics Matter?" *Sex Roles* 57 (1–2): 91–99. https://doi.org/10.1007/s11199-007-9219-z.

Hendricks, Jaclyn. 2020. " 'Cute Little White Girls' Make Soccer More Popular than Basketball: Sue Bird." *New York Post*, October 20, 2020. https://nypost.com/2020/10/20/cute-little-white-girls-make-soccer-more-popular-than-wnba-sue-bird/.

Higgs, Catriona T., and Karen H. Weiller. 1994. "Gender Bias and the 1992 Summer Olympic Games: An Analysis of Television Coverage." *Journal of Sport & Social Issues* 18 (1): 234–46. https://doi.org/10.1177/019372394018003004.

Ingraham, Chrys. 1994. "The Heterosexual Imaginary: Feminist Sociology and Theories of Gender." Sociological Theory, 12(2), 203–19. https://doi.org/10.2307/201865.

Jope, Christian. 2019. "NBA vs WNBA: Revenue, Salaries, Attendance, Ratings." *World Sports Network*, July 18, 2019. https://www.wsn.com/nba/nba-vs-wnba/.

Kane, Mary J. 1995. "Resistance/Transformation of the Oppositional Binary: Exposing Sport as a Continuum." *Journal of Sport & Social Issues* 19 (2): 191–218. https://doi.org/10.1177/019372395019002006.

Kenow, Laura J. 2010. "The All-American Professional Baseball League (AAGPBL): A Review of Literature and Its Reflection of Gender Issues." *Women in Sport and Physical Activity Journal* 19 (1): 58–69. https://doi.org/10.1123/wspaj.19.1.58.

Krane, V., K. S. Barak, and M. E. Mann. 2012. "Broken Binaries and Transgender Athletes: Challenging Sex and Gender in Sport." In *Sexual Orientation and Gender Identity in Sport: Essays from Activists, Coaches, and Scholars*, edited by G. B. Cunningham, 13–22. College Station, TX: Center for Sport Management Research & Education.

Lapchick, Richard, ed. 2019. "The 2019 Racial and Gender Report Card: Women's National Basketball Association." *TIDES*, October 16, 2020. https://docs.wixstatic.com/ugd/7d86e5_918fdf4e8051461d8f8f5f8f4180deb4.pdf.

Lumpkin, A., and Linda D. Williams. 1991. "An Analysis of Sports Illustrated Feature Articles, 1954–1987." *Sociology of Sport Journal* 8: 16–32. https://kuscholarworks.ku.edu/bitstream/handle/1808/11412/Lumpkin_an%20analysis%20of%20sports%20illustrated.pdf?sequence=1&isAllowed=y.

McCann, Michael. 2020. "Analyzing the WNBA's New CBA Deal and What It Means for the Future of the League." *Sports Illustrated*, January 14, 2020. https://www.si.com/wnba/2020/01/14/wnba-cba-labor-salary-raise-players-association.

McDonald, Mary G. 2000. "The Marketing of the Women's National Basketball Association and the Making of Postfeminism." *International Review for the Sociology of Sport* 35 (1): 35–47. https://doi.org/10.1177/101269000035001003.

———. 2012. "Out-of-Bounds Plays: The Women's National Basketball Association and the Neoliberal Imaginings of Sexuality." In *Sport and Neoliberalism: Politics, Consumption, and Culture*, edited by M. L. Silk and D. L. Andrews, 2121–24. Philadelphia: Temple University Press.

Meân, Lindsey J., and Jeffrey W. Kassing. 2008. " 'I Would Just Like to Be Known as an Athlete': Managing Hegemony, Femininity, and Heterosexuality in Female Sport." *Western Journal of Communication* 72 (2): 126–44. https://doi.org/10.1080/10570310802038564.

Megdal, Howard. 2020. "WNBA News: What We Learned from Cathy Engelbert's State of the League Talk." *Forbes*, October 5, 2020. https://www.forbes.com/sites/howardmegdal/2020/10/05/wnba-news-what-we-learned-from-cathy-engelberts-state-of-the-league-talk/?sh=66bb47741069.

Minutaglio, Rose. 2020. "The WNBA Is Wearing Breonna Taylor's Name on Jerseys. The NBA Should, Too." *Elle*, July 24, 2020. https://www.elle.com/culture/a33384408/wnba-breonna-taylor-jersey-nba/.

Musto, Michela, Cheryl Cooky, and Michael A. Messner. 2017. " 'From Fizzle to Sizzle!' Televised Sports News and the Production of Gender-Bland Sexism." *Gender & Society* 31 (5): 573–96. https://doi.org/10.1177/0891243217726056.

NBA (National Basketball Association). 2020. "WNBA and Twitter Renew Partnership to Stream Regular Season Games in 2020." *NBA Communications*, August 10, 2020. https://pr.nba.com/wnba-twitter-2020/.

Nielsen. 2011. Nielson Sports, "What Time Is Really Primetime?" September 14, 2011. https://www.nielsen.com/us/en/insights/article/2011/what-time-is-really-primetime/.

Patton, M. Q. 1990. *Qualitative Evaluation and Research Methods*. 2nd ed., 169–86. Newbury Park, CA: Sage Publications. https://doi.org/10.1002/nur.4770140111.

Perry, Alyssa J. 2020. "How Black Women Athletes Paved the Way for the NBA Strike." *npr*, September 4, 2020. https://www.npr.org/sections/codeswitch/2020/09/04/909638021/how-black-women-athletes-paved-the-way-for-the-nba-strike.

Pinchevsky, Tal. 2018. "The Women's Basketball Team That Sent Its Players to Charm School." *Wbur*, October 12, 2018. https://www.wbur.org/onlyagame/2018/10/12/california-dreams-charm-school.

Reiff, Nathan. 2020. "How the NBA Makes Money: Television Rights, Merchandising, and Ticket Sales Are Primary Revenue Sources." *Investopedia*, September 18, 2020. https://www.investopedia.com/articles/personal-finance/071415/how-nba-makes-money.asp.

Shapiro, Leonard. 1998. "WNBA Has All the Angles Covered." *The Washington Post*, June 18, 1998. https://www.washingtonpost.com/wp-srv/sports/mystics/longterm/preview98/articles/waves.htm.

Travers, Ann. 2008. "The Sport Nexus and Gender Injustice." *Studies in Social Justice* 2 (1): 79–101. https://doi.org/10.26522/ssj.v2i1.969.

UN Women. 2020. "Intersectional Feminism: What It Means and Why It Matters Right Now." July 1, 2020. https://www.unwomen.org/en/news/stories/2020/6/explainer-intersectional-feminism-what-it-means-and-why-it-matters.

USA Basketball. 2020. "Facts & Photos: 1976 to 1984 U.S. Olympic Women's Basketball Teams." July 25, 2020. https://www.usab.com/news-events/news/2020/07/1976-to-1984-women-facts-photos.aspx#:~:text=1976%20was%20the%20first%20women's,with%20a%203%2D2%20rec ord.

Vazquez, Mateo. 2020. "The Wage Gap on the Court: The WNBA v. NBA." *The Trinity Tripod*, October 19, 2020. https://tripod.domains.trincoll.edu/sports/the-wage-gap-on-the-court-the-wnba-v-nba/.

Vertinsky, Patricia, and Gwendolyn Captain. 1998. "More Myth Than History: American Culture and Representations of the Black Female's Athletic Ability." *Journal of Sport History* 25 (3): 532– 61.
https://www.researchgate.net/publication/242419674_More_Myth_than_History_American_Cu lture_and_Representations_of_the_Black_Female's_Athletic_Ability.

Walker, Matthew, Melanie Sartore, and Eric MacIntosh. 2012. "Beyond the 'Business Case' for the WNBA: A Strategic Perspectives Approach for League Sustainability." *Journal of Contemporary Athletics* 6 (1): 33–50.
https://www.researchgate.net/publication/260017685_BEYOND_THE_BUSINESS_CASE_FO R_THE_WNBA_A_STRATEGIC_PERSPECTIVES_APPROACH_FOR_LEAGUE_SUSTAI NABILITY.

Withycombe, Jenny L. 2011. "Intersecting Selves: African American Female Athletes' Experiences of Sport." *Sociology of Sport Journal* 28 (4): 478–93. https://doi.org/10.1123/ssj.28.4.478.

WNBA (Women's National Basketball Association). 2016. "History of the WNBA." May 3, 2016. https://www.wnba.com/news/history-of-the-wnba-2002/.

———. 2020. "Make Way for the 2020 Season." July 24, 2020. https://www.youtube.com/results?search_query=wnba+commerical.

Zenquis, Manuel R., and Munene F. Mwaniki. 2019. "The Intersection of Race, Gender, and Nationality in Sport: Media Representation of the Ogwumike Sisters." *Journal of Sport and Social Issues* 43 (1): 23–43. https://doi.org/10.1177/0193723518823338.

Zhang, James J., Eddie T. C. Lam, Beth A. Cianfrone, Ryan K. Zapalac, Stephen Holland, and Debbie P. Williamson. 2011. "An Importance–Performance Analysis of Media Activities Associated with WNBA Game Consumption." *Sport Management Review* 14 (1): 64–78. https://doi.org/10.1016/j.smr.2010.03.001.

Zhang, James J., Lori Pennington-Gray, Daniel P. Connaughton, Jessica R. Braunstein, Matthew H. Ellis, Eddie T. C. Lam, and Debbie Williamson. 2003. "Understanding women's professional basketball game spectators: Sociodemographics, game consumption, and entertainment options." *Sport Marketing Quarterly* 12 (4): 228–43. https:// www.researchgate.net/publication/288938901_Understanding_women's_professional_b asketball_game_spectators_Sociodemographics_game_consumption_and_entertainment_options.

CHAPTER 7

Where Equality Should Flow: Swimming as a Catalyst for Nongendered and Equality-Driven Media Coverage in Sport

Lydia Ferrari Kehoe

INTRODUCTION

The sport of swimming contains a seemingly natural parity: men and women train alongside one another and race in the same schedule of events at competitions. Significant discrepancies in events, competition, funding, training, and opportunity that exist in sports such as rugby and football are absent from swimming. One major discrepancy that was recently thrown into the spotlight once again is the difference in prize money within high-profile sporting events. A report by workplace equality group Work180 found that the winning men's team (England) of the 2020 Six Nations rugby tournament won £5 million, whereas the women's team (England) won nothing (*ITV News* 2020). Similarly, the report found that the winning men's football team in the 2020 FA Cup (Arsenal) received £3.6 million in prize money, whereas the winning women's team in the equivalent tournament (Manchester City) earned just £25,000 for their victory (Work180 2020).

The lack of such disparities in swimming means that the sport lends itself to receiving media coverage that reflects this equivalence. As swimming is not a mainstream sport, its media coverage is most accessible to audiences every four years during the Olympic and Paralympic Games.

As a recent graduate with a degree in specialist sports journalism and as a competitive swimmer of over 12 years, sport and the media have been significant pillars in both my life and my work. I have been fortunate that my personal experiences within sport have not been tainted by the sexism, discrimination, and toxic masculinity that I know permeate so many other sports and female athletes' experiences. My passion for swimming and continuous endeavours to champion women in sport within my work led me to conduct research on the portrayal of female swimmers within the media for my dissertation.

As this subject area is relatively untouched in the world of academic writing and research, my hypotheses were based solely on the bleak findings of similar analysis of other sports. Carrying out this analysis led me to realize the unique nature of the sport, the opportunity that swimming's media coverage has to be fair and equitable, and the extent to which the media is falling short of such parity.

This chapter lays bare the findings of my dissertation, the current media landscape and its power to shape perceptions of sport within society, the existing barriers facing women in sport and, most importantly, the opportunity that swimming presents in paving the way toward unbiased media coverage for female sportspeople. This is not a pipe dream for those who, like myself, advocate for equality within sports journalism. It is attainable, and it is my belief that swimming is the perfect place to start.

Dissertation

My dissertation, entitled "Media Portrayal of Female Swimmers: An Analysis of Inequalities in British Online Coverage (Case Study of The Guardian Newspaper)," explored modern media coverage of swimming, specifically, reporting produced by British daily newspaper The Guardian during the 2016 Rio Olympic Games. A corpus of 30 articles was established using the search parameters: Rio 2016 Olympic Swimming site: www.theguardian.com, and subsequently analyzed by carrying out a summative content analysis. This research method allowed me to examine the text within each article, interpret the images attached to the copy, and also gather some quantitative data, such as how many times current male and female swimmers were mentioned within each of the reports.

Similarly to research conducted about female representation in sports over the last 40 years of sport media coverage, my research confirmed one of my hypotheses, namely, that the media coverage of swimming would, like many other sports, be subject to gendered, sexist, and unequal coverage. In addition, my research disproved the second hypothesis I had established, namely, that there would be a difference in the amount of coverage afforded to male and female swimmers. Instead, the findings showed that male and female swimmers were generally afforded the same amount of coverage in the media. In simple terms, this means that there was no issue with how much reporting was done on female athletes but rather with the contents and quality of reporting.

These findings were especially significant for many reasons. The severe lack of academic research around the sport allowed me to create a picture of what swimming coverage looks like within the current media landscape, albeit restricted to a representation within the UK only. The findings provide significant insight into the pitfalls of current reporting and highlight the errors propagated by the sports journalists who feature in my research. Moreover, the format of swimming—which I discovered to be both unique and advantageous for the pursuit of parity in sports reporting—means that media personnel have a glaring opportunity to deliver fair and nongendered media coverage that focuses on the athletes and their performances alone.

Disappointingly, this was not the case. In fact, the results of the research were more damning than I first hypothesized, featuring several qualities that, in my opinion, widened the already large gap between the coverage of men and women in sport. Female swimmers were not only found to be held in lower regard than their male counterparts, but were also frequently pitted against one another. Their successes were trivialized and compared to the "male equivalent," their disappointments spoken about with less empathy and understanding, their physical appearances highlighted, and their femininity reaffirmed by the lack of use of words and phrases such as *powerful, strong,* and *dominant*. At times, these negative attributes within the reports were subtle, making their presence all the more frustrating.

The findings of my analysis were redeemed slightly by the absence of common idiosyncrasies of gendered sports reporting such as gender-marking and infantilizing, which are often found in similar academic research. However, their absence did not drastically improve the fairness of the coverage, and, instead, other characteristics, such as those outlined in the previous paragraph, littered the media reports that were analyzed.

As previously mentioned, my research was restricted to UK coverage only and, more specifically, a case study of *The Guardian* newspaper. Therefore, it cannot be said that this reflects the entirety of news coverage produced on the sport. However, examples of similar unequal coverage from other international media outlets have been noted in the last number of years, particularly surrounding the Rio 2016 Olympic Games (Xu et al. 2019; Metcalfe 2019).

The results of my research paired with the similar conclusions of other academic papers support the assumption that the coverage of men and women within swimming is not equal, fair, or genderless. This chapter expands my dissertation's work by exploring the reasons behind the type of report swimming has received to date and suggesting how the sport can act as a favourable template for equality-driven media coverage. The significance of this article lies in the fact that swimming has the potential to act as a vehicle for fair and equal reporting of women in sport. The continued propagation of new ideas and principles that promote fairness in sport media and encourage the female position within sport will bring us a step closer to shattering the glass ceiling above us.

Media and the Public Sphere

To fully grasp the importance of sport media coverage, we must first understand the role that the media plays in shaping public opinion within modern society. Extensive research has been carried out on this topic, in relation to both sport and other subject areas covered by the mass media.

When speaking broadly about the media's position within society, Kellner (2014, 7) describes the media as "a profound and often misperceived source of cultural pedagogy." Kellner notes that the media contributes to educating its audiences on behaviour, emotion, fear, desire, and thought. In respect of gender, forms of media "teach us how to be men and women" (7). This ubiquitous influence held by the media reaffirms norms and values within society and, in turn, sport.

When specifically speaking about sport, the media's influence on shaping the concept of physical activity among the public is indisputable (Puertas Molero et al. 2019). Trolan (2013, 215) concurs, reiterating that "gender differences and inequality" in sport are transmitted via broadcast and print media on a daily basis. Rowe and Brown

(1994) note not only that the media plays a crucial role in shaping society's perception of gender in sport, but that sport itself is a major sociocultural component in contemporary popular culture. The notion of gender within sport is reinforced, often subtly, through the instruments of language and imagery in the news and media. This consistently contributes to and moulds the construct of gender in sport within the minds of the people who consume it, reaffirming the "indisputable" nature of this influence (Puertas Molero et al. 2019, 1).

Kellner (2014) argues that because of this inherent influence that the media has over the portrayal of gender within sport, the public should strive to gain critical media literacy. Critical media literacy, Kellner states, refers to interpreting and criticizing the media's messages to further understand them and their impact on individuals and society at large. This level of influence held by the media means that there must be accountability on their part. Therefore, the media should not disregard their duty in reporting fairly and objectively on sport, which much academic research has consistently found to be the case. If the influence the media holds over the consensus gentium is so great, then conscious efforts should be made by media personnel and journalists alike to ensure accurate and fair reporting in sport.

Fair reporting can be achieved through simple yet effective linguistic applications. As a reporter, actively avoiding common traits of gendered reporting such as infantilizing, gender-marking, and unnecessary references to appearance and emotion, paired with a heightened level of self-awareness around how female athletes are being framed within your work will result in more balanced coverage. Reviewing your work and asking yourself: would I say this about a male sportsperson?, and will the reader be able to identify the gender of the athlete because I have unjustly made a reference to the fact that they are a mother? is crucial in creating parity within media coverage of male and female sportspeople.

History of Swimming

In the format of both competitive and noncompetitive environments, male and female athletes train and race alongside each other. In 2019, a new coed professional swimming league, known as the International Swimming League (ISL), was founded, which has coined itself as being "New. Beautiful. Equal" (ISL 2019).

The ISL claims to champion both male and female athletes, providing them with a level platform and equal opportunities to both earn money and race. Although it must be noted that a recently published paper that analyzed content on the ISL's Instagram page found that it is "far from meeting its target" of a "gender-equal media vision" (Vidotto, Collura, and Seow 2020, 20). Despite modern research findings such as that of the ISL described previously, swimming has developed drastically over the last 100 years, strengthening women's position in the sport. These developments have happened in every part of the sport: strokes have evolved, technological innovations have catapulted the quality and standard of swimsuits forward, and the opportunities for men and women within the sport have slowly aligned since the establishment of the modern Olympic Games (Morales, Tamayo Fajardo, and González-García 2019; Love 2007).

In 1896, swimming featured on the Olympic program for the first time (International Olympic Committee [IOC] 2020). However, there were only four men's events on the program. It was not until the 1912 Olympic Games in Stockholm that two women's swimming events were brought onto the schedule, by which time there were seven men's events. However, in comparison with some other sports this was a very progressive decision. For instance, gymnastics did not see an established women's program at the Games until 1952—by that time swimming contained a program of eleven events, six men and five women (IOC 2020).

Swimming was one of eight sports to feature at the first Paralympic Games in 1960, held in Rome, Italy. It has since become one of the most popular sports on the Parasport calendar (British Swimming 2016). However, research by the Women's Sports Foundation (WSF) revealed that a total of 42 National Paralympic Committees (NPCs) did not have a female athlete in their delegations for the 2016 Paralympic Games in Rio de Janeiro, Brazil (WSF 2017). Despite this severe disparity in the general participation of female athletes at the most recent edition of the Paralympics, the same research showed that female swimmers accounted for almost half (44.6%) of the total number of swimmers competing in Rio (WSF 2017).

In the modern Olympic Games, swimming has a total of 34 events: 17 men and 17 women. The only discrepancy that existed recently was the fact that previously, men swam the 1,500 m freestyle and women the 800 m freestyle. Neither sex had the option of swimming the other event because they were not on the roster. One reason for this difference could possibly have stemmed from an idea that women's abilities are inferior to men's and that therefore they would not be capable of swimming a longer-distance race. However, a concrete reason has not previously been provided by the IOC. The difference was rectified in June 2017 when the decision was taken to include the women's 1,500 m and men's 800 m freestyle on the lineup for the Tokyo Games (Gibbs 2017). For context, the Tokyo 2020 Olympic Games were officially postponed in March of last year and are due to be held in 2021 from July 23 to August 8 (*SwimSwam* 2020).

Reality of Media Coverage

A plethora of academic research (see Hardin and Shain 2005; Cooky, Messner, and Hextrum 2013; Kian, Bernstein, and McGuire 2013; Eastman and Billings 1999) has confirmed that in many sports, media coverage between male and female athletes is not equal. Common results have found that there is a severe lack of coverage of female athletes by mainstream media. It has also been found that the coverage women are afforded is often pervaded with sexist language, descriptions that position their performances as being less "impressive" than those of their male counterparts, and generally marginalizes their participation in their sport. In summary, both the quantity and the quality of the coverage for female athletes have fallen short of the male standard.

Cooky, Messner, and Hextrum (2013) conducted a longitudinal analysis of televised sport media coverage across a number of local news affiliates in Los Angeles. Their findings revealed that across a 20-year period (1989–2009), the percentage of sports coverage specific to women alone never rose above 8.7 percent (8). The average percentage across the timescale was 5.3 percent, and perhaps, most significantly, the lowest percentage of 1.6 percent was recorded in the most recent year of the study, 2009 (8). The quantitative differences found in this research provide a representation of media coverage from six different news outlets across many sports, finding that not one sport received equal coverage for men and women.

Qualitative differences recorded in the reporting of women in sport have shown that even when women are given the spotlight, it is often dimmer than that given to their male peers. This "less-than" spotlight can manifest itself in language choice, use of passive instead of active images, amount of airtime given, or the level of excitement/interest for women's sport generated by the writer or broadcaster in question.

Fink (2015, 337) describes sport as being an "institution steeped in sexism," although, importantly, noting that this does not explicitly support the notion that members of the media community are actively trying to preserve male privilege. Rather, Fink's account supports Cunningham's (2008) theory that despite opportunities existing for media personnel to present fair coverage of female athletes, the institutionalization of sexism in sport means that few media professionals even protest this ongoing prejudice (Cunningham, Ferreira, and Fink 2009).

A recent and stark example of what translated to me as a viewer as glaringly casual sexism came during the 2021 British Swimming Selection Trials. During the first day of the livestreamed event, English athlete Freya Anderson was referred to by the commentator as having a "wonderful figure for a sprint freestyler." Additionally, the commentator—a male, Olympic bronze medalist from the 1988 Olympic Games and well-seasoned sports broadcaster—said, "If you could choose [a figure] that's what you'd have: 6ft 2 I think she is." The flippant nature of his comment resonated with me as a viewer, with my first thought being "will he say the same thing for the men's race?"

This complicity of journalists, commentators, and broadcasters within the media sphere who do not actively pursue gender equity in all that they produce reinforces the notion that sport is, and will remain, a "man's game" that women play (Messner and Solomon 2007, 2). I believe this is at the core of why such a considerable amount, if not all, of sport media coverage is disproportionately balanced between men and women.

This statement is not designed to place blame on sports journalists and broadcasters alone. As the next section—*Existing Barriers*—will outline, there are several reasons why the current standard of female sports coverage is where it is. Placing blame is futile; energy would be better spent identifying and promoting measures that will raise the standard to be parallel with what male athletes receive. An opportunity exists for a complete overhaul of sports journalism to take place, an act that could start with a few changes made daily by individuals, resulting in an overarching improvement on a mass scale. An act that could also be ignited by using a favourable template like swimming.

Existing Barriers

Several mechanisms exist that continue to marginalize women in sport. Tamir, Galily, and Yarchi (2017, 7) cite these as including "women-only" Olympic sports. For instance, formerly called synchronized swimming (Butler 2017), artistic swimming is rooted within sexism. Similar to rhythmic gymnastics, these sports are designed to accentuate a woman's natural physique: flexibility, leg strength, and "grace" (Lewis 2014). Similarly, the Fédération Internationale de Natation (FINA), the world governing body for all aquatic sports, describes artistic swimming as historically being "better fitted to women who were overall more buoyant, in particular in the legs" (British Swimming, 2016).

The importance of aesthetics and physical attributes outlined in that description are features of sport that represent stark gender inequalities within the modern Olympic program, despite 126 years having passed between now and the first edition of the event in 1896. Such importance being placed on the female physique conveys a message of sport being a performance to be enjoyed by the audience, rather than representing the competitiveness, strength, and determination of the female sportspeople.

Although considerable change and progress toward gender equity in sport has occurred in that time period (i.e., levels of female participation, a move away from sport as a "male only" concept), such progress is relatively slow. Baron Pierre de Coubertin (1863–1937), founder of the modern Olympic Games, stated that women's inclusion in the Games would be "impractical, uninteresting, unaesthetic, and incorrect," as well as denouncing women's sport as being "against the laws of nature" (Hargreaves 2002, chap. 9).

Considering de Coubertin's quote in comparison with the fact that the London 2012 Olympic Games marked the first time that a woman competed from each of the 204 attending countries (Kian, Bernstein, and McGuire 2013), society has advanced markedly toward gender equivalence in sport over the last century. However, this also demonstrates that many of these advancements have only come within recent years; once again highlighting how slow-moving change has been for women in sport at the professional level. As such, total female participation in the Olympic Games can be viewed as a relatively new fact, furthering the need for the media coverage to align itself to reflect such change.

Women in Positions of Power within Sport

Issues surrounding female participation and equal pay and opportunity in swimming are not at the forefront of the sport, despite not being completely absent from it either. The starkest gender gaps can be found at the top level of the sport's governance. For 75 years (1896–1981) there were no female members in the IOC. In 2019, there were

33 female members out of a total of 144 (Katsarova 2019). Additionally, less than 20 percent of the members of affiliated bodies, such as individual National Olympic Committees, are women. According to data released by the European Institute for Gender Equality in 2015, "only 14% of all top decision-making positions in EU Member States' sports federations were occupied by women, ranging from 3% in Poland to 43% in Sweden" (2019, 4).

FINA has just two women sitting on its Bureau out of a total of 25 members. This disparity is a common trend across many, if not all, international sporting bodies, federations, and organizations, meaning that women and, in turn, the female agenda in sport, are constantly being overlooked. Similarly, this imbalance can also be found when discussing female sports journalists working in the current media sphere.

Lack of Female Sports Journalists

There are far fewer female sports journalists than male. Research has found that the introduction of Title IX in the United States in 1972 opened doors for women in sports and sports journalism alike (Hardin and Shain 2005). However, the number of women reporting on sport across the world is still frightfully low. In 2016, British journalist and former Head of Media for *Guardian News and Media Limited*, Jane Martinson, and her colleague, Chris Owen, conducted analysis on media coverage during Women's Sports Week: an annual occurrence in the UK that aims to celebrate and raise the profile of women in sport (Women's Sport Week [WSW] 2016). They assessed the by-lines of a number of national newspapers and found that of the 1,111 articles published in print press during that week, only 1.8 percent were written by women (Martinson 2016).

Similarly, my own dissertation found that of the 30 articles analyzed, not one was written by a female journalist. A paper by Strong and Hannis (2007) found that in major Australasian news outlets just 29 percent of by-lines belonged to women. In sport, specifically, Strong and Hannis (2007) found that in the same year, female journalists in Australian metropolitan newspapers accounted for only 11 percent of sports coverage. The 2011 International Press Survey analyzed the biggest national, tabloid, and regional newspapers in 22 countries across a two-week period. The results show that of the sample, 92 percent of the by-lines belonged to men and just 8 percent to women (Horky and Nieland 2011).

Although not all these examples are specific to sports journalism, they depict the worryingly broad spectrum of journalism that these inequalities span. This is one of the factors relevant to swimming that is an industry wide problem within sports journalism. Some academics have theorized the reasons behind this as being the fact that such a low percentage of sports coverage is dedicated to women's sports (see Hargreaves 2002).

Boyle (2006) contends that the "macho" culture within sports newsrooms, which is an undoubtedly male-dominated space, is off-putting for women. Nonetheless, whatever the reasoning for the paucity of female journalists, Franks and O'Neill (2014) conclude, after carrying out extensive research on the topic, that it remains difficult to see a drastic change occurring in the near future in the proportion of women reporting on sports.

Female Participation at the Olympic Games

Table 7.1 outlines various percentages of female participation in the Summer Olympic Games between the years 1894 and 2016. This details the progress made throughout more than a century of the Games being in existence, reaching a peak of 45 percent of female participation at the most recent edition of the event, the Rio 2016 Olympic Games (Lange 2020).

Table 7.1: Percentages of Female Participation at Various Olympic Games

Olympic Games	Year	Female Participation (%)
Athens, Greece—I Olympiad	1894	0 (prohibited)
Paris, France—II Olympiad	1900	2.2 (permitted for the first time)
Melbourne, Australia— XVI Olympiad	1956	11
Los Angeles, America— XXIII Olympiad	1984	23
Beijing, China—XXIX Olympiad	2008	42
Rio de Janeiro, Brazil— XXXI Olympiad	2016	45

Source(s): Data Adapted from Kian, Bernstein, and McGuire 2013; Lange 2020; Olympics.org, n.d.

Paralympics and Winter Games

Participation of female athletes, media narratives, and disparities in opportunities for female athletes are even more extensive in the Summer Paralympic Games, Winter Olympic, and Winter Paralympic Games. In 2017, the WSF provided a comprehensive report that analyzed athletic participation and leadership opportunities for women, as well as the media narratives surrounding them in the 2016 Olympic and Paralympic Games. It was the fifth report of its kind and assessed how the IOC, International Paralympic Committee (IPC), and United States Olympic Committee (USOC) are "fulfilling their stated missions with respect to fairness and gender equity" (WSF 2017, 1).

In summary, the report found that much work was needed for the aforementioned organizations to move toward their goals of gender equality at each edition of the Games. In Paralympic Games, specifically, WSF's report detailed how, out of six prominent US news broadcasters and news outlets (i.e., *ESPN, ESPNW, NBC, New York Times, Sports Illustrated, USA Today*), none of their websites contained a "Paralympic-specific portion" (WSF 2017, 62). A further study by WSF in 2018 explored female participation in both the Olympic and Paralympic Winter Games. It explained how "female Paralympians have not fared nearly as well as their Olympic counterparts" (WSF 2018, 1) in terms of increased participation in the event since the time of its establishment.

Female participation is lowest within the Paralympic Winter Games, and in the latest edition of the event, which was held in 2018, just 23.8 percent of athletes were women (see Table 7.2). In comparison, women at the 2018 Olympic Winter Games accounted for 43 percent of the athletes, much closer to the figure of 45 percent from the 2016 Rio Summer Olympics (Lange 2020). The severe disparity between male and female participation at the Paralympic Games presents even greater obstacles for the creation of equitable media coverage for those athletes. Another obstacle that runs parallel to that of participation is the lack of media coverage awarded to Paralympic athletes, both male and female alike. Maika and Danylchuk (2016, 404) describe the media interest in the Paralympic Games as being "dwarfed by the spectacle of the Olympics."

Parasport advocate Eli Wolff concurs, stating that "the reality is that the disabled sports movement is 15 years behind women's sport" (Hardin 2009,578). Importantly, these findings contribute to a broader dichotomy that exists between para-athletes and non-disabled athletes, something that is outside the scope of gender inequality but equally as important.

Media coverage of the Winter Olympic Games offers no relief from the male hegemony identified in other editions of the competition. Male hegemony is a theory within gender studies that details how stereotypical male traits are legitimized as being the *ideal* within society, therefore reaffirming male dominance in a certain field and lessening the female position (Walker and Sartore-Baldwin 2013). Daddario's (1994) research examined the 1992 Winter Olympic Games and what she deducted as the "marginalization of female athletes" within mass media coverage of the event. Her findings include female athletes being infantilized, sexist descriptors and references to familial relationships being used, and their femininity being emphasized. For the women subjected to such sexist rhetoric, these factors "diminish the athletic stature and undermine their identity as an Olympic athlete" (286).

The lack of progress and opportunity for women in sport, insufficient media coverage of Paralympic and Winter Olympic Games, and the continued use of hegemonic strategies by the media to diminish women's participation in the sporting arena all reaffirm the notion of sport as being a "man's game." They present substantial hurdles for media personnel and audiences alike to overcome in order to reach greater parity in sport and parasport. Although both the IOC and the IPC have been vocal in their mission to further women's presence within sport at all levels, more work is needed by these bodies to ensure that sport can become a level platform for men and women. In turn, this will provide the media with no excuse other than to create coverage that is representative of this strong female presence in sport, rather than the masculine hegemony within it.

The lack of some of the above factors within swimming once again substantiates my claim that it can act as a catalyst for change.

Table 7.2: Disparities in Participation across Both Summer and Winter Paralympic and Olympic Games

Event	Female Participation When First Permitted	Female Participation at Latest Edition of the Event
Summer Olympic Games	Paris 1900 - 2.2%	Rio 2016 - 45%
Winter Olympic Games	Chamonix 1924 - 4%	PyeongChang - 3%
Summer Paralympic Games	Heidelberg 1972 - 20.9%	Rio 2016 - 38.5%
Winter Paralympic Games	Örnsköldsvik - 19%	PyeongChang - 24%

Source(s): Data Adapted from Darcy 2018

Catalyst for Change

Idealistic goals, such as increasing the number of female journalists currently working within the mass media, should be set aside to make space for more tangible aims. Other areas also relevant to the sport of swimming that are more easily rectified by journalists in their day-to-day tasks should instead be targeted to improve the amount and quality of media coverage afforded to female swimmers.

I have identified these as including, but not limited to, language, portrayals of female success, comparisons between athletes, femininity, and the general narratives surrounding female swimmers. These were some of the key frameworks utilized to analyze the corpus or my dissertation, the findings of which will now be used to illustrate what I believe to be areas of *easy improvement* that would significantly better the coverage of swimming.

Language

Linguistics play a crucial part in how sportspeople are portrayed within sport media. How their performances are detailed, the adjectives and adverbs used to describe them, both as athletes and as people, is imperative to how the audience consumes news about them. Segrave, Mcdowell, and King (2006, 31) note that

> One of the mechanisms that [tend] to inferiorize women in general is language, a critical component of the social scaffolding upon which unequal gender relations are erected and perpetuated. The language of sport in particular can contribute to their cultural devaluation.

My research found a glaring disparity in the way men and women were described. Notions of male *dominance* were reinforced. Descriptors such as *dominant, powerful, bullish, smashes, stormed down, destroys* were more frequently used for male athletes. For women, the physicality of the race and the *pain* experienced was at the forefront of the accounts of their races. One headline read: "USA's Katie Ledecky fights off exhaustion and vomit for second gold," (Carpenter, 2016, 1) with the content of the article giving a detailed description of the pain she felt during the 200 m freestyle: "She was tired, she was worried." (2016, 1).

Such language is presumably used by authors to portray just how physically taxing swimming at the highest level is. However, every Olympic athlete, irrespective of gender, pushes themselves to extreme lengths. At the risk of sounding clichéd, it is just part of the job of being a high-performance athlete. As such, there is no justification, other than inherent sexism and bias, for journalists to use different language to describe female athletes or to give less thrilling accounts of their races: also identified in my research.

As Fink (2015, 334) writes, "[C]ommentators frame male and female athletic performances differently and typically in ways that minimize females' athletic abilities while proliferating male superiority." To that end, if journalists, broadcasters, and commentators alike performed an audit of the language they frequently use in their writing/commentating on swimming, greater parity could easily be achieved. As noted before, the format of swimming welcomes such equitable discourse.

Narrative

Narrative focuses on non-sport-related references, femininity, and emotional characteristics, all of which contribute to the general descriptions offered to both male and female athletes. These are part of the five techniques that Wensing and Bruce (2003, 387) state have been employed by the media to "suggest appropriate femininity." Essentially, these are aspects of writing that have no merit or place in sports journalism. Whether someone is a *mother* or a *father* should not raise the significance of their success or achievement.

References to emotion would be welcome if they occurred equally for both men and women; however, much research has found evidence to the contrary. My research found that women were referred to as *tearful, weeping, emotional* more often than men. In fact, only one reference was recorded where a male was said to have been crying.

Female Success

Success and how it is written about across gender has been found to be a consistent downfall of modern sports journalism. Female success is often trivialized (Kane 1995), further marginalizing women in sport. My research found that women were often *pitted* against one another in order to exaggerate their respective success/disappointments. When detailing the 800 m freestyle final and discussing gold medal winner Katie Ledecky and silver medalist Jazz Carlin's performance, one article read, "Carlin may as well have been an entire length of the Amazon behind her."

Similarly, women's success was written about far less sympathetically than that of their male peers. Team Great Britain (GB) swimmers Hannah Miley and Max Litchfield both finished fourth in the same event, the 400IM. The author said of Miley's performance, "Maintaining her frustrating run of near Olympic misses," (Kitson, 2016, 1) but commended Litchfield for his "gallant" (2016, 1) effort. Another entry noted the race and results of the 100 m freestyle, stating that "[Simone] Manuel and [Penny] Oleksiak's golds were made all the more remarkable by the fact that they beat the world record holder Cate Campbell of Australia" (Lutz, 2016, 1). Once again, the author here used the *pitting* technique in an attempt to highlight the significance of Manual and Oleksiak's joint win, a feat that is already a momentous achievement.

Framing of Women's Success in the Context of Men's Sport

Another common trend is the framing of women's success in a male context. For example, in an article discussing Team USA swimmer Katie Ledecky's triumphant performance in the 200-m, 400-m, and 800-m freestyle events, the author used numerous similes of male athletes and their successes to "contextualize" her achievements. *The Guardian*'s Bryan Armen Graham (2016) wrote:

> This was Tiger Woods making a mockery of Pebble Beach in 2000, finishing 12 under when no one else broke par. The equivalent of Seb Coe running in the 4·100m opposite Usain Bolt. This was Secretariat pushing the lead to 31 lengths and reducing the Belmont field to helpless specks.

Davidson (2016) highlighted this framing of women's success in terms of men's sport in a 2016 article. Ledecky is used as the case study, with Davidson writing, "It's a vestige of still seeing sports as inherently male space, and of mostly male fans and commentators unable or unwilling to consider female athletes by their merits alone" (1). In this scenario, Armen Graham (2016) subsequently went on to give a detailed account of male boxers throughout history and the sacrifices athletes such as Floyd Mayweather and Bernard Hopkins made to reach the pinnacle of their sports. He said:

> A rare few—Bernard Hopkins, Floyd Mayweather—have adopted the asceticism of camp into a 24/7/365 lifestyle. For the ordinary fighter, that proposition is impractical at best. But athletes like Hopkins and Mayweather are not ordinary. For them, the life of sacrifice and self-denial is not the cost of success nor even a natural inclination but a default state. That's Katie Ledecky, touched with no remarkable physical gift but simply a burning desire to improve. And it's why you haven't heard the last of her (2016, 1).

Template for Success: Katie Ledecky

Despite her success being framed within men's sport, Katie Ledecky was the anomaly within my research because she was the only female swimmer to receive similar descriptions to her male peers. Although this equitable coverage was not entirely consistent, I estimate that 80 percent of the media coverage afforded to her championed her successes and spoke of her incredible athleticism, speed, and strength, without unnecessarily highlighting the fact that she is a woman. The coverage could be categorized as being genderless and echoed the type of reporting her male counterparts were afforded by *The Guardian*. Her performances at the Olympic Games—which totalled four gold medals, one silver medal, two World records, and one American record—resulted in significant media coverage being centred around her.

Examples of the descriptions of Ledecky and her performances from the reports include: "destruction of the field," "smashing her personal best," "the world's most dominant athlete," and "thrashed her way to history," "A tremendous machine in flirtation with the outer limits of human performance as we know it" (Kitson 2016; Armen Graham 2016). These positive descriptions of Ledecky utilized language that was otherwise "reserved" for male athletes. Descriptors such as *dominant, smashing, destruction,* and *thrashed* appeared regularly when describing the performances of male swimmers, whereas female race descriptions received more reference to the mental and physical pain endured during a race.

One article wrote of Ledecky: "kept pushing her arms and feet, her stomach until near the end she burped. She was tired, she was worried" (Carpenter 2016). The author continued, saying: "It depends on the torture with which she has subjected her body. Will she have enough for the 800m on Thursday night?"

The above quotes illustrate how, although Katie Ledecky was *the exception* in many instances, she still received the type of gendered, sexist reporting that female sportspeople have become accustomed to. More importantly, these examples illustrate how achieving parity in sports reporting, and specifically swimming reporting, is well within the grasp of today's journalists, media professionals, news outlets, and anyone else who produces and delivers news to mass audiences.

CONCLUSION

This chapter analyzes swimming as an appropriate medium for communicating equality-driven media coverage within sport. The history of swimming is detailed, and the format of the sport is scrutinized in order to demonstrate its unique nature and ensuring opportunities for equitable media coverage to flourish. It is crucial to first understand the intricate relationship between the media and modern society and the influence the former has in shaping concepts and ideals within the latter. Current and past academic research within sports scholarship alerts us to how often women in sport are marginalized, have their position in competitive sport questioned or trivialized, and are afforded media coverage differing from what their male counterparts receive, coverage that often reaffirms notions of hegemonic masculinity within sport.

This chapter establishes the viability of swimming as a catalyst for change within modern sport media coverage. It outlines the key components at play that halt the progression of sport media toward gender equity and discusses how those same components can be utilized to make the first crack in the glass ceiling above.

It is my firm belief as a journalist, academic, and lifelong swimmer that swimming provides us with a distinct possibility of increasing the quality of and parity within sports reporting.

REFERENCES

Armen Graham, Bryan. 2016. "For the Remarkable Katie Ledecky, the Future Appears Limitless." *The Guardian*, August 13, 2016. http://www.theguardian.com/sport/2016/aug/13/katie-ledecky-swimming-2016-dominant-athlete.

Boyle, Raymond. 2006. *Sports Journalism: Context and Issues.* London: Sage. https://doi.org/10.4135/9781446247181.

British Swimming. 2016. "History of Para-Swimming." https://www.britishswimming.org/browse-sport/para-swimming/about-para-swimming/history-para-swimming/.

British Swimming. 2016. "History of Synchro." https://www.britishswimming.org/browse-sport/synchronised-swimming/learn-more-about-synchro/history-synchro/

Butler, Nick. 2017. "Name Change from Synchronised to Artistic Swimming Approved by FINA." *In Side the Games*, July 22, 2017. https://www.insidethegames.biz/articles/1053066/name-change-from-synchronised-to-artistic-swimming-approved-by-fina.

Carpenter, Les. 2016. "Rio 2016: USA's Katie Ledecky Fights off Exhaustion and Vomit for Second Gold." *The Guardian*, August 10, 2016. http://www.theguardian.com/sport/2016/aug/09/rio-2016-katie-ledecky-swimming-gold-200m-freestyle.

Cooky, Cheryl, Michael Messner, and Robin Hextrum. 2013. "Women Play Sport, But Not on TV: A Longitudinal Study of Televised News Media." *Communication & Sport* 1 (3): 203–30. https://doi.org/10.1177/2167479513476947.

Cunningham, George B. 2008. "Creating and Sustaining Gender Diversity in Sport Organizations." *Sex Roles* 58 (1–2): 136–45. https://doi.org/10.1007/s11199-007-9312-3.

Cunningham, George B., Mauricio Ferreira, and Janet S. Fink. 2009. "Reactions to Prejudicial Statements: The Influence of Statement Content and Characteristics of the Commenter." *Group Dynamics: Theory, Research, and Practice* 13 (1): 59–73. https://doi.org/10.1037/a0012967.

Daddario, Gina. 1994. "Chilly Scenes of the 1992 Winter Games: The Mass Media and the Marginalization of Female Athletes." *Sociology of Sport Journal* 11 (3): 275–88. https://doi.org/10.1123/SSJ.11.3.275.

Darcy, S. (2018). "Behemoths and the Also-Rans": the International Paralympic Movement as a Pyramid Built on Quicksand. In I. Brittain & A. Beacom (Eds.), Handbook of Paralympic Studies (pp.221-46): Palgrave Macmillan imprint is published by Springer Nature, Street, London, N1 9XW, United Kingdom

Davidson, Kavitha. 2016. "Why We Should Frame Katie Ledecky's Dominance in Terms of Women's Sports—Not Men's." *ESPN.com*, August 9, 2016. https://www.espn.com/espnw/voices/story/_/id/17251015/why-frame-katie-ledecky-dominance-terms-women-sports-not-mens.

Eastman, Susan Tyler, and Andrew C. Billings. 1999. "Gender Parity in the Olympics: Hyping Women Athletes, Favoring Men Athletes." *Journal of Sport and Social Issues* 23 (2): 140–70. https://doi.org/10.1177/0193723599232003.

Fink, Janet S. 2015. "Female Athletes, Women's Sport, and the Sport Media Commercial Complex: Have We Really 'Come a Long Way, Baby'?" *Sport Management Review* 18 (3): 331–42. https://doi.org/10.1016/j.smr.2014.05.001.

Franks, Suzanne, and Deirdre O'Neill. 2014. "Women Reporting Sport: Still a Man's Game?" *Journalism* 17 (4): 474–92. https://doi.org/10.1177/1464884914561573.

Gibbs, Robert. 2017. "Distance Events and Mixed Medley Relay Added to Tokyo Olympics." *SwimSwam*, June 9, 2017. https://swimswam.com/distance-events-mixed-medley-relay-added-tokyo-olympics/.

Hardin, Marie. 2009. "Chapter 34—Disability and Sport: (Non)Coverage of an Athletic Paradox." In *Handbook of Sports and Media*, edited by Arthur A. Raney and Jennings Bryant, 625–34. Mahwah, NJ: L. Erlbaum Associates.

Hardin, Marie, and Stacie Shain. 2005. "Female Sports Journalists: Are We There Yet? 'No.'" *Newspaper Research Journal* 26 (4): 22–35. https://doi.org/10.1177/073953290502600403.

Hargreaves, Jennifer. 2002. *Sporting Females: Critical Issues in the History and Sociology of Women's Sport*. London: Routledge.

Horky, Thomas, and J.-U. Nieland. 2011. "ISPS 2011: First Results of the International Sports Press Survey 2011." October 3, 2011. https://www.playthegame.org/fileadmin/image/PTG2011/Presentation/PTG_Nieland-Horky_ISPS_2011_3.10.2011_final.pdf.

IOC (International Olympic Committee). 2020. "Swimming Equipment and History—Olympic Sport History." November 9, 2020. https://stillmed.olympic.org/AssetsDocs/OSC%20Section/pdf/QR_sports_summer/Sports_Oly mpiques_natation_eng.pdf

ISL (International Swimming League). 2019. "New. Beautiful. Equal.—This Is ISL 2019." November 19, 2019. https://isl.global/new-beautiful-equal-this-is-isl-2019/.

ITV News. 2020. "Six Nations Tournament Worst Offender for Gender Pay Gap in Sports Prizes, Study Finds." January 31, 2020. https://www.itv.com/news/2020-01-31/six-nations-tournament-worst-offender-for-gender-pay-gap-in-sports-prizes-study-finds.

Kane, Mary Jo. 1995. "Resistance/Transformation of the Oppositional Binary: Exposing Sport as a Continuum." *Journal of Sport and Social Issues* 19 (2): 191–218. https://doi.org/10.1177/019372395019002006.

Katsarova, Ivana. 2019. "Gender Equality in Sport: Getting Closer Every Day." European Parliament, PE 635.560, March 2019: 12.

Kehoe, Lydia Ferrari. 2020. "Tokyo Olympics Officially Postponed to 2021 Over Coronavirus Pandemic." *SwimSwam*, March 24, 2020. https://swimswam.com/tokyo-olympics-postponed-to-2021-over-coronavirus-pandemic/.

Kellner, Douglas. 2014. "Chapter 1: Cultural Studies, Multiculturalism, and Media Culture." In *Gender, Race, and Class in Media: A Critical Reader*, edited by Gail Dines and Jean M. Humez, 7–19. London: Sage.

Kian, Edward M., Alina Bernstein, and John S. McGuire. 2013. "A Major Boost for Gender Equality or More of the Same? The Television Coverage of Female Athletes at the 2012 London Olympic Games." *The Journal of Popular Television* 1 (1): 143–49. https://doi.org/10.1386/jptv.1.1.143_1.

Kitson, Robert. 2016. "Katie Ledecky Breaks 800m World Record but Michael Phelps Wins Silver." *The Guardian*, August 13, 2016. http://www.theguardian.com/sport/2016/aug/12/katie-ledecky-michael-phelps-swimming-usa-olympics.

Lange, David. 2020. "Female Athletes Share at the Summer Olympics 1900–2016." *Statista*, November 19, 2020. https://www.statista.com/statistics/531146/women-participants-in-olympic-summer-games/.

Lewis, Amy. 2014. "Is Sport Sexist? Six Sports Where Men & Women Are Still Set Apart." *BBC Sport*, September 18, 2014, https://www.bbc.com/sport/golf/29242699.

Love, C. 2007. "An Overview of the Development of Swimming in England, c.1750–1918." *The International Journal of the History of Sport* 24 (5): 568–85. https://doi.org/10.1080/09523360601183095.

Lutz, Tom. 2016, "Simone Manuel makes history: 'I hope I'm an inspiration to others." *The Guardian*, https://www.theguardian.com/sport/2016/aug/11/simone-manuel-gold-medal-rio-2016-olympics-makes-swimming-history

Maika, Melinda, and Karen Danylchuk. 2016. "Representing Paralympians: The 'Other' Athletes in Canadian Print Media Coverage of London 2012." *The International Journal of the History of Sport* 33 (4): 401–17. https://doi.org/10.1080/09523367.2016.1160061.

Martinson, Jane. 2016. "Only 1.8% of Sport Articles Are Written by Women—So Much for Progress." *The Guardian*, November 15, 2016, https://www.theguardian.com/commentisfree/2016/nov/15/ignoring-womens-sport-2016-different-rochelle-clark-england-rugby.

Messner, Michael, and Nancy Solomon. 2007. "Social Justice and Men's Interests: The Case of Title IX." *Journal of Sport and Social Issues* 31 (2): 162–78. https://doi.org/10.1177/0193723507301048.

Metcalfe, Sarah Nicola. 2019. "The Development of an Adolescent Sporting Gendered Habitus: Young People's Interpretation of UK Sports-Media Coverage of Rio 2016 Olympic Games." *European Journal for Sport and Society* 16 (4): 361–78. https://doi.org/10.1080/16138171.2019.1693145.

Morales, Alfonso Trinidad, Javier Antonio Tamayo Fajardo, and Higinio González-García. 2019. "High-Speed Swimsuits and Their Historical Development in Competitive Swimming." *Frontiers in Psychology* 10 (2639): 1–11. https://doi.org/10.3389/fpsyg.2019.02639.

Puertas Molero, Pilar, Rafael Marfil-Carmona, Felix Zurita Ortega, and Gabriel González Valero. 2019. "Impact of Sports Mass Media on the Behavior and Health of Society. A Systematic Review." *International Journal of Environmental Research and Public Health* 16 (3): 486. https://doi.org/10.3390/ijerph16030486.

Rowe, David, and Peter Brown. 1994. "Promoting Women's Sport: Theory, Policy and Practice." *Leisure Studies* 13 (2): 97–110. https://doi.org/10.1080/02614369400390071.

Segrave, Jeffrey O., Katherine L. Mcdowell, and James G. King. 2006. "Language, Gender, and Sport: A Review of the Research Literature." In *Sport, Rhetoric, and Gender: Historical Perspectives and Media Representations*, edited by Linda K. Fuller, 31–41. New York: Palgrave Macmillan US. https://doi.org/10.1057/9780230600751_3.

Strong, Cathy, and Grant Hannis. 2007. "The Visibility of Female Journalists in Australian and New Zealand Newspapers: The Good News and the Bad News." *Australian Journalism Review* 29 (1): 115.

Tamir, Ilan, Yair Galily, and Moran Yarchi. 2017. "Women, Sport and the Media: Key Elements at Play in the Shaping of the Practice of Women in Sports Journalism in Israel." *Communications* 42 (4): 441–64. https://doi.org/10.1515/commun-2017-0039.

The Guardian, https://www.theguardian.com/uk/sport, accessed 2021.

Trolan, Eoin J. 2013. "The Impact of the Media on Gender Inequality within Sport." *Procedia—Social and Behavioral Sciences* 91 (October): 215–27. https://doi.org/10.1016/j.sbspro.2013.08.420.

Vidotto, Danica, Francesco Collura, and Kaitlyn Seow. 2020, p.20, "Chapter 10 p.20: New. Beautiful. Equal, But Not on Instagram: How the ISL Represents Female Athletes." In *Sport Media Vectors: Digitization, Expanding Audiences, and the Globalization of Live Sport*, edited by Laurel Walzak and Joe Recupero, Champaign, IL: Common Ground Research Networks.

Walker, Nefertiti A., and Melanie L. Sartore-Baldwin. 2013. "Hegemonic Masculinity and the Institutionalized Bias toward Women in Men's Collegiate Basketball: What Do Men Think?" *Journal of Sport Management* 27 (4): 303–15. https://doi.org/10.1123/jsm.27.4.303.

Wensing, Emma H., and Toni Bruce. 2003. "Bending the Rules: Media Representations of Gender during an International Sporting Event." *International Review for the Sociology of Sport* 38 (4): 387–96. https://doi.org/10.1177/1012690203384001.

Work180. 2020. "The Work180 Report UK: How Employers Are Attracting, Supporting and Retaining Talented Women."

WSF (Women's Sports Foundation), ed. 2017. *Women in the Olympic and Paralympic Games: An Analysis of Participation, Leadership, and Media Coverage/Women's Sports Foundation.* New York: Women's Sports Foundation. https://library.olympic.org/Default/doc/SYRACUSE/177822/women-in-the-olympic-and-paralympic-games-an-analysis-of-participation-leadership-and-media-coverage.

———. 2018. *Women in the 2018 Olympic and Paralympic Winter Games: An Analysis of Participation, Leadership, and Media Coverage/Women's Sports Foundation.* New York: Women's Sports Foundation. https://library.olympic.org/Default/doc/SYRACUSE/177820/women-in-the-2018-olympic-and-paralympic-winter-games-an-analysis-of-participation-leadership-and-me.

WSW (Women's Sport Week). 2016. "Women's Sport Week 2017 (19–25 June)." *Women in Sport* (blog). https://www.womeninsport.org/wsw2017/.

Xu, Qingru, Andrew C. Billings, Olan K. M. Scott, Melvin Lewis, and Stirling Sharpe. 2019. "Gender Differences through the Lens of Rio: Australian Olympic Primetime Coverage of the 2016 Rio Summer Olympic Games." *International Review for the Sociology of Sport* 54 (5): 517–35. https://doi.org/10.1177/1012690217710690.

The Ghost from Antigonish: The Social Construction of Disability in Our Nation

Devin Gotell

The literal definition of the Paralympics is manifested in the Greek conjugation of "para," meaning "alongside" or "beyond," and "Olympic," or the reference to Mount Olympus, a place that the Ancient Greeks revered as the home of their gods thousands of years ago. The origin of the Olympic Games is disputed, some scholars claiming that it could be well over 3,000 years old—during the murky time frame of the fabled events of Homer's *Iliad* and *Odyssey* (Hart 2018). Others prefer to agree on the date of 776 BCE as a common starting ground before being abolished during the Christianization of the Hellenistic World by the Roman Emperor Theodosius I in the year AD 393 in an attempt to suppress paganism within the empire (History.com Editors 2009). What is certain, however, is that the modern incarnation of the Olympic Games that much of this world yearns for every 2 years (or four if adhering to the seasonal variation during contemporary times) was not resurrected until 1896 when the young Pierre de Coubertin proposed its revival in 1892 (History.com Editors 2009).

According to the Canadian Paralympic Committee (n.d.), it would be within the capital remnants of another past empire where the Paralympic Games would be born over 60 years later. The first Paralympic Games took place in the city of Rome, 1960, which featured 400 athletes from 23 different countries. Since then, the Paralympic movement has grown and matured into the diamond-bit drill that may be necessary to "dismantle" (Equitable Education 2013) the barriers that those who identify within the disabled community face each and every day.

THE HERO'S JOURNEY IN PRACTICE

The Hero's Journey, or the Monomyth, was a pattern of mythology that was recognized by Joseph Campbell, an American professor of literature at Sarah Lawrence College in the year 1949. Although Campbell identified 17 stages of the Hero's Journey (Connolly 2014), the following section will engage only in the following sequence: "The call to adventure," "the mentor," "the trials," "the dragon," "the temptations," and, finally, "the ultimate boon." This more simplified sequence was used by Dr. Michael Wesch (2018), an American professor of cultural anthropology who used the Hero's Journey in his book, *The Art of Being Human*. In his book, the reader is taken into Dr. Wesch's invigorating journey to Papua New Guinea for a total of 18 months between the years of 1999 and 2003. During this time, Dr. Wesch experienced a plethora of events that ultimately led to his interrogation of what "being human" truly is (Figure 8.1).

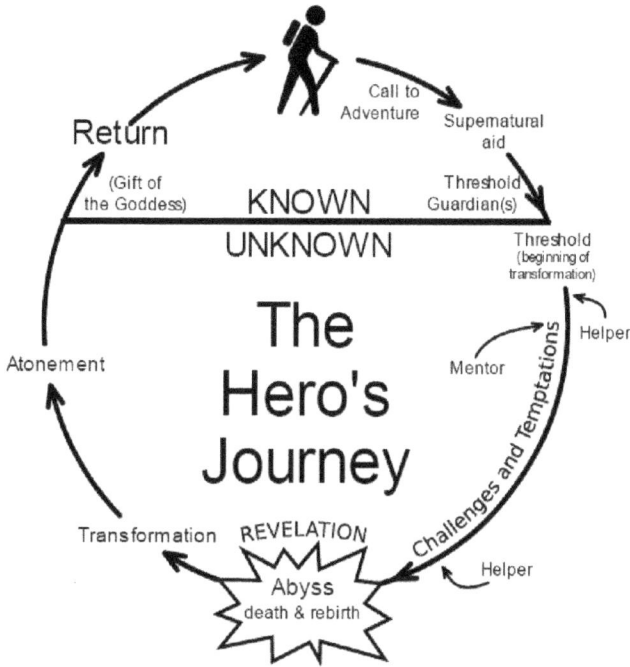

Figure 8.1: The Cycle of the Hero's Journey
Source: Wesch 2018, 328

Dr. Wesch simplifies this art of storytelling by segmenting it into a handful of key parts: The "call to adventure," "the mentor," "the trials," "the dragon," "the temptation" and finally, "the ultimate boon" (Wesch 2018, 327, 328).

"The call to adventure" is an event that triggers the beginning of any given story. It is the moment when someone or something changes from a state of mundaneness to a state of motion. The hero may be apprehensive about going on this journey, but something deep within the hero yearns for something more in their life.

"The mentor" refers to someone or something that influences the theoretical hero into gaining the courage to embark on such a journey. There may be a point of no return, or there may be a roadblock that is material or immaterial that this mentor figure is able to guide the hero past in order to go forth with the journey.

"The trials" refer to a point at which the hero faces grave difficulty. The hero may question their choices at times, but when each of these trials is completed, the hero gains resilience and vitality.

"The dragon" is something that the hero fears. The dragon can take many forms and may plug itself into the journey materially in the form of an antagonist, or immaterially in the form of doubt. However, the hero is rarely ill-equipped to deal with this theoretical dragon, because the trials endured throughout the journey thus far are often testaments that the hero is capable of eventually overcoming the dragon, however it may be represented.

"The temptations" are points within the journey where the hero is beckoned or tempted to succumb to their selfish desires. Doing so would be costly, however, and may deceive the hero into making choices that may serve to be a detriment. The pleasures that may temporarily quell the hero's selfish desires may not be worth it in hindsight.

"The ultimate boon" refers to a point where the hero manages to overcome their fear of the dragon or resist temptations that feed desire. If successful, the hero is granted revelation in some capacity. The hero may become transformative following this in a way that allows them to embark on a brand-new journey using the strength, resolve, and knowledge gained from the first.

THE HERO'S JOURNEY OF DEVIN GOTELL

The Call to Adventure

The "call to adventure" for my peculiar journey started around 20 years ago, and I suppose you could even call it an echo off the wall, because it could be argued that it was not my calling at all. It began with the realization that my older sister, Chelsey Gotell, had qualified for the 2000 Paralympic Games in Sydney, Australia. My life before this point was indeed mundane. I had a particular interest in biology as a child. Often catching the grandest of insects that lurked near the house and bringing them inside to inspect them in my book of insects to discern their taxonomic rank, much to my mother's dismay. You see, Chelsey and I have oculocutaneous albinism type I, which means that we lack pigment, or colour, in our skin, eyes, and hair. It is a rather rare phenomenon, occurring in as few as one in every 20,000 individuals in Europe and North America, but in some regions, such as Eastern Africa, figures increase to a potential one in every 1,400 (Under the Same Sun Organization, n.d.). Albinism is a genetic condition that is recessive, meaning that both parents must carry the necessary genetic material in order to manifest itself in offspring in its unique characteristics.

The Mentors

Life was not easy back then, but there was one distinct lesson that my parents taught both of us back then that continues to be key to the story changing from "mundane" to "adventurous." This was the notion that we knew ourselves best, and to settle for nothing less than that was something that our parents always stressed. Albinism was poorly understood back then, and in many ways it still is. It was believed by my neighbours, doctors, and family members alike that "we wouldn't live very long" or that we would automatically succumb to "mental illness" owing to the condition. These misguided ideas about albinism, which in reality have nothing to do with the condition, lived on as we grew older. People would stare at us, particularly adults, and everyone between as we travelled abroad where our exaggerated skin colour, or lack thereof, was considered to be nonnormative. Such as when we travelled to Durban, South Africa, for the 2006 World Championships that were held there. At a surface level, I feel that there was not a lot of difference between myself and most children that I grew up with, but the surface level is where the similarities end.

You may have read those last few sentences of the last paragraph and found them misplaced. After all, did I not just finish telling you that I have albinism and, furthermore, emphasized to you that it is a rare condition? Indeed, I did, but there are multiple layers to albinism, and one of them, which rests in the ways in which we socially construct ourselves in a society, has given me the privilege to be able to state that "there was not a lot of difference between myself and most children." This is because I grew up in a place called Antigonish County, Nova Scotia. Antigonish County lies about two hours northeast of Halifax, the province's capital. The name *Antigonish* has a very different story to tell from the majority-Caucasian demographics of the region, and it is a reminder of a dark past of erasure. It is believed to be a name of Mi'kmaq origin, understood differently depending on whom you ask as either "the place where the branches are torn off by bears gathering beechnuts" or "the meeting place of five forked rivers." These rivers being West River, South River, Brierly Brook, Wright's River, and East Wright's River (Town of Antigonish 2020).

Demographically, the region of Antigonish County is predominantly Caucasian; we are for the most part the descendants of European immigrants from as far back as the seventeenth century, and for my own lineage, it can be traced to around the mid-nineteenth century. Some of my own ancestors hailed from the British Isles, predominantly Scotland and Ireland, whereas others were from the European mainland of France in search of a better life in the new world. Since then, and of late, the town has visitors from the world over owing to the presence of its local university, St. Francis Xavier University. The scholarly institution more than doubles the sleepy and tranquil town's population during the school season, before scaling back to its native population of around 4,364 people like the ebb and flow of the nearby tides at St. George's Bay. The student population of 2019, for example, was believed to be in the region of 5,000 students. The total population of Antigonish County is around 19,301 individuals (*Statistics Canada* 2016).

The demographics of a region can tell us a great deal about it, as those who grow up in a given region tend to view themselves in a particular way. For Antigonish County as a whole, there is a great deal of pride associated with Gaelic and Celtic culture, with 46.6 percent of the population said to be traced from Scotland (*Statistics Canada* 2016). Each year, it prides itself on its Highland Games, which are disputed as being some of the oldest displays of the event outside of Scotland, having begun in Antigonish in the year 1863.

My albinism did not make me look drastically different from my peers. I have fair hair, which was at times mistaken for blonde, and blue eyes. Children would at times inquire about my nystagmus, or the rapid, involuntary shifting of my left eye, but this was the extent of it. I was taught at a very young age by my itinerant teacher, Marlies Jackson, that educating others on the features of albinism was the key to succeeding with other children, and I still believe that she was right. This was and continues to be mainly because of the various misconceptions that existed about albinism. Marlies believed that being a strong advocate for yourself held value in this respect. An itinerant teacher is simply an educator who specializes in educating children with visual impairments. Her goals were to teach us how to navigate through this world in ways that suit us. Essentially, to put it bluntly, she was preparing us for a world that was not built with us in its plan. Street signs that were much too high or too small to read were to be peered at through my monocular. I was to use the position of the sun in order to discern my cardinal direction in proximity to features of the world, and I was to adapt my method of learning to be audible as opposed to visual in the classroom, and I am to be very wary of harsh sunlight during peak hours of the day because my skin easily burns. These were my truths when navigating this world; my *normal*. We had no cell phones back in the late 1990s, no Google Maps.

As the years passed, I came to learn that my peers were actually quite malleable with regard to educating them on what albinism was, but, interestingly, it was ironically some of the adults in my life who posed the largest barriers growing up. It was noted by elementary school teachers that I took longer to tie my shoes and zip up my jacket before going outside for recess and lunch. I was no older than perhaps 4 or 5 when teachers and staff quickly decided that this was a big problem. I was whisked away to the school's library one day, where there was a room next to the computer lab. *Resource Class* was labelled across the door in an arcing fashion, in big, colourful, bubble letters. I was instructed by a teacher to sit at the table in that room, where I would practice tying my shoes until they decided that my mastery was adequate; until I could do it in a fashion that at least seemed *normal*. I suppose that this is where the *ghost* portion of this chapter's title comes into play; the duality of albinism. The phenotypic traits of my albinism happened to match with my mostly European ancestry, but for the experts in my life, such as doctors, teachers, and other figures of authority, there was caution about my albinism. This led to a feeling of liminality for me growing up, a feeling that I was neither here nor there.

> Doctors, those whom we deem experts in our lives, were just as confused as the teachers, as they squabbled among themselves over whether I needed to wear glasses or not. Over and over again they tested different lenses. I would tell them that they did not appear to make a positive impact on my eyesight, but they insisted that I wear them anyway. Finally, I asked my mum one day, Mum, why do they force me to wear these glasses?
> Do they not help you!? She replied, surprised.
> I don't think that they do. I concluded.

Then don't wear them. She replied with a thoughtful smile.

Back in 2015 at a local grocery store in London, Ontario, I was asked by a cashier whether "I had a hard life as a child." I was curious about this question, not because I took offence to it but because of my own inquisitive nature, wondering where this question stemmed from for her. When I asked her why she would ask such a question, she replied that "children can be cruel." My reply to this might have shocked her, but I simply stated that "adults are far crueler with their embedded biases and beliefs of what constitutes right and wrong in this world." I did not quite have the time to expand on what that actually meant. That adults are perhaps those in most need of an *Allegory of the Cave* so to speak in checking their ingrained beliefs versus knowledge, but looking back, I think it was a very significant statement with regard to the paragraphs I wrote previously.

The duality of albinism in some ways ties into demographics, as the condition forces us to ask tough questions about how we identify ourselves. I just so happen to have albinism and be of majority European descent. The same cannot be said, however, for those who are born with the condition as part of a family that is socially constructed to be Black, or of another race where the phenotypic traits of blue eyes, fair hair, and fair skin may raise eyebrows owing to the contrast between an individual with albinism and their family. Those who are born with albinism in Tanzania, for example, have a particularly grim reality of facing persecution and social rejection by their communities owing to their albinism (Rao 2018). The condition has been exploited by witch doctors and corrupt officials to take advantage of those who find themselves impoverished and ill. Between the years 2000 and 2016, more than 75 albinos were murdered in Tanzania alone in the name of witchcraft (Rao 2018). Superstitions surrounding the condition have led to the false belief that the organs and blood of those with albinism can cure deadly diseases such as HIV and AIDS (Rao 2018). Yet these Tanzanians who are unlucky enough to be born into such a society with albinism, who live in fear of such persecution and exploitation, were birthed from the womb of what society would label as a "Black" woman, who was likely in turn impregnated by a "Black" man. The different appearance of their new baby with albinism, however, labels that child as belonging to another category in Tanzanian society, one that is desirable for the preying eyes of witch doctors and exploiters owing to the colour of their skin and a social outcast by many others. Using this analysis, I question the social constructions of race in our societies and find it to be a rather interesting focal point when examining the effects of racialization on societies. Even those that are beyond our own in the West.

It was at the local swimming pool at the Oland Centre in Antigonish where my sister and I would build a legacy for ourselves as we trained with the local swimming team, the Antigonish Aquanauts. My sister, who is four years my senior, made waves at the local level very quickly, and by the age of 14 she had leaped from a provincial prodigy to a contender for World Champion at the 2000 Sydney Paralympic Games. It was not long before I followed suit. One of our mother's wishes was that we all learned to swim, because Grandmother was always petrified of water, and hence none of my aunts or uncles on that side of the family learned the skill very well. It was therefore imperative to her that we not follow in their footsteps. Our father also encouraged this, and so I suppose you could say that our "mentor" was our parents through their encouragement and life lessons, and for me, specifically, it was my sister, Chelsey, and her grand achievements at such a young age that set the spark. Little did they know back then just what calibrer of swimmers we would become.

So, in essence, I had to be creative with whom I called a mentor as a child, but at a social level, the adults in my life who encouraged me to question dominant ideas that created barriers in my life, such as my parents, Marlies Jackson, coaches whom I will discuss later, my older brother Shannon and, lastly, my older sister, who had very similar life experiences to mine, were my mentors. We had to be careful with whom we gave this title to, because we existed in a world where we were not understood by many.

The Trials

It was not long before I followed my sister's wake, and by the age of 15, I had found myself competing at the 2005 Canada Games in Regina, Saskatchewan, where I narrowly won the multiclass men's 100-m backstroke and achieved my first gold medal. This, in reality, was a trial, and the beginning of my high-performance athletic career, where I would become known once again by many teammates as a *ghost*, but this time, I would be referred to as the *Great Ghost*. This was a name that would stick with me throughout my career and an identity that I embraced.

In the sea of spectators at those 2005 Canada Games in Regina, some of whom were parents of swimmers, other enthusiasts who were watching the Games from the stands, lurked Head Coach Craig McCord of the Canadian Paralympic Swimming Team. The reason for his presence was simple: to find the next batch of promising youth to potentially take to the 2008 Paralympic Games in Beijing, China. Reaching beyond these types of trials eventually became human nature, particularly as I gained experience throughout what would turn out to be a 12-year-long career. We were to approach each race with stoicism. We were to have the confidence that what we had done in training thousands of times before that point would be replicated with grace, and potentially a spot on the podium. Coach Craig McCord believed in the notion that if you could step up to the plate during the toughest of times, then it would be certain that you would do it at your best.

McCord, along with other influential coaches in my life during my career such as Rob Allen of the Antigonish Aquanauts, Dave Heinbuch of the Ottawa Gee Gees, Michel Berube of Club Natation de Gatineau, and Andrew Craven of the London Aquatic Club, created something of a duality in sport politics. Their positive outlooks on life and the effects of training on an athlete in general were not always *good enough* in the grand scheme of things. Coach Dave and eventually Coach Andrew, for example, loved to use the "glass half empty or half full" philosophy in everyday life. The coaches who influence us and the reality of the politics of sport are ideologies that are actually quite incompatible. On the one hand, great coaches teach you the value of practice and repetition and create a bond that strengthens an athlete's resilience. By repeating training sessions that once seemed impossible and excelling at them the following time, we often proved to ourselves that the supposed impossible could not only be achieved but also mastered. "Sometimes you've got to travel through Hell to get to Heaven," Coach Michel often said when delivering a brutal practice. Although my connection with religious affiliation is questionable at best and I prefer to follow an agnostic model of beliefs, the message resonated loud and clear for me.

Beyond the comfort of your home and onto the world stage of the Olympic and Paralympic Games, however, the politics of sport greatly complicate these philosophies. Great coaches see their athletes as students and sometimes as good friends, but out on the world stage, high-performance athletes are simply spectacles for the masses. The balance shifts uneasily between "practice makes perfect" and "win." "Did you win!?" is one of the most dreaded and alienating questions that most high-performance athletes endure when returning from a tour. The process of the uphill battle of training, the bonds we share with our coaches and our fellow athletes, and the coaching philosophies that we follow to get to where we do are not understood or valued on the world stage. The medal that may or may not be hanging around your neck, and the colour of the alloys within those medals; gold for first, silver for second, and bronze for third place performances, respectively. These medals or lack thereof add or subtract legitimacy from your story and experience.

On the world stage at the Olympic and Paralympic Games, it is all about who wins the medals and who shatters the records, and as an athlete, it is a struggle between your values and what you can do for your nation. As you walk out on that pool deck from the comfort of the waiting room curtains and into the explosion of the crowd, you are fighting for two causes: Your own dignity as an athlete with their own unique story and values, and the nation that you represent. You are decked out from head to toe in clothing that attempts to capture the essentials of your nation. In my case, it was the maple leaf, and a vivid display of red and white in most cases. There are others too, however, that you are fighting for. Your national team's choice of sponsors, such as Speedo, the Hudson's Bay Company, to name a few in our case. Your clothing is decked with their labels as if you were a vehicle at a car show. In this way, when you walk out on that deck on display for millions of people watching worldwide, it is one of the most exhilarating and breathtaking, yet alienating, experiences you could imagine. As you stand there hopped up on the ecstasy of the environment and your own adrenalin, the administration of your team, some of whom you have never met in your life watch nervously, hoping that you do not disappoint them. They hope that you will simply "win."

This duality creates a rift between two different stories and two very different outlooks on what success and failure mean at the Olympic and Paralympic Games, and this duality can greatly distort our own views as high-performance athletes of what these terms mean. Is it *successful* to simply attend an Olympic or Paralympic Games and return without a medal? I think most high-performance athletes who have been there, including myself, would tell you that would be a resounding yes. Or is it suddenly *failure* because you did not *win*? It felt to me that the personal narrative of the experience and the story of the Olympic and Paralympic Games as a capitalist entity are not compatible.

What if I told you now that the question of disability actually amplifies this duality phenomenon? I would argue that it does so on the basis that there is an extra layer to consider once disability is brought into the equation. That layer can be best described as "inspiration porn" (Young 2014). At a TedTalk in Sydney, Australia of 2014, Stella Young described inspiration porn as the idea that one group is objectified for the benefit of another group; that is to say, the disabled experience is considered to be a "bad thing, capital B, capital T; a Bad Thing" (Young 2014). Young further emphasized her point with a childhood example, namely, that "waking up in the morning, getting good marks, having a low-key job at my mum's hair salon and watching *Buffy the Vampire Slayer* and *Dawson's Creek*" (Young 2014) were not inspirational. These activities and endeavours were things that typical people of her age were participating in. These activities were simply "life," and just because a person was disabled, it did not mean that their everyday mundane tasks should be an inspiration for anybody. "I should not be an inspiration to you for waking up and remembering my name in the morning" (Young 2014).

Stella Young passed away later in the year, on December 6, 2014, at the age of 32, but her message resonates with those of us who have experienced her tale in some capacity. The inspiration porn phenomenon can easily be seen in how media continues to address Paralympic athletes. Our narratives are at times heavily overshadowed, or totally lost, in favour of how we have *overcome* our disabilities to get to where we are. I recall this all too well as the S13 men's 400 m Freestyle Toronto Para PanAm Games Champion back in 2015, when I was asked how I "overcame" my disability's struggles in order to seize the podium. The question made for one of the most exhilarating points in my career to suddenly become one of the strangest and oddly alienating. It was a realization that to the media and those who consumed this media, all of the blood, sweat, and tears that I had shed, the 5 to 7 hours of training I completed six days of the week for years was somehow "inspirational" simply because I have a disability. To the public eye, the hard work and dedication that we exhibit during the years that precede a Paralympic Games are all for naught. What they see through the media is how we have "overcome" the features of our *non-normative* bodies to succeed.

The Dragon

The dragon in this story is deeply intertwined with its trials, and I will use the age-old proverb "It takes a village to raise a child" to justify this. This proverb is an absolute truth for professional athletes, because without mentors and influencers along the way, success is difficult to replicate, let alone conceive. Parents of high-performance athletes often change their lifestyles and commitments to ensure that their young athletes are eating only the best food, getting to their practices at absurd hours of the morning, and are there emotionally in the face of what we hardened war machines may consider "failure" from time to time. Likewise, community members such as those in Antigonish County where we called home made a difference. Naturally, this all created an exacerbated roadblock in the form of the dragon. I often felt as though there was a lot riding on my shoulders to succeed. This was indeed the dragon. I, as an athlete, was not only fighting for myself and what I stood for when I was presented behind those swimming blocks to compete against the world's best, but I also felt as though I was fighting for everyone and everything that had ever influenced where I now stood. Additional to this was the complicated international politics of sport thrown into the mix that are explained previously, and, suddenly, replicating what I have always done but better with utmost stoicism became a lot more difficult.

The dragon had also manifested itself in how disability was and continues to be perceived by those in our society who hold the dominant discourse, that is to say, those who fall under what a long, dark history of eugenic thought and the perversion of Darwinian thought in the mid- to late-nineteenth century into what is now social Darwinism believe to be aspects of "normalcy" (Chandler 2020). Such figures of power attempt to name, label, and describe us in ways that are preposterously inaccurate, and they are of no accident. They are the ways in which we have been socially constructed to be "inferior," and that disability is nothing more than tragedy, a mishap of misfortune, something that ought to be "fixed" at the first opportunity possible. In a nutshell, these are "ableist" ideas. Ableism has many forms, and even a few cousins such as sanism and audism, to name a few that adhere to the Mad and the Deaf communities respectively. These discourses fill their own hungry gullets by festering in their own biases that the disabled are figures of charity. Confirmation bias and at times disconfirmation biases are used in tandem to be reinforced by a society that continues to be built without us in its plan. Thus, as scholars such as Mia Mingus and public speakers such as the late Stella Young note, we have in many ways become more disabled by our environment than by what our own bodies could ever achieve.

The fear of the dragon, however, made me stronger over the years. Each time I managed to defy the dragon in some way through the various trials both inside and outside of the pool served as another step forward that I was able to take, both physically and intellectually. Until finally, I was standing toe to claw with the dragon, which once felt like it stood on my shoulders. It was close enough to smell its putrid breath that I once feared. It still intimidated me from time to time, but with every reminder that the journey mattered more than the outcome, the ferocity of the dragon seemed a little less dangerous, its stare a little less piercing and its intent a little less relevant to my cause. My cause can be found within this story and through my lived experiences, and this is just one of many stories that I would hope can serve to dismantle the barriers that "continue to push certain groups to the bottom of society's ranks" (Mingus, 2013).

The Temptations

There are many temptations that come with my story, and they existed almost every step of the way. I would argue that nearly all of them concerned the fact that professional athletes live a life that is incompatible with Western cultural standards of living and its cultural expectations, or lack thereof at times with regard to neglecting our bodies. I can confidently say that I have spent more time in a swimming pool during my peak than most Westerners spent at the office in a day at the time. This alone defies many aspects of Western culture, including our tendency to be very sedentary, to eat all of the wrong foods, and to drink excessively, to gawk at anything that does not resemble a "9 to 5" job and to have commitments that make a recognizable Western social life nigh impossible outside of the *athletic bubble*. When I say *athletic bubble*, I am referring to the high-performance athlete experience as a way of life as opposed to a simple profession. Dr. Wesch would probably refer to the contrast between the ways of life of a high-performance athlete and the Western qualities that I listed previously as "mismatch diseases" (Wesch 2018, 87), which, in essence, are examples of disconnects between our current environment and how we have evolved over millions of years.

It was many times over that these temptations appeared over my 12-year career, and to push against these social norms had consequences. Friends wandered astray, my various cravings and their pleasures were shoved to the sidelines, and memories among family and friends were created without my presence. Instead, I was creating my own memories thousands of kilometres away from home, in what was likely another nation, where I trained to represent my own nation alongside a Canadian Paralympic family. Abstaining from these cravings and temptations was almost always worth it. Little to this day is as memorable to me as the euphoria of letting loose with those with whom you have exerted blood, sweat, smiles, and tears with every single day for years. Those invaluable few hours of celebration that you had together after a Paralympic Games that made you feel omnipotent for just a little while before you flew back home to your corner of this sprawling planet.

The Ultimate Boon

The ultimate boon of my story may not be what those on the periphery of the high-performance athlete experience may expect. In general, most curious folk are keen to know how many medals you have won during your career and ask little else. The infamous 'did you win?!' question threatens nearly every conversation like a sudden maelstrom at sea. For me, however, it was a 12-year-long lesson. This lesson lies in the notion that the journey is what is most important in life, not the outcome. This is something that is still difficult to grasp at times during my transition into the "real world," but no less invaluable. The reason for this is the aforementioned duality of the sport world. The game of tug o' war between your own expectations as a high-performance athlete and those of your national team staff. For me the experience was about living. If winning happened to be on that agenda, as it sometimes was, then so be it, but it was not the sole reason for this journey in hindsight.

In the traditional sense, those on the periphery may understand, the boon of my career was standing atop the podium alongside two fellow Canadians after winning the S13 men's 400 m freestyle at the 2015 ParaPan Am Games in Toronto. It was not a personal best performance, and not as graceful as my past performances, owing to illness in the form of a head cold gnawing at my energy stores, but the lessons of the process allowed me to do whatever was necessary to secure the gold medal over my competitors, including two of my own teammates, my friends. A podium sweep, as they call it on home soil, is a very significant event in sport and is an event where the rare duality conflict between the athlete perspective and the political perspective both align in harmony. As an athlete, your training has pulled you into a position of victory, whereas on the political side, having three Canadian flags above the podium as the national anthem booms overhead on home soil is symbolic of *success*. It is positive publicity, and it creates stories for media coverage.

At a more complex level, however, the journey is not over, and likely never will be. The life of a high-performance athlete may be in my past, but the lessons, memories, and sense of discipline that were gained from the high-performance athlete lifestyle will continue in relevance far beyond the depths of a swimming pool. This very tale in the hands of readers like you is but a testament to that. Our stories as Paralympians are valuable beyond the pool, the track, or the boccia jack, as examples, because they serve to stand up against normalcy and the caustic discourse that comes along with normalcy. To navigate through this world differently from others is and should be perfectly fine, and to study these differences closely will aid in clearing the fog and cobwebs of the ableist narrative.

THE AFTERMATH: THE 2020 COVID-19 PANDEMIC

Campbell observed another part of the Monomyth in his analysis: the abyss, or revelation.

Referring back to the Hero's Journey (Figure 8.1), there is a point where the hero completes their journey and finds themselves in an unrecognizable place. I believe that in many ways that part of my journey is the effects of the COVID-19 pandemic on the world around me.

Telling a story can be valuable, and during the COVID-19 pandemic I have certainly taken the time to articulate my own story and discern why it matters within the world of disability movement and connect how it relates to the bigger picture. In my experience in society pre-COVID-19, it was easy to get lost in things that were in actual fact quite mundane. I have come to look at the effects of COVID-19 on Western society as a black light on a white shirt, exposing an inexorable problem that can no longer be concealed or hidden. Perhaps if you are a visually impaired reader, you can think of a different analogy: the whistle of a tea kettle on the stove. The hiss is an unmistakable reminder that the water within that kettle is boiling hot. This is to say, the blemishes that our society has succeeded in concealing for so long are now exposed in a way that is arguably inexorable. I am of the belief that there is no going back to what once was when this pandemic is over, and we will steadily head into a period of adaptation and perhaps a shift in the very fabric of society.

Some of these shifts I believe will continue to manifest themselves in how we work, in particular, how we deal with human resource management in the form of contingent workers. Simply, contingent workers are workers who do not have regular, full-time employment (Nickels, McHugh, and McHugh 2012).

The contingent workers of today could largely be seen in the same light as sixteenth century Europe's Swiss mercenaries, who were renowned for their discipline and expertise. Surrounding their mountainous abode were many gluttonous empires that at times utilized Swiss mercenaries at various points throughout their histories (Lantink 2015). Chief among them over the towering Alpines and far to the south of a fragmented Italy was the Pope of Rome, where the Swiss Guard still remains to this day in the Vatican for young, Swiss, Catholic men up to the age of 30 (Lantink 2015). Empires of the past utilized mercenary services such as those of what the Swiss had to offer, but who are the "empires" of today? I would argue that our modern corporations can be seen as such. Big businesses such as Walmart, Amazon, and Google are strikingly similar to the ambitious emperors of our past, and they engulf and dominate their surrounding competitors similarly, as small businesses cannot cope with the 2020 pandemic's dire economic effects. In order to do so, however, and similarly to an empire, these monolithic corporations have and continue to employ contingent workers, particularly during the COVID-19 crisis, which has seen millions of people shoved out of what they believed to be their traditional forms of work, and into the frontlines of these corporations as temporary workers, as mercenaries who serve these corporations for specific tasks before they are disbanded back into precarity when the job is done. Shortly after the pandemic began, back in early 2020, Walmart announced that it had planned to employ more than 150,000 contingent workers (McLean 2020). Some critics, even before the pandemic, claimed that big box stores are taking advantage of people's precarity, and promoting a "gig economy" (Willcocks 2020), arguing that such work leaves many people "lonely, powerless, and underpaid." Others, such as Noah Nickel of the *Brock Press,* claim that the gig economy has taken advantage of workers in the sense that the work is not stable. By cycling through thousands of contingent workers, big box stores are able to quickly cut ties with contingent workers by "cutting corners in regards to labour protection" (Nickel 2020). This is to say, big businesses have figured out that more than ever, they can get away with the exploitation of the occupationally precarious and avoid giving them many employee benefits while they are at it.

Another shift in the workforce is the ever-changing model of the traditional *boss.* Even prior to the effects of COVID-19, shifts in how the boss figure carries himself have changed significantly. You may have noticed that I used "himself" as an example, and that was no accident. Not only has the traditional boss shifted in the sense that there is now a "herself" and a "themself" in administrative positions, but their demeanour toward their workers has also changed. This can best be explained by Douglas

McGregor's Theory X and Theory Y theories of human work motivation back in the 1950s (Walsh 2020). The gist of the theory is that there is the authoritarian boss, or Theory X boss, and the participative boss, or Theory Y boss. The Theory X boss is traditional and far more typical for the mid-to-late twentieth century. Minimum banter with employees, an all-work-no-play attitude, the stereotypical middle-aged White man. The Theory Y boss, however, values their employees and seeks to find a balance between productivity and nurturing a sense of trust between employer and employee. In an era where many workers are either finding themselves as contingent workers or working from home owing to COVID-19, the Theory Y model certainly appears more flexible. Trust that employees will be productive at home and that they will communicate problems that they face along the way are arguably vital over the past year and may continue to be going forward in the year 2021.

Much larger shifts, such as those of total governmental upheavals, are also not uncommon. The Ancient Greek historian Polybius of Megalopolis contemplated such shifts more than 2,100 years ago during the rise of the Roman Empire around the Hellenistic World (Hart 2018) with regard to the fragility of government forms, where democracy was no exception to Polybius's model. If the lament of Polybius appears to be a far cry to you in the present day, might I suggest to you that there are scholars who contend that we may be anatomically similar to humans who lived over 165,000-195,000 years ago "in the Middle Paleolithic/Middle Stone Age" (Nowell 2010 p. 438) and behaviourally similar to those who lived around 40,000 years ago "at the start of the Upper Paleolithic" (Nowell 2010 p. 438). I believe that we are still just as capable of faltering as we are of demanding change now in 2021. The current divisive state of the United States of America is a testament to this as President Joe Biden has faced what was likely one of the most turbulent inaugurations in that nation's history. American divisiveness in itself has its own story to tell regarding political shifts, and some of Polybius's cynical views on governmental degeneration certainly hold true as America increasingly risks becoming an ochlocratic hotbed, as citizens continue to be shrouded in mistrust toward their politicians. A trend that extends far beyond the borders of just America.

One shift that I would like to see and how disability ties into what I have written previously is a Canada that is aware of disability as a way of life for the vast majority of people at a variety of points in their lives; whether it be from birth, temporary, or attained later in life. Disability is not a mishap or misfortune or a tragedy and should not be mistaken by the branding of impairments and their socially constructed implications. The stories that are told about ourselves can hold value in achieving this, because they humanize a group of people who have suffered for centuries at the hands of social Darwinism and obsessive eugenic labelling on a perverted quest to fix what is believed to be broken or not contingent with normalcy. The result of such frameworks has been a nation full of barriers that only exist because the cold hard truth of the matter is that we live in a society that was never built for those who are not "able" in mind. I suppose I can echo once more that these dominant ideas have disabled us far more than our bodies ever will.

Disability justice and social movements matter because they are part of a much larger picture. For a long time, I viewed disability as an individual problem simply because *not many others have albinism, and therefore it is my own problem to deal with*, but as time passed and I grew older and wiser, I began to see connections that I did not know existed. Disability and the barriers that the disabled community face is no accident; they are the results of a much larger, systemic, and intersectional web that connects many different groups together. Disability, race, gender, and sexual orientation all carry the ghosts and demons of social construction in our society. So no, I will not conform to normative values, and neither should you. The reality is that when I must navigate through the city, I look to the sun for guidance like a compass, as opposed to squinting at the street signs, which are much too small to read, and that is my normal.

It is my belief that one of the most valuable lessons that anthropology, and to an extent the effects of COVID-19 as a whole, have taught me is to see the bigger picture. As mentioned earlier, I once carried the belief that disability was my personal problem and that through adaptation I should find the means to live with it. Although I do still value the adaptation of tools and technologies to gain more independence and maintain control within my life, I have come to realize that I am not alone on this journey. The challenges that I face are in fact not as foreign as I once believed them to be. I had a tendency to believe that it was us and them.

I became jaded and reclusive since retirement. I tried to make sense of the new world around me but failed to realize that there were answers in fruitful abundance all around me simply because I was not *really* looking for them. I was looking for what I knew, and only what I knew. I "saw" a smaller, detailed picture in the sense that I knew the details and laws of the land within the Paralympic bubble, but was unable to connect these details to the much larger world around me. I was unable to connect, for example, our experience with a marginalized race, a different gender, or someone who may have a sexual orientation that falls beyond the "norm."

I will explain this *us versus them* phenomenon by using an analogy of Professor Eliza Chandler. I ask you, the reader, when was the last time you took a shower? When you did so and when you reflect on it, do you believe that you really took that shower independently (Chandler 2020)? There is certainly an argument that you perhaps did not. There is a strong likelihood that the expertise of carpentry and plumbing were necessary for your shower to function as it does in the form of intangible services and labour; services that were provided to you through local businesses in your community. You likely believe that you are able to take a shower independently because the frameworks that materialize capitalism allow it to be this way. We do not think of taking a shower in any other sense, because it is subconsciously normative to walk into one, turn on the water, and get on with it. Thus, there is no "us vs them," but there are certainly subconscious ideas of whom society is built for and for whom it is not when suddenly those who have bodies that fall outside of what is *normative* have difficulty taking a shower.

Who, then, experiences difficulty when taking a shower, and, more importantly, why do they experience such difficulty? If you are reading this as a wheelchair user, you will likely have no need to imagine the following scenario, but perhaps you are not a wheelchair user. I would like you to imagine yourself rolling up to a shower door, only to find that the door is not sufficiently wide for you to enter the shower. Perhaps there is even a step or two that lead to the door as well. Suppose, then, that you do manage to fumble into this shower without your wheelchair, only to then find that the showerhead, along with its temperature gauge, is too high for you to reach and that there is no form of support for you to even prop yourself in such a way that you are able to wash properly. Now ask yourself, are the obstacles that you have faced in this example a personal problem? Or would you argue that they are an environmental problem? I would certainly argue that it is the latter, and what is believed by some to be our flawless Western society is riddled with countless examples of these scenarios. My hope is that the foregoing scenario does not instill pity within you. On the contrary, my hope is, instead, that it instills in you the question of how normalcy is defined and to be critical of why it is defined this way and why such obstacles exist at all.

Let us now imagine another scenario, where you wake up one morning in a place where braille and American Sign Language were the only forms of communication to be used from now on. I would wager that a great deal of us would be left out of such a society. By identifying that much of our everyday environment actually adheres to only part of our population, and excludes the rest, we begin to understand that the disabled community is far more robust than what was once thought. In fact, the disabled make up the world's largest minority population at around a billion individuals worldwide (Chandler 2020). At the dawn of 2021, our current global population sits just shy of 7.9 billion people. This means that around 12 percent of the global population identifies as disabled. In Canada, that estimate rises to 6.25 million people, or 22 percent of the total population of individuals above 15 years of age (*Statistics Canada* 2018).

Chandler's analogy falls within the interdependent model of care, one that interrogates concepts of care within the disabled community. During another one of Professor Chandler's lectures, Chandler outlined three forms of care: dependent, independent, and interdependent. Dependent care is a form that is likely the most recognizable to most. It is the classic model that adheres to normative values that are held by the medical model. These are individuals whom we revere as "experts" in their field, and, in tandem, experts regarding the various labels that they give to the disabled community through diagnostics. They are our doctors and nurses. There is an independent form of care as well. This is one where disabled people are given resources and funding to create their own form of care through personal caregivers. The third model, interdependency, raises some interesting questions. This model believes that independence is a myth and that none of us are truly independent in the ways that we believe that we are. Hence, Chandler's analogy of the connection between the shower in your home and those who built that shower and those services that you utilized to have it built and functioning properly are an example of that myth.

Intersectionality is another hot topic within the academic world and is heavily contested among politicians and marginalized groups alike with regard to its meaning. Some individuals believe that certain groups may be "doubly oppressed" (Chandler 2020) through the multiple labels that they carry through medical, social, and cultural structures of normalcy. These labels include Black, Disabled, Gay, and Mad all in one entity. At its simplest, however, the concept of intersectionality was coined back in 1989 by Kimberlé Crenshaw, who used it to outline how these labels tend to overlap owing to intersectional societal trends that affect these groups (Coaston 2019). Back in 1989, however, Crenshaw used the term in a way that "until several years ago was a legal term in relative obscurity outside academic circles" (Coaston 2019). Intersectionality pertained primarily to the lack of visibility for Black women in the judicial system and workforce. Today, however, it has become contentious, particularly among right-leaning thinkers who have dubbed it as a victim card.

Although I do see value in intersectionality being used to draw marginalized groups closer together, I believe that the contemporary use of the term walks a tightrope of sorts and can become problematic. Crenshaw demonstrated how a more contemporary outlook of intersectionality can be used to examine the struggles of marginalized groups at her 2016 TedTalk *The Urgency of Intersectionality* by asking guests to sit down if they did not recognize the name of one of the Black individuals who had been killed in police brutality during that time. What she found was that people were far more likely to know the names of Black men who died at the hands of police rather than the names of women. Thus, being Black and a woman means that perhaps your narrative is further oppressed.

Although I can appreciate this approach, I like to see intersectionality as a "vine" (Cheuk 2021) that draws connections between different marginalized groups in ways that we can identify them and work together to address, rather than dwelling on multiple layers of oppression as if they were a "stack of pancakes" (Cheuk 2021). This vine versus pancake model is something that Professor Fiona Cheuk discussed in one of her intersectionality lectures, and she used it to emphasize the importance of seeing intersectionality through a much wider lens. By drifting away from the personal story as a "stack of pancakes," you instead see multiple stories of marginalized people who are held back by the power dynamics of our society. Identifying how power dynamics hold multiple groups back helps us not to compete against one another, as if we are at some sort of "Oppression Olympics" (Cheuk 2021) and ensures that we are not being distracted from the real issues of society, such as why it is built to exclude disabled people and reject certain bodies while accepting others, or from questioning what "race" or "gender" even mean beyond their rudimental definitions.

CONCLUSION

To conclude, I have been challenged throughout these lines of thought in their own right. In simpler terms, I suppose I could say that my outlook on life was largely ethnocentric pre-COVID-19, and most certainly before interjecting anthropological theory into disability study. I once felt that because my experience was different from what is normative, it logically followed that this was the only way in which I would navigate through the world. However, the value of "seeing big," "seeing small," and "seeing it all" (Wesch 2018, 174), or seeing the big picture lies in the ability to find similarities between my own story and that of someone who I may not initially expect to find such familiarity through the burden of knowledge. As marginalized groups, we are not doubly or triply oppressed by our labels like a "stack of pancakes" (Cheuk 2021). We are intimately connected through the vines of power dynamics in our society. By working together as disabled people, marginalized race people, members of the LGBTQ+ community, those within the Deaf and Mad community, we can together identify what power structures hold us back. Familiarity draws connection, and with connection, alienation fades.

REFERENCES

Canadian Paralympic Committee. n.d. "History of the Paralympic Movement in Canada." https://paralympic.ca/history-paralympic-movement-canada#:~:text=Origin%20of%20the%20Paralympic%20Games,1948%20Olympic%20Games%20opening%20ceremony.

Chandler, Eliza. 2020. "Rethinking Disability." Lecture VI Material, Disability Study DST 501, Ryerson University, Toronto, November, 2020.

Cheuk, Fiona. 2021. "Whose Lives Matter?" Lecture II Material, Disability Study DST 300, Ryerson University, Toronto, 2021.

Coaston, Jane. 2019. "The Intersectionality Wars: When Kimberlé Crenshaw Coined the Term 30 Years ago, It Was a Relatively Obscure Legal Concept. Then It Went Viral." *Vox Media*, May 28, 2019. https://www.vox.com/the-highlight/2019/5/20/18542843/intersectionality-conservatism-law-race-gender-discrimination.

Connolly, Sean. 2014. "Does the Presence of Joseph Campbell's Monomyth Predict any Variance in the Box Office for Big Budget Movies?" Master of Arts thesis, Indiana University.

Equitable Education. 2013. "Beyond Access: Mia Mingus on Disability Justice." Video – 15:05 Beyond Access: Mia Mingus on Disability Justice (video interview) (equitableeducation.ca)

Hart, David. 2018. "Ideas That Shape the World II." Lecture IV Material, Arts and Contemporary Study ACS 200, Ryerson University, Toronto, March, 2018.

History.com Editors. 2009. "First Modern Olympic Games." *History*, November 24, 2009. https://www.history.com/this-day-in-history/first-modern-olympic-games.

Lantink, Frans Willem. 2015. "Why Does the Vatican Have a Swiss Guard?" *Utrecht University*, October 3, 2015. https://www.uu.nl/en/news/why-does-the-vatican-have-a-swiss-guard.

McLean, Rob. 2020. "Walmart, Dollar Tree and 7-Eleven Want to Hire Nearly 200,000 Workers as the Coronavirus Pandemic Continues." *CNN Business*, March 20, 2020. https://www.cnn.com/2020/03/20/business/walmart-hiring-coronavirus/index.html.

Morris, Stuart, Gail Fawcett, Laurent Brisebois, and Jeffrey Hughes. 2018. "A Demographic, Employment and Income Profile of Canadians with Disabilities Aged 15 Years and Over, 2017." *Statistics Canada*, November 28, 2018. https://www150.statcan.gc.ca/n1/pub/89-654-x/89-654-x2018002-eng.htm.

Nickel, Noah. 2020. "The Gig Economy Is Bad News for Workers." *The Brock Press*, October 6, 2020. https://www.brockpress.com/the-gig-economy-is-bad-news-for-workers/#:~:text=The%20low%20pay%20usually%20requires,then%20your%20average%20wage%20worker.&text=As%20these%20sketchy%20practices%20seep,the%20gig%20economy%20or%20not.

Nickels, William G., James M. McHugh, and Susan M. McHugh. 2012. *Understanding Business*. 10th ed., 444–45. New York: McGraw-Hill.

Nowell, April. 2010. "Defining Behavioral Modernity in the Context of Neandertal and Anatomically Modern Human Populations." *Annual Review of Anthropology*, 39(1), 437-52. Defining Behavioral Modernity in the Context of Neandertal and Anatomically Modern Human Populations (ryerson.ca).

Rao, Pavithra. 2018. "Ending Albino Persecution in Africa." *Africa Renewal*, 2018, https://www.un.org/africarenewal/magazine/december-2017-march-2018/ending-albino-persecution-africa.

Statistics Canada. 2016. "Census Profile, 2016 Census—Antigonish, County [Census Division], Nova Scotia and Nova Scotia [Province]." https://www12.statcan.gc.ca/census-recensement/2016/dp-pd/prof/details/page.cfm?Lang=E&Geo1=CD&Code1=1214&Geo2=PR&Code2=12&SearchText=B2G2L3&SearchType=Begins&SearchPR=01&B1=All&TABID=2&type=0.

TED. 2016. "The Urgency of Intersectionality—Kimberlé Crenshaw." December 7, 2016. Video, 18:49. https://www.youtube.com/watch?v=akOe5-UsQ2o&feature=youtu.be&ab_channel=TED.

Town of Antigonish. 2020. "A Brief History." https://www.townofantigonish.ca/a-brief-history.html#:~:text=Antigonish%20is%20a%20Mi%27kmaq,place%20of%20five%20forked%20rivers.

Under the Same Sun Organization. n.d. "About Albinism." https://www.underthesamesun.com/page/about-albinism?gclid=CjwKCAjwg4-EBhBwEiwAzYAlsp9g86QJFt44nTWShXRDgpmceqfA0GxTsNqQ2ApPHo5U54NT1ie1DRoC7CIQAvD_BwE.

Walsh, Phillip. 2020. "The Growing Business: Human Resource Management." Lecture Material, Business Essentials Study BSM 200, Ryerson University, Toronto, November, 2020.

Wesch, Michael. 2018. *The Art of Being Human: A Textbook for Cultural Anthropology*, 87, 174, 325–29. Manhattan, KS: New Prairie Press. https://newprairiepress.org/ebooks/20/.

Willcocks, Paul. 2020. "Who Sticks Up for the Gig Worker?" *The Tyee*, January 7, 2020. https://thetyee.ca/Analysis/2020/01/07/Who-Sticks-Up-for-Giggers/.

Young, Stella. 2014. "I'm not your inspiration, thank you very much." TEDxSydney, April, 2014. Stella Young: I'm not your inspiration, thank you very much | TED Talk

INDEX

Page numbers in *italics* denote illustrative material.

National Basketball Association (men, NBA), 100–104, 106–108

Nike commercial, 45

professional sports team in Toronto, 56

and wearing a hijab, 44, 82

See also Hijabi Ballers (HB); Women's National Basketball Association (WNBA)

beauty, idealized, 10, 46

Bend It Like Beckham (film), 22

Benét, James, 23

Berri, David, 94, 96, 106–107

Berube, Michel, 136

Biden, Joe, 142

Bird, Sue, 94, 99

Black people

    anti-Black racism, 39–41, 43, 47, 80

    BIPOC, 22

    Black Lives Matter movement, 1, 88, 103–104

    coverage of female athletes by sport media, 99–100

    See also Black Muslim female athletes

Black Muslim female athletes

    anti-Black racism, 39–41, 42–44, 47, 78, 80

    hijab discourses, 39–40

    Islamophobia, 39–41, 47, 65–66, 74–75, 78–79

    versus male athletes, 48–49

    and media, 45–46

    resistance by, 47–48

    See also Muslim female athletes

Bouchard, Eugenie "Genie," 2, 9–11, *10*, 11–16

Boyle, Raymond, 120

branding, 13, 76

broadcasters, 24

Brown, Peter, 115

Bruce, Toni

    on portrayal of female athletes, 6, 11, 20, 34, 123

    pretty and powerful discourse, 7, 15, 16, 21, 25

    on use of social media by female athletes, 8

Brugnoli, Emanuele, 32

Bryne, Bill, 89

"Building Cultural Diversity in Sport: A Critical Dialogue with Muslim Women and Sports Facilitators" (Ahmad et al.), 66

Butler, Jimmy, 102

Butler, Judith, 8

E

F

pay

    disparity, 106–107, 113

    Equal Employment Opportunity Commission (EEOC), 25–26

    equal pay, 25–28, 119

    equal pay for work of equal value, 25–28, 119

    WNBA *versus* NBA, 94–96

people of colour, 22, 104

people with disabilities, 22, 138–139, 143–144

    See also Gotell, Devin "Great Ghost"

Pettis, Bridget, 47

pretty and powerful, 7, 15, 16, 25, 27

Q

queerness/queer erasure, 19–38

    definition, 21–22

    equal pay, 25–28

    hegemonic masculinity of sport media, 21–25

    invisibility, 22–23

    study, 28–33

    See also LGBTQIA+ issues

Qurān, 40

R

racialization, 41, 42–43, 75

Rahaman, Ruqayah, 60

el Rahman, Minara, 46

Raimondo, Analisa, 2, 4–18, vi

Rapinoe, Megan, 2, 19–38

Raptors, (Toronto, NBA), 57, 81–82

Razack, Sabrina, 2, 39–55

Richardson, F. Michelle, 45, 47

Roble, Jawahir, 82

Rooney, Art, 107

Rostom, Manal, 82, 83

Rowe, David, 115

Ryerson University. *See* "X" University

S

Sabally, Satou, 42, 47–48

Sauerbrunn, Becky, 25–26

Schultes, Peter, 33

screen time study (WNBA), 101–104

Segrave, Jeffrey O., 123

Sehlikoglu, Sertaç, 84

self-representation, 4–18

shadeism, 47

W

X

Y

.

www.ingramcontent.com/pod-product-compliance
Lightning Source LLC
Chambersburg PA
CBHW052011030426

42334CB00029BA/3181